MEMORY DISTORTIONS
AND THEIR PREVENTION

CHALLENGES AND CONTROVERSIES
IN APPLIED COGNITION

Margaret J. Intons-Peterson and Deborah L. Best, Series Editors

Intons-Peterson/Best (1998) • *Memory Distortions and Their Prevention*

MEMORY DISTORTIONS AND THEIR PREVENTION

Edited by

Margaret Jean Intons-Peterson
Indiana University

Deborah L. Best
Wake Forest University

Routledge
Taylor & Francis Group

LONDON AND NEW YORK

First published 1998 by Lawrence Erlbaum Associates

Published 2014 by Psychology Press
27 Church Road, Hove, East Sussex, BN3 2FA

and by Psychology Press
711 Third Avenue, New York, NY 10017

First issued in paperback 2014

*Psychology Press is an imprint of the Taylor & Francis Group,
an informa business*

The final camera copy for this work was prepared by the author,
and therefore the publisher takes no responsibility for consistency
or correctness of typographical style. However, this arrangement
helps to make publication of this kind of scholarship possible.

Cover design by Kathryn Houghtaling Lacey

Library of Congress Cataloging-in-Publication Data

Memory distortions and their prevention / edited by Margaret J.
Intons-Peterson, Deborah L. Best.
    p. cm — (Challenges and controversies in applied
    cognition)
Includes bibliographical references and index.
ISBN 978-0-805-83066-8 (hbk)
ISBN 978-1-138-00315-6 (pbk)

1. Memory disorders. 2. Memory. I. Best, Deborah L. II.
Intons-Peterson, Margaret Jean. III. Series.
    BF376.M47 1998
    153.1'2—dc21   98-21196
                                                CIP

This book is dedicated to the Society for Applied Research in Memory and Cognition for its timely support for the advancement of research on the applied uses of memory and cognitive theory and the reciprocal impact of such research on memory and cognitive theory. Two major purposes of its sponsorship are to facilitate the rapid presentation of new research in these areas and to highlight current controversies.

Contents

Foreword

Douglas Herrmann

This volume is the first in a series devoted to showcasing state-of-the-art applied research in memory and cognition. The series was conceived at the first meeting of the Society for Applied Research on Memory and Cognition (SARMAC), held at the 1994 Practical Aspects of Memory Conference. Those in attendance at this meeting recognized that efforts to apply cognitive psychology are growing at a fast rate. They also recognized that applications of cognitive psychology to real-world problems of society offer important, often novel solutions. The new SARMAC needed to develop more publications to serve the growing and stimulating interest in applied research.

Applied Cognitive Psychology, SARMAC's official journal, is well respected for providing an excellent outlet for articles about potential and actual applications of cognitive psychology. However, because of the substantial increase in interest in applied cognitive research, additional outlets are essential. Specifically, a form of publication is needed that would permit a more extensive examination of findings than usually is possible in a journal article. Indeed, it is desirable to have a form of publication that would permit concentrated attention from several researchers to particular research questions. Journals, such as *Applied Cognitive Psychology*, can be expected to periodically provide issues on a specific theme, but journals usually cannot present thematic issues because of their obligation to provide regular publication of refereed articles. Also, because of limitations on page length, journals are usually restricted to thematic issues concerning narrow topics or less than an in-depth examination of a broad topic.

Accordingly, SARMAC decided that applied cognitive researchers need a book series wherein each book would be devoted to cutting-edge applied-cognitive research on selected topics. The books in this series will play an extremely important role in the development of applied cognitive psychology. Substantive developments in any field require more than excellent journal articles. In addition, such developments necessitate concentrated attention to a variety of findings. Moreover, as Francis Bacon[1] noted nearly 350 years ago, nature must be understood in both basic and applied ways to be fully comprehended. Basic cognitive researchers will be able to get a better understanding of a particular applied problem from a book on a certain topic. Thus, this book series also had the goal of facilitating the synergy of basic and applied aims, findings, and methods wherever possible.

Because of the SARMAC meeting in 1994 concluded that a book series was critical to the needs of applied cognitive researchers, the Society sought two outstanding researchers to edit this series. Peggy Intons-Peterson and Debbie Best were invited and fortunately agreed to serve as the editors of this book series. The book that you are holding is the first in this series.

Peggy and Debbie decided that the topic for the first book in the series was to be memory distortion and its prevention. They have recruited some of the very best researchers in the applied cognitive field to address these issues: Valerie Reyna, Mary Ann Foley, Hugh Foley, Janine Hay, Johanna Nordlie, Larry Jacoby, Roger Dixon, Lisa Gagnon, Carolyn Crow, Mary Gauvain, Mary Beth Jensen, Alice F. Healy, Marlys Hearst Witte, Ann Kerwin, Charles Witte, Douglas Herrmann, and Carol Yoder. These authors examine distortion from several angles: fuzzy-trace theory, face identification, memory deficits with age, collaborative influences on distortion, sociocultural influences on memory, retention of procedural and declarative information, and ignorance of medical and other information. The final chapter, which, as an author, I especially recommend, addresses the issue of cognitive technology in general.

Because the surge of interest in applied cognitive psychology and in the memory distortion issue in particular, this book will be valuable to many researchers—applied and basic.

---

[1]Bacon, F. (1905). Novum organum. J. M. Robertson (Ed.). *The philosophic works of Francis Bacon*, R. C. Ellis & J. Spedding, Trans. London: George Routledge and Sons.

1

Introduction and a Brief History of Memory Distortions and Their Prevention

Margaret Jean Intons-Peterson
Indiana University

Deborah L. Best
Wake Forest University

Memory is the scaffolding upon which all mental life is constructed.
— Fischbach & Coyle (1995, p. ix).

I don't think I will ever trust my memory again.
—Undergraduate Courtney Scott after serving as an experimenter in a study of false memory.

The output of human memory often differs—sometimes rather substantially—from the input.
—Schacter (1995, p. 1).

Suppose we ask you to remember the following list: bed, rest, awake, tired, dream, wake, snooze, blanket, doze, slumber, snore, nap, peace, yawn, drowsy. After a short time, we ask you to recall the words. Chances are that you will report the word "sleep" in addition to some of the other words even though "sleep" did not appear in the list. In Intons-Peterson's laboratory, both younger (mean age = 19) and older (mean age = 70) adults recalled proportionately as many nonpresented words as presented words. Moreover, when the nonpresented words were scattered among presented ones in a recognition test, the participants were more likely to say they had heard the nonpresented words than the presented ones! Our results (Intons-Peterson,

Rocchi, West, McLellan, & Hackney, 1998) parallel those of others using the
same approach (e.g., Payne, Elie, Blackwell, & Neuschatz, 1996; Roediger &
McDermott, 1995). These false memories occur after a single hearing of the
lists, indicating that it is easy to instill such memories. False memories are a
form of distorted memories.

What are memory distortions? They may be false memories, memory
errors, perceptual illusions, false beliefs, hallucinations, and confabulations.
They may be mediated by perceptual processes, memorial processes, or
external processes. Obviously, a definition must encompass a wide range.
Probably the simplest definition is the one given at the start of the chapter by
Schacter, "the output of human memory often differs . . . from the input."
(1995, p. 1). This definition does not mean that memory is invariably
inaccurate. Fortunately, most of the time memory operates accurately and
effectively, allowing us to pursue our daily lives with confidence and
adaptability. Nevertheless, the impact of memory distortions can be
staggering, as in inaccurate eyewitness testimony, hallucinations, and
confabulations. Moreover, memory can be fallible, fragile, and
inaccurate—discouraging and potentially dangerous attributes for one of our
most important abilities. Hence, we want to know when distortions occur and
how to prevent them. These issues are the topics of this book. Specifically,
the chapters address the processes that produce memory distortions and their
prevention.

Furthermore, the emphasis in the book is on memory distortion in daily
activities of normal adults and not on drug-induced, psychotic, or hypnotic
distortions. The book also does not include some areas of memory distortions
that already have received substantial attention, such as eyewitness testimony
(e.g., Loftus, 1979; Loftus & Doyle, 1987; Wells, 1988), jury manipulation
(e.g., Pennington & Hastie, 1990), or repressed memories (e.g., Freyd, 1996;
Lindsay & Read, 1994; Loftus & Ketcham, 1994; Pope, 1996). Instead, we
explore memory distortions in such everyday situations as memories for events
(chapters 2 and 4), faces (chapter 3), collaboration and false beliefs (chapter
5), space (chapter 6), motor or procedural information (chapter 7), and in
normal aging (chapters 4 and 5). Each of these chapters also addresses
possible preventive measures. The last two chapters describe specific
approaches for aiding memory. Chapter 8 introduces an exciting and novel
method for making material memorable, the method of ignorance! In this
method, people are challenged to think of what they do not know about a
particular topic. This requires them to think of what they do know in an active
and engaging way. The net result is likely to be memory enhancement.
Chapter 9 details various techniques that have been developed by using
principles of cognitive psychology in a new area called cognitive technology.
The central focus of cognitive technology is to harness technology in the
service of cognitive performance.

FIG. 1.1. The tops of the two tables are identical in size and shape in the plane of the picture. From *Mind Sights* by Shepard ©1990 by Roger N. Shepard. Used with permission of W.H. Freeman and Company.)

Let us return to the issue of memory distortions. In the example given at the beginning of this chapter, we described a method for eliciting false memories. Strictly speaking, the learners are remembering something that did not happen rather than distorting a memory representation of an actual event. Perhaps false memories should be called memory errors, which they are in the sense that the participants are requested to recall or recognize only the words they had heard. From another perspective, the list was constructed to represent a concept such as sleep. The words were all words that are frequently given as free associates to the stimulus word "sleep." The underlying rationale is that hearing the words activates a network of associations. This network contains the concept word, "sleep," so that when the person subsequently tries to retrieve items from a memory search, "sleep" will likely be encountered along with other presented words. In this sense, then, the retrieval of "sleep" tells us about the structure of memory and about the ability of the people to distinguish between the presented and nonpresented items. In our everyday

FIG. 1.2. The two monsters are identical in size. As Shepard noted, we may interpret their identical faces as expressing different emotions—such as rage on the part of the pursuer and fear on the part of the pursued. (From *Mind Sights* by Shepard ©1990 by Roger N. Shepard. Used with permission of W.H. Freeman and Company.)

lives, we face similar distinctions when we forget whether we did something or simply thought about doing it.

If memory distortions are deviations from the input, we need to consider the input. Typically, the input is mediated by the senses, making perception a major building block of memories. How veridical are perceptions? Again, most of the time they serve us well. We are able to see, hear, smell, and taste in biologically adaptive ways. But some perceptual illusions are so powerful that we cannot escape them even if we know about them. Consider Fig. 1.1. Do the two tables have the same top surfaces? Yes, but about the only way for most of us to convince ourselves is to place a drawing or template of one table top on the other table.

Figure 1.2 shows another other powerfully persuasive visual illusion. Are the two figures the same size? Again, they are, but they certainly look different, even when we know they are the same size. Are our eyes playing tricks on us? As cognitive psychologists we know that it is our brain, not our eyes, that is responsible. As the brain integrates information across optical input and previous experiences, the output leads us to draw the wrong conclusions. Thus, even seemingly straightforward physical events may induce memory distortions. Similar outcomes occur with verbal and other sensory input and with imagined events or objects. Given their pervasiveness, it is not surprising that memory distortions have interested scholars and others for a long time.

A BRIEF HISTORY

Curiosity about memory distortions and attempts to understand their origins has an extensive and prescient history. Philosophers of history might well consider Aristotle's laws of association as establishing the argument that items experienced in close temporal or spatial contiguity will tend to be remembered together. This idea, however, had little experimental support until Ebbinghaus (1885/1964) introduced a method to determine whether a memory was true or false, accurate or inaccurate. In effect, he established the foundation of the experimental method in psychology. His approach was to learn a series of nonword trigram letters (the famous nonsense syllables). Because the trigrams were not standard words, any intrusion of a word or of nonstudied combinations of letters could be detected when he tested himself for retention at a later time. By using unfamiliar learning materials, Ebbinghaus could ascertain whether a response was right or wrong.

At about the same time, other European scientists were finding that the use of misleading or vague information could affect the accuracy of memories. In France, Binet (1900) noted that asking misleading questions about objects children had seen led them to produce systematically distorted recollections whereas in Germany, Munsterberg (1908) demonstrated the unreliability of eyewitness testimony. It is amazing to contemplate the faith still placed in eyewitness testimony given Munsterberg's well-known treatise on the subject and the extensive, confirmatory research that has been done since then (e.g., Loftus, 1979; Loftus & Doyle, 1987; Wells, 1988). Freud's (1896) early work also addressed memory distortions. He posited that the distortions were produced as a way to defensively exclude painful memories from consciousness (repression), a theory he derived from his clinical experience. Such painful memories were thought to come from sexual abuse or trauma, a view Freud subsequently abandoned, saying that the reports of such memories were actually confabulations or fantasies. Memory distortions also were reported about this time in brain-damaged alcoholic patients by Korsakoff (1889a, 1889b). These distortions are known today as Korsakoff's syndrome. Korsakoff sufferers have severely impaired memory for recent and remote events and often produce substantial confabulations.

As we move further into the 20th century, the research comes closer to the sorts of memory distortions considered in this book. In 1932, Bartlett published his classic monograph, *Remembering*. In the book, Bartlett reported that memories of a story changed with successive retellings. Although Bartlett's original work is not always replicable (Gauld & Stephenson, 1967; Roediger, Wheeler, & Rajaram, 1993), contemporary researchers are still influenced by his view that memories are reconstructions of past events guided by the rememberer's knowledge of the world. At the time, another view, a behavioristic–associationistic one, flourished in the United States.

The behavioristic–associationistic models assumed that forgetting of an association occurred when another association interfered with it. Interference could occur in both a forward—prospective—direction or in a backward—retrospective—direction. Associations or memories do not exist in a vacuum. Instead they exist in a universe of other potentially competing memories. Memories are particularly vulnerable to interference from subsequent events, the retroactive interference previously identified. For some 50 years, research investigated the conditions under which proactive and retroactive interference occurred. This massive attack led to the realization that memories are fragile. The probability that a particular association will be retained declines precipitously unless the association is rehearsed, preferably in an active, elaborative manner, and related to existing knowledge. It became apparent that networks of associations are constructed, and this latter knowledge led Deese (1959), who constructed the example given at the beginning of this chapter, to offer a novel, associationistic explanation of Bartlett's work. His argument was that when parts of the associational network are activated, other parts also are activated. At the time of retrieval, the rememberer may retrieve a nonpresented, but nevertheless activated item. Also see Estes (1997) for a recently published, sophisticated version of this general approach.

The extensive attention to associationism also suggested that misleading information may be incorporated in memory representations, which leads to changes in recollection (e.g., Loftus, Feldman, & Dashiell, 1995). As Loftus et al. related, participants first view a simulated crime or accident. Later, half of the people receive misleading information about the situation; the other half do not receive the information. Then the participants attempt to recall the original event. Typically, the misled participants induce systematic errors in recall. In fact, as Loftus et al. (1995) noted:

> subjects have recalled seeing stop signs when they were actually yield signs, hammers when they were actually screwdrivers, and curly-haired culprits when they actually had straight hair. Subjects have also recalled nonexistent items such as broken glass, tape recorders, and even something as large and conspicuous as a barn in a scene that contained no buildings at all. (p. 48)

Today, controversy still rages about whether memories are ever lost or simply have not been retrieved (Atkinson & Shiffrin, 1968), about whether memory distortions actually impair memory representations or interfere with retention of the original accurate memories (e.g., Belli, Windschitl, McCarthy, & Winfrey, 1992; Brainerd, Reyna, Howe, & Kingma, 1990), about whether trauma produces indelible memories (Brewin, 1989; Pillemer, 1992; Terr, 1988) or modifiable ones (e.g., Freyd, 1996), or about the accuracy of our knowledge of the source of our memories (source monitoring, e.g., Johnson, Hashtroudi, & Lindsay, 1993). These issues continue to swirl about us and to engender research such as the work reported in the chapters in this book. Simultaneously, theoretical issues also guide applied approaches and are influenced, in turn by applied work (e.g., Herrmann & Raybeck, 1997; Intons-Peterson, 1997; Payne, Conrad, & Hager, 1997).

This brief historical review was designed to set the stage for the chapters in the book. Each reports contemporary research on topics that are timely, challenging, and often contentious. If the chapters spark controversy in both basic and applied research, our efforts are successful.

ORGANIZATION OF THE BOOK

Suppose you are confronted by a student and a dean. The dean accuses the student of cheating because the student gave different responses during two interviews. How would you handle the situation? This is essentially the same situation that confronts police officers as they interview witnesses. Is the witness telling the truth? In chapter 2, Reyna uses this example to dissect a hypothetical student's testimony, showing how memory lapses, distortions, and even the questions themselves can affect responses. Reyna then shows how knowledge of memory theory, such as the fuzzy-trace model, can be used to explain memory operations as well as to make counterintuitive predictions. For example, the fuzzy-trace model correctly predicts that repeated questioning of what happened (the gist of a memory) may contribute to memory distortions that outlast true memories (based on verbatim recall). The general discussion of memory lapses in this chapter sets the stage for considering memory distortions in specific areas, such as visual perception (chapter 3), intentional versus automatic processes (chapter 4), collaborative memory (chapter 5), spatial distortions (chapter 6), and fact learning (declarative memory; chapter 7).

Chapter 3 focuses on the veridicality of visual perception when a familiar object is partly occluded. For example, witnesses of a crime are often asked to describe suspects. Typically, the viewing conditions are not ideal. The event often happens quickly, the observer is not prepared to scrutinize the suspect, and the suspect may vanish quickly from view. The suspect might not be seen from the front. The suspect may be wearing a mask, hat, scarf, glasses, or even a beard as a disguise. How can witnesses be expected to deliver reliable testimony under such circumstances? In fact, there are parallels in our daily lives when we do quite well. We are able to recognize people with their hats pulled down against the wind, with sunglasses on, and when we catch only a fleeting glimpse of them in a crowded area. These successful efforts to see beyond such occlusions (disguises) led Foley and Foley to ask if we have a tendency to complete objects that are actually presented as incomplete or as partly covered. In chapter 3, they note that in daily life, objects or items are often obscured and yet we cope—most of the time. People tend to recognize incomplete or occluded visual information as complete, but they then cannot distinguish between items presented as complete and those that were incomplete. For example, when they see a profile, they may fill in the full face and then, if questioned later, remember the experience as having seen the person's full face. Presumably, an imaginal closure or filling in occurs. Thus, imaginal closure may lead to the misidentification of the source of memory, from imagined to actually seen.

Quite a different type of memory distortion comes in the form of repeatedly asking questions. Amnesiacs and others suffering from serious memory deficits often repeat questions even though their questions have been answered. In chapter 4, Hay, Nordlie, and Jacoby discuss the origins of such memory distortions and possible remedies that have implications for the understanding of the functioning of normal memory. Hay et al. distinguish between intentional memory processes, derived from deliberate attempts to remember information (recollection), and automatic processes, delivered without conscious awareness. The former appear to decline with age, whereas the latter are preserved. For example, retention of a deliberately learned list of words or a story may decline with age or brain insults, but retention in the form of indirect tests, such as word completion, after previous exposure to the target words remains unimpaired. Hay et al. describe the development of an opposition technique that serves as a sensitive diagnostic tool for elderly adults who are beginning to show signs of dementia. In one variant of the opposition technique, people are shown faces of nonfamous people. Then they are shown another list of faces composed of the faces of some famous individuals and some nonfamous ones. Finally, they are asked to identify only the famous faces when shown a list containing some of both of the first two lists. Before seeing the final list, the people are told that all of the faces shown in the first list were not famous. Presumably, if they can remember the origins of their memories of the faces, they should be able to correctly exclude all of the List 1 nonfamous faces. Opposing this perspective, however, is the automatic familiarity gained by the List 1 nonfamous faces during their viewing. This familiarity is likely to be interpreted as adding to the perceived fame of the nonfamous words, and may result in the incorrect identification of the List 1 nonfamous faces as famous ones. Thus, intentional memory processors use the knowledge to exclude List 1 faces, whereas automatic processes foster inclusion of these faces. Older adults have more difficulty excluding the List 1 faces than younger adults, suggesting that intentional memory processes have declined although automatic ones remain intact. These automatic processes may have potential for aiding memory.

Another approach to helping memory and avoiding memory distortions is to use other people as memory collaborators. In chapter 5, Dixon, Gagnon, and Crow describe how memory collaboration aids accuracy and reduces distortion, although its effectiveness depends on beliefs about cognitive collaboration. Older adults appear to perform quite competently when they collaborate with well-known partners (namely their spouses). Collaboration with unfamiliar individuals is less effective. In fact, the older couples, who had been married at least 40 years, produced better story recall with fewer errors than older stranger pairs, or younger couples or stranger pairs. Dixon et al. note that beliefs about cognition are very important. If people believe that memory declines with age, they may interpret every groping for a word as a confirmation of this belief, even though the incidence of word groping may be no higher than when they were young. Beliefs may reduce expectations and lower cognitive engagement.

The influence of social and cultural beliefs emerges in chapter 6, as well. In this chapter, Gauvain discusses spatial distortions of distance, spatial relations, and directions as functions of practical activity and culture. Human spatial thinking reflects social and cultural influences. For example, the Alaskan Inuit draw geographic maps that contain objects in relation to each other but that do not accurately represent distance between objects in contrast to the kinds of geographic maps typically used in many countries to describe the country's layout. It is the case, however, that the latter countries also use schematic maps to depict subway systems. Gauvain reports that, in general, the longer the distance the greater the underestimation of the distance, one form of spatial memory distortion. Another form is distortion of spatial relations. When asked what direction one goes to get from San Diego to Reno, people are likely to say, "Northeast," when the actual direction is northwest. Still another form is a distortion of direction. This is particularly likely to occur when people infer directions to an out-of-sight location. In general, these distortions reflect two sources of bias: internal ones like simplification and regularization and external sources like past experience and context (familiarity, relational groupings). A theme running through this chapter is that the active exploration of a space leads to better memory for that space than a more passive approach. We could liken the active approach to what has been called procedural memory and the passive approach to declarative memory, a topic pursued by Jensen and Healy in chapter 7.

Declarative memory or the learning of facts carries with it the seeds for disaster. These memories begin to decline after relatively short intervals of time. An obvious antidote, if one wants to construe it that way, is to involve the person in active rehearsal, production, or actual carrying out of activities to be learned. This type of procedural learning produces longer lasting retention. In chapter 7, Jensen and Healy describe numerous studies that have compared the efficacy of the two forms of memory, with the typical result being that procedural is more durable than declarative memory. Jensen and Healy show that this is even true when applied to a common situation, such as taking a driver's test. They devised a series of questions to test procedural or declarative memory while using the same correct answer for each kind of memory, a clever control. This control means that any differences between the two forms of memory cannot be attributed to differences in the answers. Although the research did not have enough participants to provide extensive power, the results generally supported the superiority of procedural memory.

Measures to guard against memory distortions appear in chapters 2 through 7. For example, memory is usually accurate for a short time after input; metaphors are remembered better than duller prose (Reyna, 1996), false recognition of gist can be reversed by priming verbatim memory before testing (Brainerd, Reyna, & Kneer, 1995). Hay et al. (chapter 4) describe a training program to aid recollection. Dixon et al. (chapter 5) cite the use of compensatory mechanisms to minimize memory declines. These mechanisms include substitution (using alternate pathways to task completion), accommodation (adjusting or devaluing blocked goals), remediation (investing more time in performing the declining skill), and assimilation (modifying the environment or expectations of others). Jensen and Healy (chapter 7) emphasize the procedural-motoric aspects of learning, noting that undergraduates remembered where a class was held better than who taught the class, the class title, and when the course met. In chapters 8 and 9, the authors develop specific approaches to aid in the prevention of memory distortions and loss.

In chapter 8, Witte, Kerwin, and Witte introduce a method that we believe is new to psychology: the method of ignorance. In this technique, participants ask questions about unknowns at increasingly abstract levels. To do so, the participants must learn what is known. They have to organize their knowledge effectively enough to be able to generate questions about unknowns that differ in levels of abstractness. This technique is very clever, for it immediately sets into action many memory processes known to be highly advantageous, such as active rehearsal, building on familiar knowledge, self-testing, and generating schemata. The intent of the method is to address errors in reasoning in which individuals are reluctant to rethink an idea or test evidence that may contradict a previously accepted truth (Wason & Johnson-Laird, 1972) and to help overcome the pronounced tendency to prefer to deal with affirmative instances (examples of what a concept is) rather than negative or exclusionary evidence (what a concept is not), even when the latter strategy is more effective than the first (e.g., Bourne, et al., 1976; Haygood & Bourne, 1965). The method of ignorance approach is so versatile that it could be adapted to almost any setting, although it needs to be handled by individuals prepared to accept that not all information may be knowable. We hope that this chapter will initiate the use of the ignorance method throughout psychology.

The last chapter concludes our treatment of memory distortions by identifying devices, techniques, and applications of memory enhancers and rehabilitators. This burgeoning area of work is becoming known as cognitive technology. It includes the assessment of memory capabilities, memory improvement systems, and ways to deal with prospective and retrospective memory. Prospective memory is memory for things we need to do in the future, whereas retrospective memory involves information from the past. The chapter also describes the mutual dependencies and inspiration that applied memory problems and basic cognitive research provide to each other. The applied problems drive a researcher to seek a solution, which typically involves general principles enunciated by basic cognitive research. The solution and its implementation often raise additional questions that guide the development of future basic research. This synchrony may connect industry and academia or may be initiated primarily in one or the other place. The synchrony is a testament to human ingenuity, which we expect to be harnessed in the service of improving our memories.

REFERENCES

Atkinson, R. C., & Shiffrin, R. M. (1968). Human memory: A proposed system and its control processes. In K. W. Spence & J. T. Spence (Eds.), *The psychology of learning and motivation: Advances in research and theory* (Vol. 2, pp. 89–105). New York: Academic Press.

Bartlett, F. C. (1932). *Remembering*. Cambridge, England: Cambridge University Press.

Belli, R. F., Windschitl, P. D., McCarthy, T. T., & Winfrey, S. E. (1992). Detecting memory impairment with a modified test procedure: Manipulating retention interval with centrally presented event items. *Journal of Experimental Psychology: Learning, Memory, and Cognition, 18,* 356–367.

Binet, A. (1900). *La suggestibilité.* Paris: Schleicher Freres.

Bourne, L. E., Jr., Ekstrand, B. R., Lovallo, W. R., Kellogg, R. T., Hiew, C. C., & Yaroush, R. (1976). Frequency analysis of attribute identification. *Journal of Experimental Psychology: General, 105,* 294–312.

Brainerd, C. J., Reyna, V. F., Howe, M. L., & Kingma, J. (1990). The development of forgetting and reminiscence. *Monographs of the Society for Research in Child Development, 55,* (3, Whole No. 222).

Brainerd, C. J., Reyna, V. F., & Kneer, R. (1995). False recognition reversal: When is similarity distinctive? *Journal of Memory and Language, 34,* 157–185.

Brewin, C. R. (1989). Cognitive change processes in psychotherapy. *Psychological Review, 96,* 379–394.

Deese, J. (1959). On the prediction of occurrence of particular verbal intrusions in immediate recall. *Journal of Experimental Psychology, 58,* 17–22.

Ebbinghaus, H. (1885/1964). *Memory: A contribution to experimental psychology.* New York: Dover.

Estes, W. K. (1997). Processes of memory loss, recovery, and distortion. *Psychological Review, 104,* 148–169.

Fischbach, G. D., & Coyle, J. T. (1995). Preface. In D. L. Schacter (Ed.), *Memory distortion: How minds, brains, and societies reconstruct the past* (pp. ix–xi). Cambridge, MA: Harvard University Press.

Freud, S. (1896). The aetiology of hysteria. In J. Strachey (Ed.), *The standard edition of the complete psychological works of Sigmund Freud.* London: Hogarth.

Freyd, J. (1996). *Betrayal trauma theory: The logic of forgetting abuse.* Cambridge, MA: Harvard University Press.

Gauld, A., & Stephenson, G. B. (1967). Some experiments related to Bartlett's theory of remembering. *British Journal of Psychology, 58,* 39–49.

Herrmann, D., & Raybeck, D. (1997). A clash of cultures: Basic and applied cognitive research. In D. G. Payne & F. G. Conrad (Eds.), *Intersections in basic and applied memory research* (pp. 25–44). Mahwah, NJ: Lawrence Erlbaum Associates.

Haygood, R. C., & Bourne, L. E., Jr. (1965). Attribute and rule learning aspects of conceptual behavior. *Psychological Review, 72,* 175–195.

Intons-Peterson, M. J. (1997). How basic and applied research inform each other. In D. G. Payne & F. G. Conrad (Eds.), *Intersections in basic and applied memory research* (pp. 3–24). Mahwah, NJ: Lawrence Erlbaum Associates.

Intons-Peterson, M. J., Rocchi, P., West, T., McLellan, K., & Hackney, A. (1998). Aging, optimal testing times, and negative priming. *Journal of Experimental Psychology: Learning, Memory, and Cognition, 24,* 362–376.

Johnson, M. K., Hashtroudi, S., & Lindsay, D. S. (1993). Source monitoring. *Psychological Bulletin, 114,* 3–28.

Korsakoff, S. S. (1889a). Etude medico-psychologique sur une forme des maladies do la memoire [Medical-psychological study of a form of diseases of memory]. *Revue Philosophique, 28,* 501–530.

Korsakoff, S. S. (1889b). Über eine besondre Form psychischer Störung, Kombiniert mit multiplen Neuritis [On a particular form of psychic disorder combined with multiple neuritis] (H. Victor & P. I. Yakovlev, Trans.). *Archiv für Psychiatrie und Nervenkrankheiten, 21,* 669–704.

Lindsay, D. S., & Read, J. D. (1994). Psychotherapy and memories of childhood sexual abuse: A cognitive perspective. *Applied Cognitive Psychology, 8,* 281–338.

Loftus, E. F. (1979). *Eyewitness testimony.* Cambridge, MA: Harvard University Press.

Loftus, E. F., & Doyle, J. M. (1987). *Eyewitness testimony: Civil and criminal.* New York: Kluwer.

Loftus, E. F., Feldman, J., & Dashiell, R. (1995). The reality of illusory memories. In D. L. Schacter, (Ed.), *Memory distortion: How minds, brains, and societies reconstruct the past* (pp. 47–68). Cambridge, MA: Harvard University Press.

Loftus, E. F., & Ketcham, K. (1994). *The myth of repressed memory: False memories and allegation of sexual abuse.* New York: St. Martin's Press.

Munsterberg, H. (1908). *On the witness stand. Essays on psychology and crime.* New York: Clark, Boardman, Doubleday.

Payne, D. G., Conrad, F. G., & Hager, D. R. (1997). Basic and applied memory research: Empirical, theoretical, and metatheoretical issues. In D. G. Payne & F. G. Conrad (Eds.), *Intersections in basic and applied memory research* (pp. 45–68). Mahwah, NJ: Lawrence Erlbaum Associates.

Payne, D. G., Elie, C. J., Blackwell, J. M., & Neuschatz, J. S. (1996). Memory illusions: Recalling, recognizing and recollecting events that never occurred. *Journal of Memory and Language, 35,* 261–285.

Pennington, N., & Hastie, R. (1990). Practical implications of psychological research on juror and jury decision making. *Personality and Social Psychology Bulletin, 16,* 90–105.

Pillemer, D. B. (1992). Remembering personal circumstances: A functional analysis. In E. Winograd & U. Neisser (Eds.), *Affect and accuracy in recall: Studies of flashbulb memories* (pp. 236–269). New York: Cambridge University Press.

Pope, K. S. (1996). Memory, abuse, and science. *American Psychologist, 51,* 957–974.

Reyna, V. F. (1996). Meaning, memory and the interpretation of metaphors. *Annals of Child Development, 12,* 87–117.

Roediger, H. L., III, & McDermott, K. B. (1995). Creating false memories: Remembering words not presented in lists. *Journal of Experimental Psychology: Learning, Memory, and Cognition, 21,* 803–814.

Roediger, H. L., III., Wheeler, M. A., & Rajaram, S. (1993). Remembering, knowing and reconstructing the past. In D. L. Medin (Ed.), *The psychology of learning and motivation: Advances in theory and research,* (Vol. 30, pp. 97–134). New York: Academic Press.

Schacter, D. L. (1995). Memory distortion: History and current status. In D. L. Schacter (Ed.), *Memory distortion: How minds, brains, and societies reconstruct the past* (pp. 1–46). Cambridge, MA: Harvard University Press.

Shepard, R. N. (1990). *Mind sights.* New York: Freeman.

Terr, L. (1988). What happens to early memories of trauma? A study of 20 children under age five at the time of documented traumatic events. *Journal of the American Academy of Child and Adolescent Psychiatry, 27,* 96–104.

Wason, P. C., & Johnson–Laird, P. N. (1972). *Psychology of reasoning: Structure and content.* Cambridge, MA: Harvard University Press.

Wells, G. L. (1988). *Eyewitness identification: A system handbook.* Toronto: Carswell Legal Publications.

2

Fuzzy-Trace Theory and False Memory

Valerie F. Reyna
University of Arizona

To a surprising degree, verdicts in U.S. courtrooms depend on memory. In this chapter, the case of Jennifer (a student accused of cheating) is used to illustrate how the ordinary properties of memory can make the innocent appear guilty, and vice versa. Cherished truisms—for example, that witnesses who contradict themselves must be lying—are challenged by scientific data showing that false testimony may be more consistent than truthful testimony. As Jennifer's case unfolds, the reader is introduced to recent findings in false-memory research, including autosuggestion, external suggestion, forgetting and recovery of verbatim details, the mere-memory-testing effect, the false-memory persistence effect, and source misattribution, as well as constraints on suggestibility. The findings are explained in terms of fuzzy-trace theory, which assumes that gist and verbatim representations of events are remembered independently.

When students recall material for a test, patients report their history to a physician, pilots remember their training in an emergency, or witnesses recount a crime to a police officer, and in many other circumstances, accurate memory is crucial. But how accurate is memory? Some psychologists believe that experience is accurately and indelibly etched in memory, although retrieval can vary. Others believe that remembering inevitably distorts experience, that memories are constructed from a mixture of experience, knowledge, inference, and, perhaps, motivation. Evidence has accumulated on both sides.

Recently, a new approach to memory—fuzzy-trace theory—has attempted to reconcile these divergent views (for a review, see Reyna & Brainerd, 1995a). The aim of the theory is to explain demonstrations of memorial accuracy and of distortion, and to predict conditions under which each of these will be observed. In the attempt, we have discovered some surprising facts about memory and how it works. This chapter is about those facts and their implications for the nature of memory.

EVERYDAY FALSE MEMORIES: AN EXAMPLE

In order to understand those facts, consider the following case of a student accused of cheating on an examination. Although this combination of events is not true, each event is an example of those that have occurred in real cases.

Dr. Maryland calls the Dean of Students to report that he suspects that one of his students, Jennifer James, has cheated on an examination. He found a set of cards near her desk with many of the answers copied on them. A university official interviews Jennifer and asks her numerous questions. Jennifer cannot explain why her score was 85% on this examination but was below 65% on the other four examinations. Suspicious, the official interviews her a second time. This time he surreptitiously tape records the interview. The official notices a number of inconsistencies between the first and second interviews. In the first interview, Jennifer indicated that she studied for the examination "the night before, about 10 o'clock." However, in the same interview, she said that she started studying about 7:45. At first, she said that there was no particular reason why she put the cards on the floor. In the second interview, she said that she put them there because then they would be too far away to see. When she was asked whether she studied more than usual for this examination, she said no. Later, she said that she had studied more than usual. At first, she said that she had asked the teaching assistant whether she could sit in the back. Later, she said she did not speak to anyone. At first, she specifically denied that she told a friend before the examination that she was going to flunk. Later, she said that she thought that she'd said something like that. During both interviews, however, Jennifer acknowledged that she had been "nervous" about the examination. She vividly remembered feeling rushed and out of sorts that day. The official concluded that Jennifer had made false statements to him and had probably cheated on the examination.

Do you think Jennifer is guilty? Her statements certainly make her seem guilty; they make it appear that she is either lying or, at best, unreliable. However, the inconsistencies in Jennifer's statements are predictable based on normal properties of memory. Each of the phenomena illustrated here have been produced in the laboratory (albeit under different conditions and with different materials). Moreover, because the laboratory investigator controls the events, he or she can be sure about what really happened. Therefore, true memories can be clearly distinguished from false ones, an advantage that is typically not enjoyed outside the laboratory.

ANALYSIS OF THE EXAMPLE

Verbatim–Gist Independence

How could someone contradict herself like Jennifer did and not be lying or unreliable? Consider the first inconsistency, between studying at 7:45 p.m. versus 10 p.m. This inconsistency illustrates the verbatim–gist independence effect (Brainerd & Reyna, 1992; Reyna, 1992). In laboratory experiments, it has been shown that people will respond to one question based on their memory for the gist of an event, whereas another question might cue their verbatim memory, especially if it is presented shortly after the event occurred (e.g., Reyna & Brainerd, 1995a; Reyna & Kiernan, 1994, 1995; Reyna & Titcomb, 1997). Therefore, Jennifer's gist memory could be that she studied well after dinner and before the news. When asked when she started studying, however, she might have been reminded that she began at precisely 7:45 p.m. At the level of gist, Jennifer has not contradicted herself, although legal matters often turn on memory for precise details such as the time that events took place.

Suggestion and Autosuggestion

The second inconsistency involved the reason for the cards being placed on the floor. At the first interview, Jennifer responds truthfully that she put the cards on the floor for no particular reason. Later, however, she infers that she must have put the cards on the floor so that she could not see them; this inference explains the behavior. This is an example of *autosuggestion*, namely the belief that events were experienced that are actually only consistent with experience (e.g., Brainerd & Reyna, 1995; Ceci & Bruck, 1993; Reyna, 1995). The effect is called autosuggestion because it is the product of internal cognitive processes. If someone says, "There's cake in the refrigerator," you may remember that you were offered some cake, that is, what was meant rather than what was said (Ackerman, 1992; Beal, 1990). Even when pressed about whether those exact words were used, people will claim that they have specific memories for such meaning-consistent implications. When the question concerns verbatim events, this kind of incorrect response based on gist is an example of cognitive interference (Dempster, 1992; Reyna, 1995; Schneider & Bjorklund, 1998).

The next inconsistency concerned whether Jennifer had studied "more than usual." Suppose that, after hearing about the higher grade, one of Jennifer's friends praised her for studying more than usual. If the friend's praise occurred weeks after the first interview (and the original events), but before the second interview, Jennifer could be the victim of a misinformation effect, a postevent misleading suggestion from an external source (e.g., Loftus & Hoffman, 1989; Titcomb & Reyna, 1995). Although not all misleading suggestions take, exposed subjects accept misinformation as having occurred reliably more often than nonexposed subjects. Because both children and adults are susceptible to such misinformation effects, despite having been witnesses to the true events, care must be exercised in interviewing to avoid implanting false memories (Brainerd, 1997; Brainerd & Ornstein, 1991; Poole & Lindsay, 1995; Warren, Hulse-Trotter, & Tubbs, 1991). As in autosuggestion, postevent suggestion can produce claims of specific memories for events that never occurred (Payne, Elie, Blackwell, & Neuschatz, 1996; Schacter, 1995; Schacter, Verfaellie, & Pradere, 1996).

Ironically, Jennifer could be more vulnerable to (auto- and postevent) suggestion because she is innocent: Jennifer was not on guard against her friend's casual suggestion that she studied more than usual, nor is she trying to recall critical events verbatim. (Recall that she is unaware that she is being tape-recorded.) Rather than aiming for verbatim accuracy, Jennifer tries to answer each question truthfully, based on what she thinks she remembers. This is why, at the second interview, she says that she "did not speak to anyone" before the examination. Jennifer might not remember speaking to anyone, for instance to the teaching assistant, because of the normal processes of forgetting (Brainerd, Reyna, Howe, & Kingma, 1990). If Jennifer were interviewed after several weeks, as is typical in legal matters, a great deal of detail would have already been forgotten. However, if Jennifer were questioned repeatedly, or reminded about the conversation with the teaching assistant, she might be able to retrieve or redintegrate some of the details despite the delay (Brainerd et al., 1990; Poole & White, 1991, 1993, 1995; Reyna & Titcomb, 1997; Warren & Lane, 1995).

Mere-Memory-Testing Effects

Jennifer's remaining statements seem particularly damning. Jennifer initially denies that she told a friend that she was going to flunk, and subsequently reverses herself. If Jennifer anticipated flunking, she would be motivated to cheat, and she ultimately admits to expressing that fear. However, this inconsistency, too, can be recognized as one produced in the laboratory: the mere-memory-testing effect (found in children by Brainerd & Reyna, 1996; subsequently replicated in adults by McDermott, 1996b). Recall that the interviewer asked Jennifer numerous questions, including this one about telling a friend that she was going to flunk. It has been shown that merely asking subjects about events that never occurred increases the probability that, on a subsequent occasion, they will then claim that the event occurred.

The mere-memory-testing effect differs from the misinformation effect because there is no implication that the false event occurred; the initial questions are neutral, as when a police officer asks whether a perpetrator had any scars or other distinguishing marks. Of course, most neutral questions do not produce false memories. However, it is easy to see that if many questions are asked about the same events (as is typically the case in legal matters), inconsistencies should eventually be produced: Witnesses will come to accept as true events that were initially denied, simply as a result of exposure to questions.

Persistence and Source Confusion

Although Jennifer's memory for many events seems to shift, she remembers being nervous before the examination during both interviews. Common sense and most theories of memory would suggest that her memory of being nervous is more likely to be authentic, compared to the memories that shifted. It is generally assumed that untruthful testimony has inconsistencies (and will break down during cross-examination, Perry Mason style). It is also assumed that memories for real events must be stronger than memories for events that never happened. Recent research indicates, however, that false memories can be as persistent, or more persistent, than true memories (Brainerd, Reyna, & Brandse 1995; McDermott, 1996a). Thus, Jennifer might forget that she talked to the teaching assistant, a true memory, but falsely remember being nervous before the examination across multiple interviews. Once again, consistency by itself is not diagnostic of truth-telling.

Finally, Jennifer vividly remembered feeling rushed and out of sorts on the day of the examination. This statement contributes to the incriminating perception that she was especially agitated prior to the examination, and might have been driven to do something desperate, such as cheat. However, despite the vividness of this memory, it could be misleading. Research has indicated that people sometimes confuse the sources of their memories. False memories can result when the substance of an event is accurately recalled, but it is attributed to the wrong person, location, or time (Belli, Lindsay, Gales, & McCarthy, 1994; Lindsay, 1990; Lindsay & Johnson, 1991; Reyna & Titcomb, 1997). For example, Jennifer could have been genuinely agitated and rushed on the day after the examination, and wrongly attributed that memory to the day of the examination. If the days differed arbitrarily at the time (although which day was which might later take on crucial significance), such a confusion would be more likely (Reyna & Titcomb, 1997; Titcomb & Reyna, 1995).

In general, research has suggested that fragments of real experience can become connected to inappropriate true memories (e.g., so that sources are misattributed) or even to false memories (e.g., so that memories of gist that did not actually occur take on specific attributes of person, location, time, and so on). Jennifer might distinctly remember being rushed on the day of the examination, she might recollect specific details such as her sweaty palms, but, nevertheless, this memory would be false because those events occurred on the following day.

In addition, source confusion and misattribution offer new ways to characterize traditional misinformation effects, that is, as failures to attribute memories to the correct experimental context, event versus postevent. This source misattribution explanation for misinformation effects does not rule out other explanations—current research suggests that there are many ways in which new information can impair memory for old information (e.g., see Titcomb & Reyna, 1995).

At the outset, I noted that the phenomena illustrated in Jennifer's case have each occurred in real cases. One might argue that by combining these phenomena into a single case, I have misrepresented the extent to which the normal workings of everyday memory could lead to such a guilty-appearing characterization. Although that argument would be valid for a psychological profile of Jennifer, it does not hold in an investigatory context. First, Jennifer's true statements would not have mitigated her false ones; she would have remained guilty of having made those statements. A report of her investigation would have summarized the subset of evidence that was incriminating, as the basis for a finding, as was done here. The fact that it might have taken hundreds of questions to "uncover her guilt" would be immaterial. This investigatory perspective contrasts with psychological research and, for that matter, with probability theory. Based on the latter, after many questions, inconsistencies would be expected because of the cumulative probabilities of various memory errors. Thus, by selecting the "relevant" responses from many questions, an impression of overwhelming guilt can be created.

CONSTRAINTS ON THE CREATION OF FALSE MEMORIES

Jennifer's story is disturbing because it illustrates how the normal workings of memory could make an innocent person appear to be a liar and a cheat. Loftus and Ketcham (1994) provided additional examples of seemingly false accusations based on the workings of memory (although, again, because the examples are not from the laboratory, it is impossible to know for certain whether the accusations are false). Does this mean that memory can be manipulated easily, that false memories are the norm? Because research does not represent a random sample of everyday memory, it is difficult to answer such a question definitively. However, there do seem to be constraints on the suggestibility of memory (e.g., Reyna & Titcomb, 1997).

First, research generally shows that, a short time after presentation, subjects are more likely to spontaneously recall and recognize true events rather than false ones (e.g., Reyna & Kiernan, 1994). Under these conditions, they are also more likely to attribute specific details to true events (e.g., Gardiner & Java, 1991; Reyna & Kiernan, 1994). These generalizations are qualified, however, by age, delay, exposure to misinformation, instructions (e.g., the cognitive interview; emphasis on truth, or gist, versus just the facts, or verbatim, memories, Reyna & Titcomb, 1997), the relative cuing of gist versus verbatim memories (Brainerd, Reyna, & Kneer, 1995; Roediger & McDermott, 1995), and the material to be remembered (e.g., pictures versus words; metaphorical versus literal sentences, Reyna & Kiernan, 1995), among other factors (Reyna & Brainerd, 1995a, 1995b). For example, under verbatim instructions, young adults can recognize virtually the exact wording of metaphorical sentences even after a substantial delay (Reyna & Kiernan, 1995). Duller prose is not nearly so memorable (Reyna, 1996a).

In addition, fuzzy-trace theory suggests that false memories can be reported without necessarily distorting original memories. For instance, as illustrated in Jennifer's case, some questions can cue gist memories, whereas other questions can cue verbatim memories for actual events. To be sure, subjects claim that the gist was actually experienced, that they remember it verbatim, although an experimenter can verify that such a memory is false (Brainerd & Reyna, 1996; Reyna & Kiernan, 1994). Moreover, false memory effects, such as false recognition of gist (Bransford & Franks, 1971), can be reversed by priming verbatim memories prior to testing (Brainerd, Reyna, & Kneer, 1995). Similarly, source misattribution does not require that original memories be forgotten, only that they be misplaced. Thus, in these instances, memory is not irretrievably falsified; false memory is potentially constrained because various testing and interviewing techniques can sometimes recover the original memories (Brainerd & Hill, 1997).

Finally, although gist memories are false in the sense that they do not represent direct experience, they represent the truth as individuals understand it. Often, such memories are consistent with the facts. For instance, it is possible to construct memory for the time of an event using memory for gist as a foundation, as in the inference that an event took place in the morning because of a clear memory that breakfast was on the table. If you followed such a rule, that is, that breakfast implies morning, you would generally be right. Indeed, verbatim memory can be used to reject the truth, as when preschoolers claim that an inference is not true because it differs from what was said (Brainerd & Reyna, 1993; Reyna & Kiernan, 1994). For witnesses, however, and for many others, it is crucial to avoid inference and interpretation. Our system of jurisprudence requires that the responsibility for the latter rests with the jury. Admittedly, the nature of memory suggests that such an ideal will never be fully realized. By understanding the nature of memory, however, techniques can be developed that enhance accuracy.

EXPLAINING FALSE MEMORIES

Research on false memories has yielded many surprising findings, some of which have been reviewed here, including the verbatim–gist independence effect, autosuggestion (gist interference), external suggestion, forgetting and recovery of verbatim details, the mere-memory-testing effect, the false-memory persistence effect, and source misattribution. Considering these findings, it would be difficult to think of memory as anything like a tape recorder. On the other hand, as discussed, the falsification of memory is subject to constraints: The events we remember are not random, and, under limited circumstances, we are capable of verbatim accuracy. How do theories of memory explain these findings?

The dominant views of memory are that it is essentially veridical and indelible, or that it is constructed out of an understanding of experience. The veridical view springs from both the Freudian concept that unconscious and temporally distant memories influence current behavior, and from the information-processing idea that once long-term memories are formed, forgetting is merely a matter of retrieval failure (Schwartz & Reisberg, 1991). The constructive view of memory was championed by Bartlett and Piaget (see Schwartz & Reisberg, 1991; Siegler, 1991). Indeed, the conventional account of false-memory effects in the experimental literature is that they demonstrate that memory is constructive (e.g., Loftus, 1995).

Neither of these approaches, veridical or constructive memory, can explain the range of phenomena reviewed in this chapter (for fuller discussions, see Reyna & Brainerd, 1995b; Reyna & Lloyd, 1997). For example, constructivism indicates that verbatim and gist memories are integrated to form semantic representations. Thus, people will falsely recognize semantically consistent sentences (e.g., inferences) as having been presented (e.g., Bransford & Franks, 1971; Paris & Carter, 1973). This fundamental tenet of constructivism predicts that the recognition of presented sentences and of inferences should be positively dependent, at least to some degree. Although this prediction was made explicitly by constructivists for many years, it was not tested until relatively recently. The test disconfirmed the conventional wisdom: Recognizing verbatim sentences was independent of recognizing inferences. These tests provided evidence that verbatim experience and semantic gist are represented independently (Reyna & Kiernan, 1994).

Additional effects, such as the false-memory persistence effect, the mere-memory-testing effect, recovery of verbatim details after a delay, and verbatim–gist interference, are difficult to reconcile with the constructivist view. The veridical approach suffers from complementary weaknesses. Although it can account for the sometimes remarkable accuracy of memory, it has difficulty explaining the many demonstrations of false memory, nor can it predict the specific properties of such memories (for a prescient discussion of these issues, see Hasher & Griffin, 1978).

According to fuzzy-trace theory, the strengths of both memory traditions can be brought together without sacrificing clear prediction. Relatively few core assumptions are required to explain the data, together with knowledge about how empirical conditions map onto the assumptions. The relevant assumptions of fuzzy-trace theory are that verbatim and gist representations of experience are stored and retrieved independently, that these representations differ in specificity and in forgetting rates, and that forgetting consists of the disintegration of these representations (e.g., Reyna & Brainerd, 1992, 1995a; Reyna & Titcomb, 1997). These assumptions bring contradictory data, both the gist and verbatim aspects of memory, under one explanatory umbrella.

Most important, systematic theory leads to new and unexpected predictions. For example, the assumption that gist memories are forgotten more slowly than verbatim memories led to the counterintuitive prediction that false memories, based on gist, could be more persistent than true memories (based, at least in part, on labile verbatim memories). The mere-memory-testing effect showed that cuing false memories increases their acceptance on subsequent memory tests. According to fuzzy-trace theory, then, we can expect that repeatedly cuing gist memories, but failing to cue verbatim memories, will increase the tendency to accept those false memories on subsequent tests (Brainerd & Reyna, 1996; McDermott, 1996b; Payne et al., 1996; Roediger, Jacoby, & McDermott, 1996; Roediger & McDermott, 1995; Zaragoza & Mitchell, 1996). Thus, fuzzy-trace theory predicts and explains cue-repetition effects on false memories (Reyna, 1996b). Finally, fuzzy-trace theory predicts surprising interactions between social and cognitive factors, specifically, how social motivational factors can affect reliance on gist versus verbatim memories in different contexts (Davidson, 1995; Klaczynski & Fauth, 1997). In short, by emphasizing theoretical explanation, we can move beyond demonstrations and address the causal factors that underlie false memory.

REFERENCES

Ackerman, B. (1992). The sources of children's source errors in judging causal inferences. *Journal of Experimental Child Psychology, 54,* 90–119.

Beal, C. R. (1990). Development of knowledge about the role of inference in text comprehension. *Child Development, 61,* 1011–1023.

Belli, R. F., Lindsay, D. S., Gales, M. S., & McCarthy, T. T. (1994). Memory impairment and source misattribution in postevent misinformation experiments with short retention intervals. *Memory & Cognition, 21,* 40–54.

Brainerd, C .J. (1997). Children's forgetting, with implications for memory suggestibility. In N. L. Stein, P. A. Ornstein, B. Tversky, & C. J. Brainerd, (Eds.), *Memory for everyday and emotional events* (pp. 209-235). Mahwah, NJ: Lawrence Erlbaum Associates.

Brainerd, C. J, & Hill, D. (1997). Voices of children. [Review of the book, *Jeopardy in the Courtroom: A scientific analysis of children's testimony.*] *Contemporary Psychology, 42,* 7–11.

Brainerd, C. J., & Ornstein, P. A. (1991). Children's memory for witnessed events: The developmental backdrop. In J. Doris (Ed.), *The suggestibility of children's recollections* (pp. 10-20). Washington, DC: American Psychological Association.

Brainerd, C. J., & Reyna, V. F. (1992). Explaining "memory free" reasoning. *Psychological Science, 3,* 332–339.

Brainerd, C. J., & Reyna, V. F. (1993). Memory independence and memory interference in cognitive development. *Psychological Review, 100,* 42–67.

Brainerd, C. J., & Reyna, V. F. (1995). Autosuggestibility in memory development. *Cognitive Psychology, 28,* 65–101.

Brainerd, C. J., & Reyna, V. F. (1996). Mere memory testing creates false memories in children. *Developmental Psychology, 32,* 467–478.

Brainerd, C. J., Reyna, V. F., & Brandse, E. (1995). Are children's false memories more persistent than their true memories? *Psychological Science, 6,* 359–364.

Brainerd, C. J., Reyna, V. F., Howe, M. L., & Kingma, J. (1990). The development of forgetting and reminiscence. *Monographs of the Society for Research in Child Development, 53,* Nos. 3–4 (Serial No. 222).

Brainerd, C. J., Reyna, V. F., & Kneer, R. (1995). False-recognition reversal: When is similarity distinctive? *Journal of Memory and Language, 34,* 157–185.

Bransford, J. D., & Franks, J. J. (1971). The abstraction of linguistic ideas. *Cognitive Psychology, 2,* 331–380.

Ceci, S. J., & Bruck M. (1993). Suggestibility of the child witness: A historical review and synthesis. *Psychological Bulletin, 113,* 403–439.

Davidson, D. (1995). The representativeness heuristic and the conjunction fallacy effect in children's decision making. *Merrill Palmer Quarterly, 41,* 328–346.

Dempster, F. N. (1992). The rise and fall of the inhibitory mechanism: Toward a unified theory of cognitive development and aging. *Developmental Review, 12,* 45–75.

Gardiner, J. M., & Java, R. I. (1991). Forgetting in recognition memory with and without recollective experience. *Memory & Cognition, 19,* 617–623.

Hasher, L., & Griffin, M. (1978). Reconstructive and reproductive processes in memory. *Journal of Experimental Psychology: Human Learning and Memory, 4,* 318–330.

Klaczynski, P., & Fauth, J. (1997). Developmental differences in memory-based intrusions and self-serving statistical reasoning biases. *Merrill-Palmer Quarterly, 43,* 539–565.

Lindsay, D. S. (1990). Misleading suggestions can impair eyewitnesses' ability to remember event details. *Journal of Experimental Psychology: :earning, Memory, and Cognition, 16,* 1077–1083.

Lindsay, D. S., & Johnson, M. K. (1991). Recognition memory and source monitoring. *Bulletin of the Psychonomic Society, 29,* 203–205.

Loftus, E. F. (1995). Memory malleability: Constructivist and fuzzy-trace explanations. *Learning and Individual Differences, 7,* 133–137.

Loftus, E. F., & Hoffman, H. G. (1989). Misinformation in memory: The creation of new memories. *Journal of Experimental Psychology: General, 118,* 100–104.

Loftus, E. F., & Ketcham, K. (1994). *The myth of repressed memory: False memories and allegations of sexual abuse.* New York: St. Martin's Press.

McDermott, K. B. (1996a). The persistence of false memories in list recall. *Journal of Memory and Language, 35,* 212–230.

McDermott, K.B. (1996b, November). *Testing enhances the illusion of remembering.* Poster presentation at the 37th annual meeting of the Psychonomic Society, Chicago.

Paris, S. G., & Carter, A. Y. (1973). Semantic and constructive aspects of sentence memory in children. *Developmental Psychology, 9,* 109–113.

Payne, D. G., Elie, C. J., Blackwell, J. M., Neuschatz, J. (1996). Memory illusions: Recalling, recognizing, and recollecting events that never occurred. *Journal of Memory and Language, 35,* 261–285.

Poole, D. A., & Lindsay, D. S. (1995). Interviewing preschoolers: Effects of nonsuggestive techniques, parental coaching, and leading questions on reports of nonexperienced events. *Journal of Experimental Child Psychology, 60,* 129–154.

Poole, D. A., & White, L. T. (1991). Effects of question repetition on the eyewitness testimony of children and adults. *Developmental Psychology, 27,* 975–986.

Poole, D. A., & White, L. T. (1993). Two years later: Effects of question repetition and retention interval on the eyewitness testimony of children and adults. *Developmental Psychology, 29,* 844–853.

Poole, D. A., & White, L. T. (1995). Tell me again and again: Stability and change in the repeated testimonies of children and adults. In M. Zaragoza, J. R. Graham, G. N. N. Hall, R. Hirschman, & Y. S. Ben-Porath, (Eds.), *Memory, suggestibility, and eyewitness testimony in children and adults* (pp. 24–43). Thousand Oaks, CA: Sage.

Reyna, V. F. (1992). Reasoning, remembering, and their relationship: Social, cognitive, and developmental issues. In M. L. Howe, C. J. Brainerd, & V. Reyna (Eds.), *Development of long-term retention* (pp. 103–127). New York: Springer-Verlag.

Reyna, V. F. (1995). Interference effects in memory and reasoning: A fuzzy-trace theory analysis. In F. N. Dempster & C. J. Brainerd (Eds.), *Interference and inhibition in cognition* (pp. 29–59). San Diego, CA: Academic Press.

Reyna, V. F. (1996b, November). *Repetition dissociates verbatim and gist memory for narratives.* Paper presented at the annual meeting of the Psychonomic Society, Chicago.

Reyna, V. F. (1996a). Meaning, memory and the interpretation of metaphors. In J. Mio & A. Katz (Eds.), *Metaphor: Implications and applications,* (pp. 39–57, Mahwah, NJ: Lawrenwce Erlbaum Associates.

Reyna, V. F., & Brainerd, C. J. (1992). A fuzzy-trace theory of reasoning and remembering: Paradoxes, patterns, and parallelism. In A. F. Healy, S. M. Kosslyn, & R. M. Shiffrin (Eds.), *From learning processes to cognitive processes: Essays in honor of William K. Estes* (pp. 235–259). Hillsdale, NJ: Lawrence Erlbaum Associates.

Reyna, V. F., & Brainerd, C. J. (1995a). Fuzzy-trace theory: An interim synthesis. *Learning and Individual Differences, 7,* 1–75.

Reyna, V. F., & Brainerd, C. J. (1995b). Fuzzy-trace theory: Some foundational issues. *Learning and Individual Differences, 7,* 145–162.

Reyna, V. F., & Kiernan, B. (1994). The development of gist versus verbatim memory in sentence recognition: Effects of lexical familiarity, semantic content, encoding instructions, and retention interval. *Developmental Psychology, 30,* 178–191.

Reyna, V. F., & Kiernan, B. (1995). Children's memory and metaphorical interpretation. *Metaphor and Symbolic Activity, 10,* 309–331.

Reyna, V. F., & Lloyd, F. (1997). Theories of false memory in children and adults. *Learning and Individual Differences, 9,* 95–123.

Reyna, V. F., & Titcomb, A. L. (1997). Constraints on the suggestibility of eyewitness testimony: A fuzzy-trace theory analysis. In D. G. Payne & F. G. Conrad (Eds.), *Intersections in basic and applied memory research,* (pp. 157–174). Mahwah, NJ: Lawrence Erlbaum Associates.

Roediger, H. L. III, Jacoby, J. D., & McDermott, K. B. (1996). Misinformation effects in recall: Creating false memories through repeated retrieval. *Journal of Memory and Language, 35,* 300–318.

Roediger, H. L. III, & McDermott, K. B. (1995). Creating false memories: Remembering words not presented in lists. *Journal of Experimental Psychology: Learning, Memory, and Cognition, 21,* 803–814.

Schacter, D. L. (1995). Memory distortion: History and current status. In D. L. Schacter, J. T. Coyle, G. D. Fischbach, M. M. Mesulam, & L. E. Sullivan (Eds.), *Memory distortion: How minds, brains, and societies reconstruct the past* (pp. 1–43). Cambridge, MA: Harvard University Press.

Schacter, D. L., Verfaellie, M., & Pradere, D. (1996). The neuropsychology of memory illusions: False recall and recognition in amnesiac patients. *Journal of Memory and Language, 35,* 319–334.

Schneider, W., & Bjorklund, D. F. (1998). Memory. In D. Kuhn & R. S. Siegler (Eds.), *Handbook of child psychology: Cognitive perception and language* (Vol. 2; pp. 467–521). New York: Wiley.

Schwartz, B., & Reisberg, D. (1991). *Learning and memory*. New York: Norton.

Siegler, R. S. (1991). *Children's thinking*. Englewood Cliffs, NJ: Prentice-Hall.

Titcomb, A. L., & Reyna, V. F. (1995). Memory interference and misinformation effects. In F. N. Dempster & C. J. Brainerd (Eds.), *Interference and inhibition in cognition* (pp. 263–294). San Diego, CA: Academic Press.

Warren, A., Hulse-Trotter, K., & Tubbs, E. C. (1991). Inducing resistance to suggestibility in children. *Law and Human Behavior, 15,* 273–285.

Warren, A. R., & Lane, P. L. (1995). Effects of timing and type of questioning on eyewitness accuracy and suggestibility. In M. Zaragoza, J. R. Graham, G. N. N. Hall, R. Hirschman, & Y. S. Ben-Porath, (Eds.), *Memory, suggestibility, and eyewitness testimony in children and adults* (pp. 44–60). Thousand Oaks, CA: Sage.

Zaragoza, M., & Mitchell, K. J. (1996). Repeated exposure to suggestion and the creation of false memories. *Psychological Science, 7,* 294–300.

3

A Study of Face Identification:
Are People Looking Beyond Disguises?

Mary Ann Foley
Hugh J. Foley
Skidmore College

Object recognition is often quite good even under conditions of incomplete visual information (e.g., when portions of the objects are deleted or occluded from view). Nonetheless, people are confused about the way they actually saw objects, often reporting that incomplete objects were seen as complete. In this chapter, we focus on the basis of this confusion, using new research on face identification as a case in point. This line of research points to the activation of imaginal filling-in processes, a form of closure, as a mediating mechanism for object recognition under conditions of partial viewing. Implications of this line of research for theories about developmental differences in face identification and for approaches to the assessment of eyewitness identification are considered.

On many occasions, the perception of an object is incomplete because portions of the object are occluded. Whether attempting to read a sign partially occluded by the branches of a tree, or to find a friend in a busy train station, people are able to accomplish their goals remarkably well. Similarly, catching glimpses of perpetrators dashing from the scene of accidents or crimes often involves viewing conditions that are visually incomplete. In these instances, face identification can be difficult, particularly when deliberate attempts are made by the perpetrators to disguise themselves.   How are people able to identify objects or faces under conditions of incomplete visual information?

Several explanations suggest mechanisms for how these identification processes might be accomplished (e.g., Bruce & Humphreys, 1994; Snodgrass & Feenan, 1990), but one of particular interest to us invokes the activation of closure processes. From this point of view, people are described as filling in missing visual information in their mind's eye, closing missing lines to render visually incomplete forms as complete (Gollin, 1962; Hearst, 1991; Leeper, 1935; Murray & Kennison, 1989; Ramachandran, 1992; Snodgrass & Feenan, 1990; Snodgrass & Surprenant, 1989).   In picture-fragmentation tasks, for example, when people are shown a series of pictures of incomplete objects that are made increasingly complete, they are able to identify these objects before the final, complete version is presented (e.g., Gollin, 1962; Snodgrass & Feenan, 1990). Similarly, in priming tasks, incomplete pictures of objects, including those created by occlusion, are effective for priming the targets (Sekuler & Palmer, 1992; Sekuler, Palmer, & Flynn, 1994). Performance on both picture-fragmentation and priming tasks of this sort is thought to be mediated by filling-in closure processes (Sekuler et al., 1994; Snodgrass & Feenan, 1990).

IMPLICIT IMAGINAL PROCESSING: ANY EVIDENCE?

But is there any direct evidence suggesting that what mediates such performance here is some sort of imaginal filling-in process?   Studies of source monitoring do suggest that information about imaginal processing is represented in memories and serves as a cue for source-monitoring judgments. For example, when orienting tasks involve explicit requests to generate images of objects presented as pictures or words, both adults and children are quite good at remembering the way in which the information was originally presented (Foley, Durso, Wilder, & Friedman, 1991). They experience little confusion when asked to remember whether an item had been previously presented as a picture or a word (Foley et al., 1991). According to the source-monitoring framework, cognitive operations that accompanied the deliberate creation of the images in response to the presentation of words are represented in memories for the words. Later, these cues help people distinguish between pictures and words.   Evidence for the role of these kinds of operations in source monitoring is also observed in contexts involving anagram solving and word-association tasks (e.g. Johnson, Hashtroudi, & Lindsay, 1993; Johnson, Raye, Foley, & Foley, 1981).

More important for present purposes, studies of source monitoring also suggest that implicit imaginal processing occurs under some viewing conditions, and its occurrence leads to subsequent memory confusions. When asked to describe the function of objects presented as pictures or words, for example, adults and children subsequently report that they had seen pictures of objects when the items had actually been presented as words (Foley et al., 1991). This increase in confusion after describing the function of objects leads to a reduction in source-monitoring performance relative to situations in which orienting tasks involve explicit requests to generate images. On average, performance is 70% versus 90% for the two kinds of orienting tasks, respectively. This reduction in performance is interpreted as evidence that words automatically elicited images of the objects to which they referred in the function condition, and these images were later misremembered as presented pictures (Durso & Johnson, 1980; Foley et al., 1991). In these cases, imaginal activations occurred in the absence of pictorial referents. Indeed, the results of a number of studies of source monitoring support the conclusion that a mental image may be mistaken for a perception, particularly when the image is elicited in a relatively automatic fashion (e.g., Finke, Johnson, & Shyi, 1988; Johnson, 1991, in press; Johnson, Foley, & Leach, 1988; Johnson, Foley, Suengas, & Raye, 1988; Johnson et al., 1993; Johnson, Raye, Foley, & Kim, 1982; Kimer, Foley, & Quiros, 1996; Markham & Hynes, 1993).

IMPLICIT IMAGINAL PROCESSING:
A MECHANISM FOR CLOSURE?

If implicit imaginal processing is evoked in the absence of pictorial referents, it might also be expected to occur in response to the presence of incomplete pictorial information. In the presence of incomplete visual information, people may fill in the information that is missing from incomplete pictures, seeing completed images in their mind's eye. This line of reasoning leads to a specific prediction about the direction of source monitoring errors. If people are filling in missing visual information, then, when later asked to report how they had seen pictures originally, they should be likely to report that incomplete pictures were presented as complete rather than the reverse.

In a new series of studies, we tested this possibility by using a variation of a source-monitoring task to index potential confusion (Foley, Foley, Durso, & Smith, 1997). In all of our studies in this series, participants experienced two kinds of visual information, that is, pictures of readily identifiable objects presented either in complete or incomplete form. After responding to these pictures (e.g., describing the functions of objects portrayed in the pictures), people were surprised by requests to report on the way in which they experienced the pictures originally (either in complete or incomplete form). Indeed, when we asked participants to remember the way in which they saw pictures initially, they experienced confusion, claiming incomplete pictures were presented as complete, rather than the reverse (Foley et al., 1997). This bias to report complete is robust, observed across a range of visual materials (e.g., visually simple and visually complex pictures) and orienting tasks (e.g., describing objects' functions, rating faces for their distinctiveness, rating faces for their resemblance to familiar persons).

In our initial studies, incomplete pictures were created explicitly by deleting the left or right half of the pictures. We wondered whether a similar bias would be observed when incomplete pictorial information was created more naturalistically, by occluding objects by other objects. We considered this question in the context of search tasks. Adult participants were asked to locate pictures of objects embedded in complex scenes. Whether asked to search for several pictures embedded in one complex scene (Foley et al., 1997) or to search for pictures of objects, each embedded in a different scene (Foley, Korenman, & Foley, 1998), adults were more likely to claim they experienced the incomplete pictures as complete rather than the reverse when locating them in the scenes. Thus, in these hidden-picture tasks, people seem to look beyond the occluding objects in the scenes, representing the targets as visually complete.

We have eliminated several alternative explanations for this bias to claim incomplete pictures were presented as complete, showing that the bias is not simply an index of poor memory. That is, recognition was comparable and generally good for both complete and incomplete pictures. A number of other findings weaken the persuasiveness of the second alternative that the bias is an expression of a more general response bias to say complete. First, the bias was only evident when pictorial renderings of familiar objects looked like the kinds of renderings we typically experience for these referents (Snodgrass & Vanderwart, 1980). Furthermore, the bias was not observed when people mistakenly claimed a new picture was one they saw before, nor when a naming task preceded the source-monitoring test (Foley et al., 1997). Finally, and perhaps most important, the bias to report complete was not more pronounced when test items were all completed pictures. In all of the studies reported in our first series, the test items were presented as words. But, in a new study, after seeing pictures of complete and incomplete pictures, during test the participants were shown pictures, all of which were complete in form. The bias to report complete was comparable in magnitude to that reported previously (Foley, Foley, & Smith, 1998).

In sum, the evidence from our first series of studies is strong in its suggestion that implicit imaginal processing occurs in response to the presentation of incomplete pictorial information, with people filling in missing information in thought. And, this occurrence subsequently leads people to mistakenly claim they saw complete pictorial information when, in fact, they did not.

FACE IDENTIFICATION:
ARE PEOPLE LOOKING BEYOND DISGUISES?

Findings in the face identification literature suggest that similar filling-in processes might also be at work when people view incomplete pictures of faces. In priming tasks, for example, partial photographs of unfamiliar faces are effective primes whether the portions deleted are internal or external portions of the faces (Brunas, Young, & Ellis, 1990). These priming effects suggest that the incomplete pictures of faces may activate more complete representations for the faces (e.g., Brunas et al., 1990; Sekuler et al., 1994), leading us to expect that people might claim incomplete pictures of faces were presented complete in form.

To test this idea, we showed undergraduates photographs of faces of men and women (Foley et al., 1997). All of the faces were presented from the frontal perspective, but half were incomplete in form. Incomplete photographs were created by deleting the left or right half of the faces. Initially, participants made judgments about each face, indicating whether each was distinctive, had a distinctive feature, or resembled someone they knew. On a surprise source-monitoring task, participants were more likely to claim an incomplete face was originally viewed in its complete form, independent of the way in which the faces were processed originally, replicating our findings for pictures of objects. This bias suggests that people were completing incomplete faces in their mind's eye during the encoding task, later misclassifying their memory for the completed image as a memory for a photograph (Foley et al., 1997). In this study of face identification, the removal of half of each of the faces was clearly intentional on the part of the experimenter. But what happens under more naturalistic viewing conditions? We are often asked to identify unfamiliar faces under conditions of partial viewing. We may catch a glimpse of what someone looks like as she dashes across our field of view, showing only one side of her face. Or we may be asked to help locate a guest speaker in a crowded airport, with many other faces and objects partially occluding our view. Of course, the guest speaker may also be bundled up with a warm hat, heavy scarf and sunglasses, concealing portions of his face.

The literature on face identification includes many variations of the study of incomplete visual information. For example, the effects on face identification of the deletion of facial features have clearly been identified by comparisons of consequences of removing internal (eyes, nose, and mouth) or external (hairline, chin) facial features (Brunas et al., 1990; Campbell, Walker, & Baron-Cohen, 1995). Similarly, the effects of the addition (or deletion) of features that might function as disguises (e.g., beards, eyeglasses, mustaches, hats) have also been studied. The addition or deletion of paraphernalia associated with faces such as hats, eye glasses, and scarves as well as changes in perspective detract from recognition performance (e.g., Bruce, 1982, 1988; Bruce & Humphreys, 1994; Bruce & Young, 1986; Ellis, 1992; Patterson & Baddeley, 1977), and the disruptive effects of these sorts of features are not comparable (e.g., McKelvie, 1993; Patterson & Baddeley, 1977; Terry, 1994). Further, the presence of full-face masking diminishes performance as well (e.g., Costen, Shepherd, Ellis, & Craw, 1994; Davies & Flin, 1984).

When explaining the ways in which adults recognize faces in these sorts of situations, investigators often invoke explanations based on holistic or configurational processing. Two versions of configurational processing are currently attracting the attention of such researchers, namely, first- and second-order configurational processing (e.g., Carey, 1992; Carey & Diamond, 1977, 1994; Chung & Thomson, 1995; Diamond & Carey, 1977; Rhodes & Tremewan, 1994; Tanaka & Farah, 1993). First-order configurational processing involves the abstraction of holistic or gestalt-like representations for faces (Carey, 1992; Tanaka & Farah, 1993). From this perspective, when faces are partially concealed by disguises, adults are thought to abstract holistic or gestalt-like representations. Second-order configurational processing is more precise in nature, suggesting that adults notice relationships among features that are relatively invariant (e.g., "large wide-set eyes for such a long narrow face," Diamond & Carey, 1986, p. 108). Some investigators have suggested that first-order and second-order configurational processes represent perceptually based and cognitively based encoding, respectively (Carey, 1992; Ellis, 1992), but the independent contributions of these two kinds of processes to face identification remain to be specified (e.g., Carey & Diamond, 1994; Chung & Thomson, 1995).

What intrigues us about explanations invoking configurational processing, however, is their suggestion that adults may look beyond surface features associated with faces. If adults are processing faces configurationally, it suggests that they are looking beyond disguises to see whole faces (or seeing relationships among features) partially covered by facial disguises. This looking beyond to see the shape of the face (or relations among its features) may well be mediated by closure processes. From our point of view, some facial features (e.g., beards, mustaches) or other features attached to faces (e.g., large floppy hats, scarves) represent a special group of occluders. We know that these kinds of occluders affect adults' face identification, but we actually know very little about adults' specific memory for the presence (or removal) of these occluders. Would adults remember the ways in which they originally saw faces (e.g., noticing the face now is complete? Noticing the face is disguised by a different set of features?) The bias to claim incomplete faces were presented as complete in form is at least consistent with the prediction that adults may not remember the exact way in which they experienced faces. If presented with a partially covered face the second time they see a picture, would they notice the change in presentation mode? The answers to these kinds of questions should inform our theories of face identification, but, equally important, they should also inform the ways in which we guide witnesses in the process of facial reconstructions for perpetrators. We are exploring these questions in a new series of studies on face identification, one of which we report in this chapter.

For the most part, when incomplete information is presented either during encoding or test (e.g., by deleting portions of faces), researchers are interested in the effects on recognition of these kinds of variations (Bruce & Humphreys, 1994; Faw, 1992; Hole, 1994; Shapiro & Penrod, 1986). In the context of traditional recognition paradigms, people report "yes" or "no" to indicate whether they think they saw a face before or not. In the context of forced-choice recognition paradigms, people choose among a few alternatives to indicate the face they saw previously (e.g., Faw, 1992; Matthews, 1978). When researchers go beyond simple questions of recognition to ask people for more precise information (e.g., "Does this face look the same or different as it did the first time you saw it?") face identification may improve (e.g., Pezdek & Chen, 1982; Reynolds & Pezdek, 1992). However, in the small number of studies that have asked people to make these kinds of precise judgments, often people see only the original set of faces, without new faces serving as distractors, making it difficult to interpret the basis for their performance.

FACE IDENTIFICATION: DO PEOPLE LOOK BEYOND DISGUISES?

In our new studies of the effects of disguise, adults saw unfamiliar computer-generated faces (Mac-a-Mug). The faces were presented in full frontal view or they were partially covered by disguises. After completing an orienting task in which participants estimated the extent to which each face was criminal looking, they were surprised by a source-monitoring test. At test, some faces were experienced in the same way as they were originally seen, but others were changed. Some faces that were presented in full view were partially concealed at test. Some faces that were partially concealed initially were uncovered at test. On the source-monitoring test, people were asked whether each test face was a face they had seen earlier in the session. When they reported that they had seen a face during the encoding phase, participants were asked whether the face looked the same or different from the way it had looked the first time they saw it. In the study we report here, if a face was disguised at encoding and at test, the specific occluders remained unchanged from encoding to test (e.g., the same eyeglasses were used at presentation and test).

If adults are looking beyond disguises, what kind of source-monitoring performance might we expect? If they initially see unfamiliar faces, some disguised and some not, they should later be confused about the ways in which they originally experienced those faces. Furthermore, confusion should be greater for faces that were initially disguised, independent of the way the faces were presented at test. The logic underlying this prediction is that when presented with a disguised face initially, if adults look beyond the disguises, they should encode the face holistically. When later presented with an undisguised version of the face at test, presumably this face will resemble the memory representation for the original version that they saw. This resemblance could lead adults to report "the face looks the same as it did earlier," an incorrect response. This kind of error would reduce source-monitoring performance. Along similar lines, if presented with the same disguised face at test, if its memory representation does not include the disguise, adults should report "it looks different," an incorrect response, again leading to a reduction in source-monitoring performance. For undisguised faces, we would also expect some source-monitoring confusion, with people making mistakes about whether faces look the same or different. We know that recognition for photographs or composites of unfamiliar faces is not particularly good (e.g., Faw, 1992). Thus, we would not expect particularly good recognition of faces in this study, nor would we expect excellent source-monitoring performance. But because the representations for undisguised faces seen at test would resemble the original versions adults actually saw, there should be less confusion about the way in which undisguised faces were viewed initially, producing better source-monitoring scores for these types of faces. In contrast, if features serving as disguises are encoded as part of the memory representations for faces, then when participants see the same face twice, disguised in an identical manner, source monitoring should be quite good. The study we report in this chapter is a preliminary test of these possibilities.

Method

Participants. Forty-eight college-age adults attending Skidmore College participated in this study, each receiving credit toward the completion of course requirements for their introductory psychology classes.

Materials. Eighty composite faces were created using Mac-a-Mug Pro software. The composite faces were created in various ways, combining six kinds of facial features (eyes, nose, chin, mouth, hair, and ears) along with nonfacial features (mustaches, beards, glasses, and hats). Except for repeating the use of a few of the noses and ears available in the software package, the facial features selected were unique to each composite face. For each composite face, two versions were constructed, that is, full view (undisguised) or partially concealed by secondary facial features (e.g., moustache, beard) and/or nonfacial features (e.g., eyeglasses, hats). Partially concealed versions were disguised by either one or two features. Examples are shown in Fig. 3.1.

Forty of the 80 composite faces, along with 4 practice items, were included in the first part of the session. All 40 composite faces were presented from the frontal perspective, but half were partially concealed by facial disguises. Of the 20 partially covered composite faces, 10 were minimally concealed (i.e., covered partially by one additional feature) and 10 were more fully concealed (i.e., covered partially by two features). Each version of the composite faces was presented equally often across participants.

For the test phase, these 40 composite faces were randomly presented along with 40 new composite faces (half of which were partially concealed). Of the 40 original composite faces, 20 were presented in exactly the same way in which they were presented previously. Twenty other original composite faces were presented differently. Of the 10 faces that were originally presented in full view, 5 were now partially covered by one feature and 5 were partially covered by two. For the remaining 10 faces that were originally experienced partially covered by one or two features, all 10 were now presented undisguised. For the 40 distractors, half were disguised. Of the 20 disguised distractor faces, 10 were partially covered by one feature and 10 were partially covered by two. Virtually none of the features on the distractor faces had been used to partially conceal the target faces.

Apparatus. A Macintosh Quadra 800 computer running Super Lab software presented the composite faces and recorded responses.

Procedure. Undergraduates were initially told that the purpose of the experiment was to create a set of norms for composite faces to express impressions of criminality. They were asked to use a 7-point scale to rate the extent to which each composite face looked like a criminal face, with higher ratings indicating greater criminality. The rating task was self-paced, and both the ratings and time to respond were recorded automatically. During a 5-minute retention interval, participants were then asked to search for number series embedded in a complex array of numbers. Finally, they were surprised with the source-monitoring task. They were shown 80 test composite faces, and asked to indicate whether or not each face was one they had seen earlier in the session. For those faces classified as previously presented, participants were also asked whether they looked the same or different from the way in which the faces looked originally.

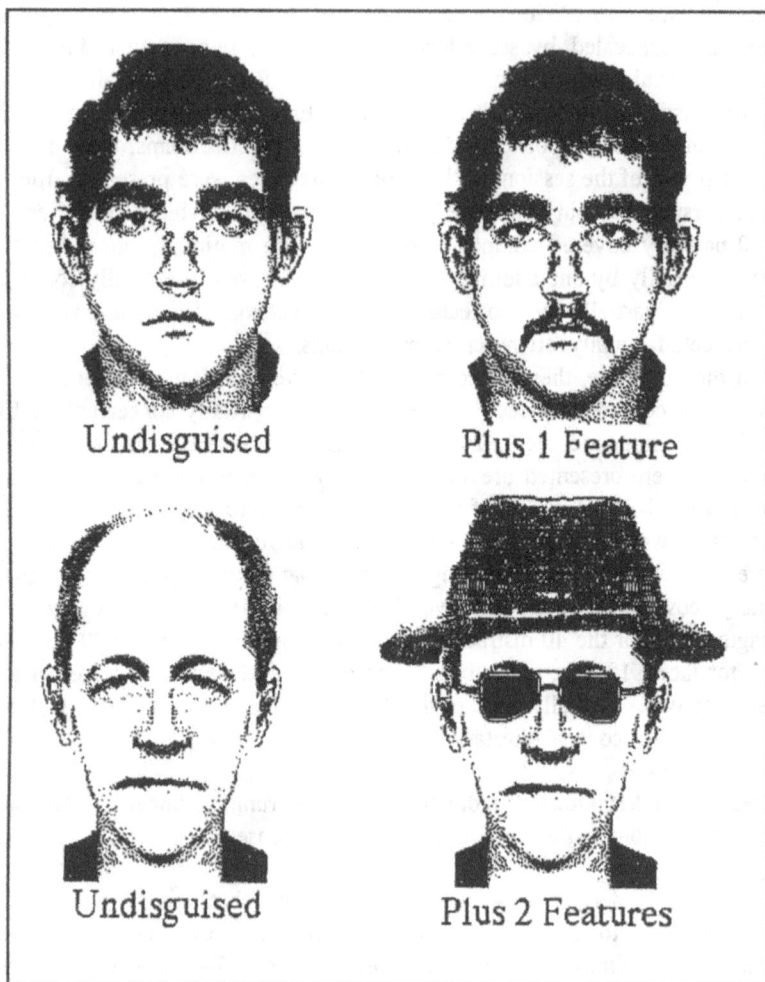

Fig. 3.1. Examples of composite faces.

Results and Discussion

Source-Monitoring Performance. Responses on the source-monitoring tests were assessed by computing a proportion, that is, the number of targets whose presentation/test combination was correctly classified (i.e., as same or different) divided by the number recognized as old. For example, when faces were presented as undisguised during encoding, the numerator for the source-monitoring score was the number of undisguised faces correctly called same if they were presented the same way at encoding and test or the number correctly called different if their presentation was changed at test. The denominator in each of these examples was the number of undisguised faces recognized as old (whether classified as same or different in terms of encoding/test match). An analysis of variance was calculated on these scores, including as factors Presentation Mode at Encoding (Full view vs. Disguised) and Presentation Mode at Test (Full view vs. Disguised).

As shown in Table 3.1, participants were confused about the way in which they originally saw the faces, producing relatively low source-monitoring scores. This pattern produced a significant main effect for Mode of Presentation at Encoding, but no other effects were significant. The source-monitoring scores were significantly lower for faces that were originally disguised ($M = .51$) than for those that were not ($M = .72$), independent of the way the faces were presented at test. In fact, performance was close to chance for composite faces originally seen as disguised. As the analysis on recognition will show, however, this poor source-monitoring performance is not simply a reflection of poor memory for the faces. As mentioned earlier, disguised faces were partially covered by either one or a few features. For disguised faces only, source-monitoring performance was worse for maximally disguised faces ($M = .40$) than for minimally disguised ones ($M = .58$), independent of the way in which faces were presented at test.

Recognition of Faces. The source-monitoring test was rescored to create a measure of recognition, that is, the proportion of faces correctly recognized as target composite faces, ignoring whether or not they were correctly classified as looking the same or different. In an analysis including Presentation Mode at Encoding (Full view vs. Disguised) and Presentation Mode at Test (Full view vs. Disguised), three effects were significant. There was a main effect for Mode at Encoding, a main effect for Mode at Test, and a significant interaction. Subsequent tests showed that if the version of the faces participants saw the second time was the same as the version they saw initially, participants were equally good at recognizing undisguised and disguised faces ($Ms = .84$ and $.80$, respectively). However, recognition was hurt when faces were changed to look different at test, particularly when they were originally experienced as undisguised, consistent with a previous finding (e.g., Carey & Diamond, 1977). These findings are summarized in Table 3.2. Our results for recognition of target faces replicate previous effects on recognition memory, showing a decrement in performance when the way in which faces are presented at test differs from the way in which they were

TABLE 3.1

Proportion of Faces Correctly Classified as Looking Same or Different
at Encoding and Test (Source Monitoring Performance)

	Presentation Mode at Test	
	Same	Changed
Presentation Mode at Encoding		
Face in Full View	.68	.76
Face Disguised (in Partial View)	.49	.53

presented initially (e.g., Carey & Diamond, 1977; Davies & Flin, 1984; Patterson & Baddeley, 1977). Interestingly, although the source-monitoring scores were lower for faces covered by more than one disguise, the proportion of hits was equivalent for faces covered by one or more disguises (.82 and .86, respectively).

Could our source-monitoring results simply reflect poor recognition memory for disguised faces? This seems highly unlikely because recognition of both disguised and undisguised faces was relatively good if the faces were experienced in the same way during encoding and test (about 80%, see Table 3.2). Furthermore, although recognition performance was comparable for faces experienced in the same way at encoding and test (whether or not the faces were disguised initially, about 82%, see Table 3.2), people were particularly confused about the way in which they had seen the disguised faces, producing low source-monitoring scores for these faces compared to those that were not disguised (see Table 3.1 again).

Do the recognition data suggest that adults are processing faces configurationally? If adults do process faces in this manner, should we expect recognition performance to be comparable independent of the versions seen at encoding and test? We think not. If people strip away the facial coverings in their mind's eye, they should be seeing undisguised faces even when disguised. But when those unfamiliar faces were initially disguised, the versions people saw in their mind's eye (e.g., the relation between the eyes and nose) may have differed from the version actually partially covered by disguises. Thus, at least some of the undisguised faces they see at test may not match the faces they saw when stripping away the partial coverings. In this case, then, recognition performance should be particularly reduced for disguised faces

TABLE 3.2
Proportion of Faces Correctly Recognized as Seen During Encoding
(Without Regard for Correctness of Classification
as Looking the Same/Different)

| | Presentation Mode at Test | |
	Same	Changed
Presentation Mode at Encoding		
Face in full view	.84	.55
Face disguised (in partial view)	.80	.71

undisguised at test. And, this was indeed the case (see Table 3.2). A similar pattern was also reported by Davies and Flin (1984) who examined the effects of stocking masks on face identification. Of course, if the faces were familiar, we would expect this pattern to change considerably.

Recognition of New Faces: False Positives. Responses to new faces serving as distractors are important because they provide guidance in the interpretation of source-monitoring performance. In our previous studies, responses to new items provided convincing evidence that the bias to call an incomplete picture complete was not a general response bias to say complete. When misclassifying new objects as old, adults were more likely to report incomplete if any bias was observed (Foley et al., 1997).

In the present study, responses to new faces misidentified as old were analyzed in a similar way to see if there was any bias to report "looks the same" or "looks different." In an analysis of variance including Mode of Presentation of New Faces (Disguised or not) and Type of Response Error (Same vs. Different), participants were more likely to say a new face looked different if it was misrecognized as old than they were to say it looked the same. This bias was more pronounced for new faces that were partially disguised, producing an interaction between Mode of Presentation at Test and Type of Response Error. These results are summarized in Table 3.3. Notably, the same tendency to say "different" more often than "same" was not evident in the source-monitoring errors on old faces. Had such a bias been present, then source-monitoring performance on faces presented differently at encoding and test would have appeared to be better because the bias to say "different" would have inflated performance. But this was not the case.

TABLE 3.3
Proportion of New Faces Incorrectly Classified as Seen During Encoding

	Mode at Test	
	Disguised	Not Disguised
Type of Response Error		
"Saw and looks the same"	.04	.14
"Saw but looks different"	.38	.24

GENERAL DISCUSSION

The results of our new study of face identification are intriguing because they suggest that people are looking beyond disguises when processing faces—expressing confusion later when asked to remember the ways in which they saw those faces. In particular, they were more confused about disguised faces than undisguised ones, producing lower source-monitoring scores for disguised faces, independent of the way in which faces were presented at test. This pattern suggests that adults may have represented disguised faces without the occluding disguises. This line of work should help inform our choices among theoretical explanations for face identification. If people are looking beyond disguises when processing faces, what are they seeing? As we suggested earlier, two possibilities can be gleaned from the face identification literature. Adults may be seeing gestalt-like representations for the shapes of the faces, generating first-order configurations, or they may be seeing relations among features of faces (e.g., the eyes in relation to the nose and mouth), generating second-order configurations (Carey & Diamond, 1994; Chung & Thomson, 1995; Tanaka & Farah, 1993). The present study does not allow us to choose between these alternative versions of configurational processing, nor was it intended to do so. However, the study does suggest that the source-monitoring framework is a promising heuristic for exploring the bases of configurational processing. Because the representations resulting from configurational processing have not been fully specified, this is a worthy direction for future research. Currently, with several of our students, we are examining the effects on source monitoring of changes in disguise from encoding to test, rather than simple addition or deletion of disguise from encoding to test. Simultaneously, we are looking to see if the nature of the object serving as the occluder (e.g., floppy hat covering the side of a face, or a magazine functioning in the same manner) affects performance.   If adults are indeed processing faces configurationally, they should be less sensitive than children to the type of occluder (e.g., kind of hat, kind of magazine).

The logic guiding our face identification studies also points to a provocative speculation about the basis for developmental differences in face identification. Developmental differences in the identification of unfamiliar faces are striking (Carey, 1981; 1992; Carey & Diamond, 1977, 1994; Carey, Diamond & Woods, 1980; Chance, Goldstein, & Schict, 1967; Diamond & Carey, 1977; Ellis, 1990, 1992; Ellis, Ellis, & Hosie, 1993; Ellis, Shepherd, & Davies, 1979; Flin & Dziurawiec, 1989).   One explanation for these developmental differences posits encoding shifts with age, with children processing faces in a piece-meal fashion initially and shifting to configurational processing around 10 years of age (Carey & Diamond, 1977, 1994; Chung & Thomson, 1995; Diamond & Carey, 1977; Flin, 1985). Thus, young children are thought to focus on facial features, noticing details like bushy eyebrows (pieces of the face) rather than abstracting more configurational characteristics like "large wide-set eyes for such a long, narrow face" (Diamond & Carey, 1986, p. 108). Older children and adults, on the other hand, are thought to be better at identifying faces concealed by disguises because they are able to see beyond the disguises, abstracting representations for complete faces. Whether young children are incapable of configurational processing or are less likely than older individuals to process faces in this way is still a matter of some debate (Carey & Diamond, 1994; Chung & Thomson, 1995).   In either case, if young children are indeed less likely to process faces configurationally, they may actually be less confused about the way in which they originally saw pictures of faces—especially when the target face is occluded with the same distinctive disguise at test. We are currently exploring this possibility in two new developmental studies (Foley, Foley, & Cormier, 1998).

Finally, the practical import of the line of work we report here should not go unnoticed. The discrepancy is often striking between what a perpetrator actually looks like once arrested and the composite faces circulated to attempt to find this person. These composite faces are reconstructed from people's reports of what perpetrators looked like or from their own selection of facial features available in reconstructive kits for representing faces. When people are asked to process faces by focusing on specific features (e.g., the size of noses), they are better able to provide accurate descriptions of these faces, but if asked to identify faces previously seen, this advantage is not observed (Wells & Turtle, 1989). In the latter context, people are better able to identify faces if they have first processed those faces configurationally (e.g., indicating whether a face looks like that of an honest person; Wells & Turtle, 1989). Could the very process of reconstructing faces contribute to the failure in the identification process, particularly when reconstructed faces include baseball caps and dark glasses? When asked to choose between two uncovered faces, one of which was originally seen and one of which is the reconstructed composite (without the occluders), will people pick the person who they actually saw? Does the collaborative nature of the reconstructive process also bear on the quality of the identification process? Answers to these kinds of questions should lead to a clearer understanding of the specific kinds of information that people remember about unfamiliar faces. Recommendations for designing effective techniques for face reconstruction should follow as well.

REFERENCES

Bruce, V. (1982). Changing faces: Visual and non visual coding processes in face recognition. *British Journal of Psychology, 73,* 105–116.

Bruce, V. (1988). *Recognizing faces.* Hove, UK: Lawrence Erlbaum Associates.

Bruce, V., & Humphreys, G.W. (Eds.). (1994). *Object and face recognition.* Hillsdale, NJ: Lawrence Erlbaum Associates.

Bruce, V., & Young, A. (1986). Understanding face recognition. *British Journal of Psychology, 77,* 305–327.

Brunas, J., Young, A. W., & Ellis, A. W. (1990). Repetition priming from incomplete faces: Evidence for part to whole completion. *British Journal of Psychology, 81,* 43–56.

Campbell, R., Walker, J., & Baron-Cohen, S. (1995). The development of differential use of inner and outer face features in familiar face identification. *Journal of Experimental Child Psychology, 59,* 196–210.

Carey, S. (1981). The development of face perception. In G. Davies, H. Ellis, & J. Shepherd (Eds.) *Perceiving and recognizing faces* (pp. 9–38). New York: Academic Press.

Carey, S. (1992). Becoming a face expert. *Philosophical transactions of the Royal Society of London, Series B, 335,* 95–103.

Carey, S., & Diamond, R. (1977). From piecemeal to configurational representation of faces. *Science, 195,* 312–314.

Carey, S., & Diamond, R. (1994). Are faces perceived as configurations more by adults than by children? *Visual Cognition, 1,* 253–274.

Carey, S., Diamond, R., & Woods, B. (1980). The development of face recognition: A maturational component? *Developmental Psychology, 16,* 257–269.

Chance, J., Goldstein, A. G., & Schict, W. (1967). Effects of acquaintance and friendship on children's recognition of faces. *Psychonomic Science, 7,* 223–224.

Chung, M. & Thomson, D. M. (1995). Development of face recognition. *British Journal of Psychology, 86,* 55–87.

Costen, N. P., Shepherd, J. W., Ellis, H. D., & Craw, I. (1994). Masking of faces by facial and non-facial stimuli. *Visual Cognition, 1,* 227–251.

Davies, G., & Flin, R. (1984). The man behind the mask—disguise and face recognition. *Human Learning, 3,* 83–95.

Diamond, R., & Carey, S. (1986). Why faces are and are not special: An effect of expertise. *Journal of Experimental Psychology: General, 115,* 107–117.

Diamond, R., & Carey, S. (1977). Developmental changes in the representation of faces. *Journal of Experimental Child Psychology, 23,* 1–22.

Durso, F. T., & Johnson, M. K. (1980). The effects of orienting task on recognition, recall and modality confusion of pictures and words. *Journal of Verbal Learning and Verbal Behavior, 19,* 416–429.

Ellis, H. D. (1990). Developmental trends in face recognition. *The Psychologist: Bulletin of British Psychological Society, 3,* 114–119.

Ellis, H. D. (1992). The development of face processing skills. *Philosophical Transactions of the Royal Society, Series B, 335,* 105–111.

Ellis, H. D., Ellis, D. M. & Hosie, J. A. (1993). Priming effects in children's face recognition. *British Journal of Psychology, 84,* 101–110.

Ellis, H. D., Shepherd, J. W., & Davies, G. M. (1979). Identification of familiar and unfamiliar faces from internal and external features: Some implications for theories of face recognition. *Perception, 8,* 431–439.

Faw, H. W. (1992). Recognition of unfamiliar faces: Procedural and methodological considerations. *British Journal of Psychology, 83,* 25–37.

Finke, R. A., Johnson, M. K., & Shyi, G. (1988). Memory confusions for real and imagined completions of symmetrical visual patterns. *Memory & Cognition, 16,* 133–137.

Flin, R. H. (1985). Development of face recognition: An encoding switch? *British Journal of Psychology, 76,* 123–134.

Flin, R. H. & Dziurawiec, S. (1989). Developmental factors in face recognition. In A. Young & H. Ellis, (Eds.), *Handbook of research on face processing* (pp. 335–378). North Holland: Elsevier.

Foley, H. J., Foley, M. A., Smith, S. (1998). *How closely do images resemble pictorial referents: Further investigations of closure processes.* Manuscript in preparation.

Foley, H. J., Foley, M. A., & Cormier, K. (1998). *Remembering how you saw a face: Are there developmental differences?* Manuscript in preparation.

Foley, M. A., Durso, F. T., Wilder, A., & Friedman, R. (1991). Developmental comparisons of explicit versus implicit imagery and reality monitoring. *Journal of Experimental Child Psychology, 51,* 1–13.

Foley, M. A., Foley, H. J., Durso, F. T., & Smith, K. (1997). Investigations of closure processes: What's closing. *Memory & Cognition, 25,* 140–155.

Foley, M. A., Korenman, L., & Foley, H. J. (1998). *Investigations of closure processes: Developmental comparisons.* Manuscript in preparation.

Gollin, E. S. (1962). Factors affecting the visual recognition of incomplete objects: A comparative investigation of children and adults. *Perceptual and Motor Skills, 15,* 583–590.

Hearst, E. (1991). Psychology and nothing. *American Scientist, 79,* 432–443.

Hole, G. J. (1994). Configurational factors in the perception of unfamiliar faces. *Perception, 23,* 65–74.

Johnson, M. K. (in press) Source monitoring and memory distortion. In L. Squire & D. Schacter (Eds.), *Biological and psychological perspectives on memory and memory disorders.* New York: American Psychiatric Press.

Johnson, M. K. (1991). Reflection, reality monitoring and the self. In R. G. Kunzendorf (Ed.), *Mental imagery* (pp. 3–16). New York: Plenum.

Johnson, M. K., Foley, M. A., & Leach, K. (1988). The consequences for memory of imagining in another person's voice. *Memory & Cognition, 16,* 337–342.

Johnson, M. K., Foley, M. A., Suengas, A., & Raye, C. L. (1988) Phenomenal characteristics of memories for perceived and imagined autobiographical events. *Journal of Experimental Psychology: General, 117,* 371–376.

Johnson, M. K., Hashtroudi, S., & Lindsay, D. S. (1993). Source monitoring. *Psychological Bulletin, 114,* 3–28.

Johnson, M. K., Raye, C. L., Foley, H. J., & Foley, M. A. (1981). Cognitive operations and decision biases in reality monitoring. *American Journal of Psychology, 94,* 37–64.

Johnson, M. K., Raye, C. L., Foley, M. A., & Kim, J. (1982). Pictures and images: spatial and temporal information compared. *Bulletin of the Psychonomic Society, 19,* 23–26.

Kimer, K., Foley, M. A., & Quiros, L. (1996, April). *Individual differences in source-monitoring: Focusing on imaginal experiences.* Paper presented at the Eastern Psychological Association meetings, Philadelphia.

Leeper, R. (1935) A study of a neglected portion of the field of learning—the development of sensory organization. *Journal of Genetic Psychology, 46,* 41–75.

Markham, R., & Hynes, L. (1993). The effect of visual imagery on reality-monitoring. *Journal of Mental Imagery, 17,* 159–170.

Matthews, M. L. (1978). Discrimination of Identi-kit constructions of faces: Evidence for a dual-processing strategy. *Perception and Psychophysics, 23,* 153–161.

McKelvie, S. J. (1993). Effects of spectacles on recognition memory for faces: Evidence from a distractor-free test. *Bulletin of the Psychonomic Society, 31,* 475–477.

Murray, F. S., & Kennison, E. L. (1989) Degree of fragmentation and number of distinctive features in the recognition of pictured objects by children and adults. *Bulletin of the Psychonomic Society, 27,* 121–124.

Patterson, K. E., & Baddeley, A. D. (1977). When face recognition fails. *Journal of Experimental Psychology: Human Learning and Memory, 3,* 406–417.

Pezdek, K., & Chen, K. (1982). Developmental differences in the role of detail in picture recognition memory. *Journal of Experimental Child Psychology, 33,* 207–215.

Ramachandran, V. S. (1992). Blind Spots. *Scientific American, 267* (5), 86–91.

Reynolds, J. K., & Pezdek, K. (1992). Face recognition memory: The effects of exposure duration and encoding instruction. *Applied Cognitive Psychology, 6,* 279–292.

Rhodes, G., & Tremewan, T. (1994). Understanding face recognition: Caricature effects, inversion, and the homogeneity problem. In V. Bruce & G. W. Humphreys (Eds.), *Object and face recognition: Special issue in visual cognition* (pp. 275–313). Hillsdale, NJ: Lawrence Erlbaum Associates.

Sekuler, A. B., & Palmer, S. E. (1992). Perception of partly occluded objects: A microgenetic analysis. *Journal of Experimental Psychology: General, 12,* 95–111.

Sekuler, A. B., Palmer, S. E., & Flynn, C. (1994). Local and global processes in visual completion. *Psychological Science, 5,* 260–267.

Shapiro, P. N., & Penrod, S. (1986). Meta-analysis of facial identification studies. *Psychological Bulletin, 100,* 139–156.

Snodgrass, J. G., & Feenan, K. (1990). Priming effects in picture fragmentation completion: Support for the perceptual closure hypothesis. *Journal of Experimental Psychology: General, 119,* 276–296.

Snodgrass, J. G., & Surprenant, A. (1989). Effect of retention interval on implicit and explicit memory for pictures. *Bulletin of the Psychonomic Society, 27,* 607–617.

Snodgrass, J. G., & Vanderwart, M. (1980). A standardized set of 260 pictures: Norms for name agreement, image agreement, familiarity, and visual complexity. *Journal of Experimental Psychology: Human Learning and Memory, 6,* 174–215.

Tanaka, J. W. & Farah, M. J. (1993). Parts and wholes in face recognition. *Quarterly Journal of Experimental Psychology, 50,* 367–372.

Terry, R. L. (1994). Effects of facial transformations on accuracy of recognition. *Journal of Social Psychology, 134,* 483–492.

Wells, G. L., & Turtle, J. W. (1989). What is the best way to encode faces? In M. M. Gruneberg, P. E. Morris, & R. N. Sykes (Eds.), *Practical aspects of memory: Current research and issues* (pp. 163–168). New York: Wiley.

4

Assessing Memory Deficits in Elderly Adults: Repetition Errors, Misattributions, and Memory Slips

Janine F. Hay
McMaster University

Johanna W. Nordlie
New York University

Larry L. Jacoby
McMaster University

To understand errors such as the repeated asking of questions, it is necessary to distinguish between intentional memory processes (recollection) and automatic influences of memory. This distinction is important because there is evidence that elderly adults possess preserved automatic abilities in the presence of significant recollection deficits. We investigate misleading effects of memory that can arise when automatic influences are unopposed by recollection. Standard memory tests fail to separate out contributions to performance of these two bases of responding that can lead to an overestimation of memory abilities in older adults. We describe an opposition procedure used to assess recollection deficits in elderly adults and discuss the advantages of such a procedure as a diagnostic tool. Finally, some preliminary results from a training procedure designed to rehabilitate recollection are presented.

"Where are your kids now?" When visiting our aging parents some of us will be repeatedly asked a question like this. Most striking and frustrating is the repetition. The first asking of the question is viewed as concern for the children and is gladly answered. However, for our parent, it is as if asking the question and having it answered does not allow the question to be put to the side but, instead, increases the probability of its being repeated. Later askings of the question create annoyance that turns into concern as we realize the tragedy that our parents might be suffering. As the aging population continues to grow in society, it is inevitable that a significant proportion of people will suffer devastating effects on memory as a result of Alzheimer's disease (AD). Among the most obvious memory deficits that will be apparent is the repeated asking of questions.

Although frustrating, repeatedly asking a question gives reason for hope because it provides evidence of preserved memory abilities of the sort measured by indirect tests. Indirect tests reveal automatic influences of memory by demonstrating, for example, that a word is used more often as a completion for a word stem or fragment if it was seen earlier, regardless of whether participants were aware of its presentation (for a review, see Moscovitch, Vriezen, & Goshen-Gottstein, 1993). Such demonstrations are striking because they illustrate the effects of the past in the absence of conscious remembering. Findings of dissociations between performance on indirect and direct tests of memory have been cause for a great deal of excitement in cognitive psychology over the last few years. Even very dense amnesics show evidence of memory on indirect tests although they are impaired in their performance on direct tests (Roediger & McDermott, 1993). Similarly, when applied to an elderly population, it is recollection, the intentional use of memory, that shows a dramatic decline with age. In contrast, indirect tests generally show an absence of age-related differences in performance, although small effects are sometimes found (Light, 1991).

We have been very interested in separating out automatic and intentional bases of responding in order to examine the effects of aging on specific aspects of memory. One of our recent research objectives has been to develop a diagnostic device that is particularly sensitive to differences in recollection, in hopes that we might be able to identify elderly adults who are experiencing early signs of dementia. Moreover, we intend to extend our diagnostic measure into a memory rehabilitation program for elderly adults, as well as other special populations. Baddeley and Wilson (1994) exploited preserved automatic influences of memory as a means of rehabilitating the performance of those who are memory impaired. Our goal is somewhat more ambitious in that we want to measure and train intentional uses of memory. Our hope is that we can return control of memory to the memory-impaired individual rather than place the control of memory in the environment. At the end of this chapter, we report some preliminary results from a new procedure that has been designed to rehabilitate recollection.

FALSE FAME AND OPPOSITION

The story of our search for a diagnostic device begins with experiments showing that one can become famous overnight, or even sooner if the audience is not paying sufficient attention (Jacoby, Kelley, Brown & Jasechko, 1989; Jacoby, Woloshyn, & Kelley, 1989). In these experiments, automatic influences of memory (familiarity) were placed in opposition to recollection, allowing us to infer recollection deficits through the errors that people commit. In the first phase of the experiment, participants read a list of names that they were told were nonfamous; next they were given a fame-judgment test consisting of old nonfamous names mixed with new famous and new nonfamous names. The prior presentation of nonfamous names serves to increase their familiarity, which in turn, makes it more likely that the names will later be mistakenly identified as being famous. However, if participants can remember the source of the name correctly, then any automatic influence of familiarity will be opposed, allowing them to be certain that the name is nonfamous. Therefore, to the extent that one is able to recollect, one can avoid undesirable effects of the past.

Fame-judgment tests were performed either immediately after Phase 1 or 24 hours later. Results of this experiment revealed a false-fame effect after the delay in that young adults frequently judged old nonfamous names to be famous. In contrast, when participants performed the fame-judgement task immediately after Phase 1, the false-fame effect did not appear. These findings suggest that young adults were able to escape misleading effects of automatic influences of memory by recollecting source information. However, when recollection was reduced by extending the retention interval, or dividing attention at study or test, then the false-fame effect became very apparent. These results have implications for special populations who are impaired in their ability to recollect because it is these memory-impaired people who will be most susceptible to misleading effects of familiarity. Indeed, elderly adults do show a pronounced false-fame effect (Dywan & Jacoby, 1990; Jennings & Jacoby, 1993a), as do amnesics (Cermak, Verfaellie, Butler, & Jacoby, 1993; Squire & McKee, 1992) and patients who have sustained a closed-head injury (Dywan, Segalowitz, Henderson, & Jacoby, 1993). We have made use of the misleading effects of automatic influences of memory, similar to the false-fame effect described here, to diagnose deficits in recollection in elderly adults. Furthermore, the logic of this opposition procedure serves as the basis of our memory training procedure described later.

TWO EFFECTS OF REPETITION

What effect might earlier askings of a question have on the probability that the question is later repeated?   Answering this question requires that one separately examine the effects of repetition on both automatic and intentional memory processes. A friend whose mother is suffering symptoms of AD tells the story of taking her mother to visit a nursing home. On arriving at the home, the rules and regulations were explained, one of which regarded the dining room. It was mentioned that the dining hall was set up in a restaurant style except that tipping was not required. The lack of tipping in the dining hall was emphasized and reiterated several times. In a meeting that followed later that day, the friend's mother was asked if she had any unanswered questions about the nursing home. She replied that she only had one question: She wondered if she was supposed to tip in the dining room!

This example again illustrates an opposition condition. Repeatedly hearing about tipping practices in the dining room should make that information more familiar and, therefore, it should be more likely to come to mind. In contrast, recollection of the earlier discussion should prevent one from asking about tipping practices again later. The two bases of responding lead to different outcomes but when recollection fails, as it often does with aging, or more dramatically with AD, then automatic influences are left unopposed and repetition errors result. We attempted to investigate the effects of repetition on memory performance in elderly adults in a similar situation in the lab.

In the initial phase of the experiment (Jacoby, in press), first-year university undergraduates and elderly volunteers over the age of 60 years read words on a computer screen either one, two, or three times. Following the initial study list of read words, participants were then presented with a second study list in which different words were heard on a tape recorder only once. Participants were instructed to remember the heard words for a later memory test. At test, they were presented with words that were earlier read in List 1 (once, twice, or three times), earlier heard in List 2, or were new words that had not been encountered before. Although instructed to report the words that were earlier heard in List 2, participants were warned that the test list would also include words that were earlier read. Read words were meant to be excluded and thus they were not supposed to be reported. Furthermore, participants were told that none of the words in the read list appeared in the heard list and vice-versa. Because repeated presentation of a read word increases its familiarity, participants could misattribute this familiarity to it being earlier heard and mistakenly identify read words as heard words. If participants could recollect the source of the read word, then the automatic influence of familiarity would be opposed and participants would correctly identify the word as being read at study. Relying on familiarity alone would produce one type of response, whereas recollection would lead to a different response.

The probability of mistakenly identifying an earlier read word (repeated once, twice, or three times at study) as a heard word was determined across short and long deadline manipulations. In the short deadline condition, a test word was exposed for 750 msec and participants were expected to respond during that interval. In contrast, for the long deadline condition, each word was exposed for 1,250 msec before participants were allowed to respond and then they too were required to respond in a 750 msec interval.

The effects of repetition on performance are summarized in Table 4.1. The results demonstrated that as the number of repetitions increased for read items, young participants were less likely to confuse read words with words that were earlier heard. This finding suggests that young participants were better able to recollect read words the more often they were repeated. However, when young participants were forced to respond at a faster rate, the opposite pattern of results was obtained. At a short deadline, the read items that were most often repeated in the study list were the ones that were most likely to be confused for heard words. The pattern of results with the elderly at a long deadline looked very similar to the pattern shown by young adults when they were pressed to respond quickly. That is, as the number of repetitions increased, elderly adults were more likely to confuse read words with words that were heard. These repetition errors produced by elderly adults are similar to the earlier "Should I tip?" example. Why does repetition increase the likelihood of errors by older adults and by young adults at short deadlines? The dissociations in performance that emerged as a function of age and deadline condition can be taken as evidence for two effects of repetition on memory performance: Repetition increases recollection, as well as familiarity. Given that recollective abilities have been shown to be diminished in older adults (Jacoby, Jennings, & Hay, 1996; Jennings & Jacoby, 1993a, 1997), as well as at short as compared to longer deadlines (Hay & Jacoby, 1996; Yonelinas & Jacoby, 1994), automatic influences of memory are frequently left unopposed in these situations, and thus attribution errors often result. When recollection is reduced, the unopposed effects of familiarity become more apparent with increasing repetition because familiarity also increases with the number of presentations. These results provide support for the anecdotal suggestion that as one becomes older, unwanted repetitions become more common.

DIAGNOSING RECOLLECTION DEFICITS IN OLDER ADULTS

The evidence thus far suggests that elderly adults experience pronounced declines in recollection, which in turn can lead to repetition errors. But are

TABLE 4.1
Probability of Identifying Words as Earlier Heard

Age Group	Response Deadline	Read Presentations				Heard
		1x	2x	3x	New	
Young	Long (1,250 + 750 ms)	.32	.26	.20	.18	.56
	Short (750 ms)	.24	.35	.38	.16	.37
Elderly	Long (1,250 + 750 ms)	.27	.35	.38	.13	.35

we able to identify individuals who are most likely to produce such errors and therefore, detect the severity of memory deficits present? For example, one would be less concerned about a parent who repeats the question, "Where are your kids now?" 1 month later than a parent who repeats the question after only a few minutes. In order to differentiate normal elderly from those in the early stages of dementia, we need a diagnostic measure to reveal the degree of memory impairment.

An opposition procedure was devised by Jennings and Jacoby (1997) to provide a more diagnostic index of age-related deficits in recollection. They measured severity of recollection deficits in a situation where unwanted repetition had to be avoided, similar to the repeated asking of a question. This type of error may occur if automatic influences of memory, which compel such a repetition, are not successfully opposed by recollecting that the question was already asked and answered. The length of interval required to demonstrate age differences in repetition errors was determined in the expectation that it would provide a more sensitive measure of memory deficits than that shown by standard, direct tests of memory that are typically used in neuropsychological assessments. Their experiments were modeled after the situation of avoiding repeating oneself across increasing delays.

In Jennings and Jacoby's (1997) opposition paradigm, young and elderly participants studied a list of words and then performed a recognition test for those words. The recognition test consisted of old, studied words intermixed with new words, with the catch being that each new word was repeated in the test list at various intervals (e.g., 0, 1, 3, 4, 7, 12, 24, or 48 intervening items between repetitions of new, nonstudied words). Participants were instructed to report only the old items from the earlier list, each of which was presented once and thus never repeated. However, they were also cautioned about the repetitions of new items in the test list and were instructed *not* to report these catch items during the recognition test. Repeated items served a function similar to that of repeatedly asking the same question of the same person. Recollection of the first presentation of a new item should allow participants to reject the item although familiarity gained from its earlier presentation would have the opposite effect and lead to erroneously categorizing a new item as an old item. Jennings and Jacoby were interested in determining the extent to which participants were able to avoid reporting catch items. It was expected that this type of repetition error would be more pronounced with age and would increase as the interval between presentations was lengthened.

The results of this experiment revealed that elderly adults showed striking age-related deficits in detecting repeated items after only four items intervened between the first and second presentations! In contrast, there were no age differences detected on a standard test of recognition memory that was incorporated into the earlier opposition task. Jennings and Jacoby (1997) argued, as we do here, that an opposition procedure provides a more sensitive measure of memory deficits in elderly adults than does a direct test and sometimes may lead to very different conclusions about the effects of aging on memory. That is, the striking age-related impairments revealed by repetition errors in an opposition paradigm contrast a great deal with findings that elderly adults sometimes do not even demonstrate impairments on standard tests of recognition memory, as shown by Jennings and Jacoby as well as others (e.g., Craik & McDowd, 1987; Rabinowitz, 1984).

Repetition errors, as defined here, can be viewed as a failure in source memory. Most studies investigating source memory have relied on tasks that explicitly instruct participants to report source information. In contrast, our approach entails source monitoring while engaging in other activities and therefore may offer a more sensitive measure of source errors than has been traditionally used. For example, consider the difference between the task of avoiding repeatedly asking the same question while engaging in conversation, compared to the task of listing all the occasions on which one has asked that question. Guiding the responding of participants through direct questioning can alter the nature of the task in important ways, as demonstrated in an experiment by Multhaup (1995). Multhaup increased the structure of a false-fame task by explicitly asking participants about source information. During the fame-judgment test, participants were instructed to categorize each name as a famous name, a nonfamous name seen earlier, or a new nonfamous name. It was found that this additional support benefited performance in older adults to such an extent that the typical false-fame effect was eliminated. Although this finding is encouraging, it also suggests that the severity of memory impairments in older adults can be underestimated if they are tested in highly structured situations. Tasks that require participants to explicitly make source judgments may overlook a critical difficulty experienced by elderly adults—an inability to monitor in unstructured situations. We propose that the opposition procedure just outlined offers a more sensitive measure for assessing memory deficits than either standard source-monitoring tests or standard recognition tasks. Furthermore, this diagnostic measure provides a useful means for determining the severity of recollection deficits and thus promises to be an important tool for diagnosing memory impairments in special populations in the future.

ASSUMPTIONS, ESTIMATES, AND CONTROVERSY

It is possible that deficits in recollection, measured by repetition errors, could be underestimated if elderly adults also experience a decline in automatic influences of memory. To ensure that this is not the case, one must have a means of separately examining estimates of automatic and intentional influences of memory. Using Jacoby's (1991) process dissociation procedure, we have been able to estimate the contribution of these processes to performance for both young and elderly adults. The results we have obtained across several experiments have consistently shown that aging produces impairments in recollection but does not affect the automatic component of memory (see Jacoby, Jennings, & Hay, 1996; Jennings & Jacoby, 1993a, 1997).

However, the utility of the process dissociation procedure has been somewhat controversial because of the assumptions it makes about the nature of the relationship between automatic and intentional influences (for a review, see Yonelinas & Jacoby, in press). In particular, it is the assumption that recollection and automatic influences make independent contributions to performance that has received some criticism. These difficulties can be avoided altogether if one's goal is to demonstrate the existence of recollection deficits rather than estimate the contribution of the underlying processes. That is, by making use of the opposition task alone, one is able to obtain an effective and sensitive measure of recollection capable of diagnosing age-related deficits in memory performance. Nevertheless, we believe many of the current criticisms of the process dissociation procedure are unfounded and have presented evidence in support of independence elsewhere (for a review, see Jacoby, Yonelinas, & Jennings, 1996).

MEMORY SLIPS: SEPARATING HABIT AND RECOLLECTION

We have seen that automatic influences of memory can arise from a single presentation of an item (e.g., Jennings & Jacoby, 1997) and that these influences can become stronger when items are repeated on two or three prior occasions (Jacoby, in press). The effects of repetition can also be demonstrated on automatic influences that have been built up by multiple presentations of stimuli, as in the case of a habit. For example, we (Hay & Jacoby, 1996) created habits of specific strengths during an experimental session and then examined how these habit strengths affected likelihood of making errors, or memory slips, when automatic responding dominates over the ability to recollect a prior event.

Hay and Jacoby (1996) separated the contribution of recollection and habit to cued recall performance. In their experiments, responses were made typical or atypical by an initial training session designed to create habits of specific strengths. During this initial phase, participants were exposed to pairs of associatively related words with the probabilities of the pairings being varied. For example, a stimulus word "knee" was paired with a response word "bend" on 75% of occurrences (typical response), whereas for the other 25% of occurrences, it was paired with the response "bone" (atypical response). In another condition, pairings appeared with a 50-50 probability. Once these habits were established, the second phase of the experiment presented participants with specific items to study (e.g., knee - bend) for a cued recall test that followed. At test, participants received a stimulus word and fragment (knee - b_n_) and were asked to complete the fragment with the response they remembered from the study list (bend or bone). Word fragments were constructed such that both responses could always be used as completions. Participants could respond at test by recollecting the previously presented item, by relying on their habit for the typical item, or both. We made use of Jacoby's (1991) process dissociation procedure to separate out and measure these different bases of responding.

To understand the rationale underlying the process dissociation procedure as used in this paradigm, consider the example of searching your home for the keys to your car. The typical place you keep your keys is on a table near the front door of your home. However, sometimes you leave your keys on the dresser in your bedroom, which is what happened on this occasion. Given a failure in recollection, is it likely that you will mistakenly begin the search for your keys at their typical location? One factor that influences the likelihood of this memory slip is the past probability of leaving the keys in their typical place. The higher that probability, the stronger the habit of searching for them at that location will be and, consequently, the more likely one will be to commit an error, or memory slip, when the keys are elsewhere.

The results of our experiments indeed showed that participants were more likely to make memory slips when habit was strong (75%) as compared to weak (50%), suggesting that a strong habit is difficult to overcome. However, in situations where habit and recollection worked in concert to produce the same response, automatic responding was a basis for correct responding rather than a source of errors. Under these conditions, performance was assisted to a greater extent when habit was stronger (75% vs. 50%). Furthermore, the estimates of habit reflected the probability with which items were presented in the training session and thus probability matching was revealed (e.g., Estes, 1976). It has been suggested that probability matching, producing responses at a rate that matches their occurrence, occurs without awareness and intention and therefore qualifies as implicit learning (Reber, 1989). Our procedure allowed us to separate the contributions of habit and recollection so that habit could be examined uncontaminated by intentional influences of memory. In doing so, we found that only estimates of the automatic component reflected probabilities from training: Recollection was not affected by this habit strength manipulation. In another experiment (Jacoby & Hay, 1993), we compared young and elderly adults on this task and found that recollection was impaired in older adults but estimates of habit did not differ by age. Furthermore, probability matching was demonstrated for both young and elderly groups. The previous two experiments in combination show opposite dissociations and thus provide support for independent bases of responding in memory.

These results have implications for training automatic retrieval processes. Several recent memory rehabilitation techniques have focused on creating habits or automatic responses through repeated rehearsal, allowing memory-impaired individuals to acquire a limited amount of new information (e.g., Camp & Schaller, 1989). Although our findings suggest that elderly adults are very capable of developing habits in this manner, these rehabilitation techniques nevertheless have some shortcomings. Automatic responding may assist performance under certain conditions but it can also be a source of errors: Strong habits can increase the likelihood of producing memory slips if automatic influences are not successfully opposed by recollection. Given that recollection is impaired in older adults, the elderly are particularly at risk for memory slips. Furthermore, creating highly structured, routinized environments to support automatic responding can limit the potential stimulation for active information processing and thus lead to self-induced dependence and perceived loss of control (Langer, 1981). Rather than create highly structured environments where automatic responding aids memory, we favor a more internal rehabilitation approach that attempts to restore controlled uses of memory to the individual.

REHABILITATING RECOLLECTION

Is it possible to rehabilitate the elderly's ability to use recollection as a means of avoiding unwanted repetition? We believe that training recollection may be possible in older adults, as well as other memory-impaired populations who show some degree of spared recollective abilities. Jennings and Jacoby (1993b) presented some preliminary results from a procedure they devised to improve memory performance in elderly adults. The rationale that underlies their approach attempts to train recollection in situations where it is easy, and then gradually increase the difficulty to shape recollective processing. Moving elderly adults slowly through situations of increasing difficulty may allow them to adapt their recollective abilities to more demanding situations. The logic of this approach can be understood in terms of older adults' propensity to repeatedly ask the same question. Even if memory is significantly impaired, one would not expect an elderly adult to repeatedly ask the same question immediately after asking it the first time. However, after some time has passed, the question is more likely to be repeated. Is it possible to train people to extend the delay before which they might repeat themselves?

Jennings and Jacoby (1993b) adapted the opposition condition from the recognition lag paradigm described earlier for their rehabilitation procedure.

Participants studied a list of 30 words, followed by a recognition test in which 30 new words appeared and were repeated at one of two lags. The task required participants to respond "yes" to items that were old and "no" to new items at their first presentation and when they were repeated. Recollection deficits were inferred by measuring errors (responding "yes" to repeated words), as this task put recollection and automatic influences in opposition. Initially, participants had to recollect repeated words after a brief interval following their presentation (one intervening item) and thus the task was quite easy. However, a shaping procedure was used to increase the lag intervals between repeated test words as performance improved across the training sessions and thus the task gradually became more difficult. Improvements in performance were assessed by comparing the length of the interval in which participants reached criterion performance. If the interval length increased across training, recollection was considered to be improved.

Ten elderly adults received four training sessions a day for 7 days. Preliminary results using this procedure suggested some significant improvement in recollection. Initially, elderly participants performed to criterion when only one item intervened between repeated presentations, however, after the training sessions, these adults performed to criterion with 28 intervening items! Furthermore, the benefits of training appeared to be intact at a 3-month follow-up session (Jennings & Jacoby, 1993b). Control participants, who performed the same lag intervals but did not receive the shaping procedure, did not show the same level of improvement found with the experimental group. These preliminary results appear encouraging and suggest that it may be possible to improve recollection in older adults. Future work will strive to further increase these training effects, produce positive transfer to everyday life, and maintain long-term performance.

CONCLUDING COMMENTS

To understand errors such as memory slips and the repeated asking of questions, it is necessary to distinguish between automatic and intentional influences of memory. This distinction is an important one, especially if one's goal is to identify deficits in controlled responding in the presence of preserved automatic abilities, a pattern typical of elderly adults. Standard memory tests used in neuropsychological batteries, as well as in many experimental paradigms, fail to separate out the contributions to performance of two bases of responding. This omission can lead to an overestimation of the memory abilities of elderly adults and may result in professionals missing early warning signals for dementia. We suggest a task that places recollection and automatic influences in opposition is better suited to detect age-related deficits in memory and, furthermore, should serve as a very useful tool in the diagnosis and treatment of memory disorders.

REFERENCES

Baddeley, A., & Wilson, B. A. (1994). When implicit learning fails: Amnesia and the problem of error elimination. *Neuropsychologia, 32,* 53–68.

Camp, C. J., & Schaller, J. R. (1989). Epilogue: Spaced retrieval memory training in an adult day-care center. *Educational Gerontology, 15,* 641–648.

Cermak, L. S., Verfaellie, M., Butler, T., & Jacoby, L. L. (1993). Attributions of familiarity in amnesia: Evidence from a fame judgment task. *Neuropsychologia, 7,* 510–518.

Craik, F. I. M., & McDowd, J. M. (1987). Age differences in recall and recognition. *Journal of Experimental Psychology: Learning, Memory, and Cognition, 13,* 474–479.

Dywan, J., & Jacoby, L. L. (1990). Effects of aging on source monitoring: Differences in susceptibility to false fame. *Psychology and Aging, 5,* 379–387.

Dywan, J., Segalowitz, S. J., Henderson, D., & Jacoby, L. L. (1993). Memory for source after traumatic brain injury. *Brain and Cognition, 21,* 20–43.

Estes, W. K. (1976). The cognitive side of probability learning. *Psychological Review, 83,* 37–64.

Hay, J. F., & Jacoby, L. L. (1996). Separating habit and recollection: Memory slips, process dissociations and probability matching. *Journal of Experimental Psychology: Learning, Memory, and Cognition, 22,* 1323–1335.

Jacoby, L. L. (in press). Ironic effects of memory: Should I tip? *Journal of Experimental Psychology: Learning, Memory, and Cognition.*

Jacoby, L. L. (1991). A process dissociation framework: Separating automatic from intentional uses of memory. *Journal of Memory and Language, 30,* 513–541.

Jacoby, L. L., & Hay, J. F. (1993, November). *Action slips, proactive interference, and probability matching.* Paper presented at the 34th annual meeting of the Psychonomic Society, Washington DC.

Jacoby, L. L, Jennings, J. M., & Hay, J. F. (1996). Dissociating automatic and consciously-controlled processes: Implications for diagnosis and rehabilitation of memory deficits. In D. J. Herrmann, C. L. McEvoy, C. Hertzog, P. Hertel & M. K. Johnson (Eds.), *Basic and applied memory research: Theory in context* (Vol. 1, pp. 161–193). Mahwah, NJ: Lawrence Erlbaum Associates.

Jacoby, L. L., Kelley, C. M., Brown, J., & Jasechko, J. (1989). Becoming famous overnight: Limits on the ability to avoid unconscious influences of the past. *Journal of Personality and Social Psychology, 56,* 326–338.

Jacoby, L. L., Woloshyn, V., & Kelley, C. M. (1989). Becoming famous without being recognized: Unconscious influences of memory produced by dividing attention. *Journal of Experimental Psychology: General, 118,* 115–125.

Jacoby, L. L., Yonelinas, A. P., & Jennings, J. M. (1996). The relation between conscious and unconscious (automatic) influences: A declaration of independence.

In J. Cohen, & J. W. Schooler (Eds.), *Scientific approaches to the questions of consciousness* (pp. 13–47). Mahwah, NJ: Lawrence Erlbaum Associates.

Jennings, J. M., & Jacoby, L. L. (1993a). Automatic versus intentional uses of memory: Awareness, attention and control. *Psychology and Aging, 8,* 283–293.

Jennings, J. M., & Jacoby, L. L. (1993b, August). *The effect of aging on consciously-controlled memory processing.* Paper presented at the annual American Psychological Association Conference, Toronto.

Jennings, J. M., & Jacoby, L. L. (1997). An opposition procedure for detecting age-related deficits in recollection: Telling effects of repetition. *Psychology and Aging, 12,* 352–361.

Langer, E. J. (1981) Old age: An artifact? In J. L. McGaugh & S. B. Kiesler (Eds.), *Aging, biology and behavior* (pp. 255–281). New York: Academic Press.

Light, L. L. (1991). Memory and aging: Four hypotheses in search of data. *Annual Review of Psychology, 43,* 333–376.

Moscovitch, M., Vriezen, E. R., & Goshen-Gottstein, Y. (1993). Implicit tests of memory in patients with focal lesions or degenerative brain disorders. In F. Boller & J. Grafman (Eds.), *Handbook of neuropsychology* (Vol. 8, pp. 133–173). Amsterdam: Elsevier Science Publishers.

Multhaup, K. S. (1995). Aging, source, and decision criteria: When false fame errors do and do not occur. *Psychology and Aging, 10,* 492–497.

Rabinowitz, J. C. (1984). Aging and recognition failure. *Journal of Gerontology, 39,* 65–71.

Reber, A. S. (1989). Implicit learning and tacit knowledge. *Journal of Experimental Psychology: General, 118,* 219–235.

Roediger, H. L., & McDermott, K. B. (1993). Implicit memory in normal human subjects. In F. Boller & J. Grafman (Eds.), *Handbook of neuropsychology* (Vol. 8, pp. 63–131). Amsterdam: Elsevier Science Publishers.

Squire, L. R., & McKee, R. (1992). Influence of prior events on cognitive judgments in amnesia. *Journal of Experimental Psychology: Learning, Memory, and Cognition, 18,* 106–115.

Yonelinas, A. P., & Jacoby, L. L. (1996). Response bias and the process dissociation procedure. *Journal of Experimental Psychology: General, 125,* 422–439.

Yonelinas, A. P., & Jacoby, L. L. (1994). Dissociations of processes in recognition memory: Effects of interference and of response speed. *Canadian Journal of Experimental Psychology, 48,* 516–534.

5

Collaborative Memory Accuracy and Distortion: Performance and Beliefs

Roger A. Dixon
Lisa M. Gagnon
Carolyn B. Crow
University of Victoria

Collaborative cognition refers to a common form of cognitive activity occurring in the context of more than one individual. We contend that collaborative cognition may be of special interest to cognitive developmental researchers, especially those focusing on cognitive development in adulthood. By examining collaborative cognition and aging, researchers may resolve some theoretical puzzles (e.g., identifying mechanisms through which individual aging-related losses may be mitigated) and practical challenges (e.g., promoting further effectiveness at everyday cognitive tasks by older adults). We therefore review evidence pertaining to issues of accuracy and distortion in (a) cognitive performance in younger and older collaborating units, and (b) beliefs about collaborative effectiveness and aging. Regarding performance, some evidence supports the notion that accuracy is enhanced for selected older collaborating units, especially such presumed interactive experts as long-term married couples. Regarding beliefs, initial evidence suggests that adults believe that collaborative experience is an important component of cognitive effectiveness; collaborative experts, such as married couples, are believed to be more efficient and productive than are collaborating units of lesser experience and working alone. Further research on accuracy and distortion in collaborating units of adults could benefit from integrating cognitive performance and metacognitive beliefs.

Collaborative cognitive activity is a common fact of everyday life for many adults. For older adults it may even represent a mechanism for compensating for individual-level cognitive decline. The extent to which collaboration promotes accuracy (and reduces distortion) in memory performance is an important issue that has received considerable attention in a variety of literatures. Just as important and far less studied in aging research are beliefs about collaborative accuracy or distortion. In general, knowledge and beliefs about cognition are of considerable concern in aging research (Hertzog & Dixon, 1994). Regarding collaboration, such beliefs may play a critical role in the extent to which (a) participants will engage in collaborative cognitive activity with a sense of cognitive efficacy, and (b) observers will invest products of collaborative memory performance with confidence. Because beliefs about cognitive collaboration are virtually unexamined in the research literature, we present some new data pertaining to this issue.

In order to make this case in the present chapter, we address three major points. First, we summarize recent arguments concerning the theoretical and practical utility of examining collaborative memory performance in normal adults, especially older adults. Second, we describe some research indicating that, in some circumstances, collaborative memory accuracy is relatively high whereas distortion is relatively low. Finally, we present some recent data pertaining to beliefs about collaborative memory accuracy and distortion.

COLLABORATIVE COGNITION IN ADULTHOOD: THEORETICAL AND PRACTICAL UTILITY

Collaborative cognition refers to cognitive activity that occurs in the context of more than one individual, where that activity is typically directed at an identifiable set of tasks, usually in pursuit of common goals, and performed cooperatively (although not necessarily optimally or effectively). As we use the term, *collaborative cognition* is neutral with respect to quality or quantity of outcome and characteristics of process (Dixon, 1996). That is, collaborative cognition refers to working together on a problem, but it does not imply that the process is efficient nor that the product is accurate or complete. Historically, many researchers have investigated characteristics of the group and task that affect collaborative processes and performance (e.g., Hill, 1982; Paulus, 1989; Steiner, 1972). More recently, several collections of writings have focused attention on a variety of methodological, theoretical, and practical implications of cognitive collaboration, cooperation, transaction, or teamwork (e.g., Galegher, Kraut, & Egido, 1990; Resnick, Levine, & Teasley, 1991). Numerous areas in psychology have explored such issues, including cognitive science, social cognition, industrial/organizational, educational, and child developmental. In addition, for both theoretical and practical reasons, researchers in cognitive aging have begun to explore collaborative cognition with a variety of tasks and group compositions (see reviews by Baltes & Staudinger, 1996; Dixon, 1996; Dixon & Gould, 1996). In the next two sections, we summarize the theoretical and practical reasons for this surge of interest in the area of cognitive developmental psychology.

Theoretical Issues

The study of cognitive development throughout adulthood is frequently referred to as *cognitive aging*. This term carries no particular implication about the direction or magnitude of aging-related change. That is, it is neutral with respect to whether cognitive development in adulthood is characterized by gains, losses, or both (e.g., Baltes, 1987). Nevertheless, it is clear that there is considerable normal aging-related loss in cognitive functioning, especially in the late years. Memory processes are among those for which aging-related decline is most comprehensively documented (e.g., Craik & Jennings, 1992). Such decline may be linked to (or indexed by) normal neurological and sensory changes occurring with advancing age (e.g., Salthouse, 1991). For example, neurological slowing, loss of sensory acuity, and possible diminution of processing resources have been shown to affect cognitive decline in late adulthood (e.g., Craik & Jennings, 1992; Lindenberger & Baltes, 1994; Salthouse, 1994). In memory and aging research, typical results include aging-related decreases in accurate recall, and increases in errors of omission and commission—phenomena that representatives of one perspective might view as reflecting increases in memory distortion.

Despite the negative manifold of losses occurring with cognitive aging, a provocative theoretical riddle is often presented to (and by) cognitive aging researchers (e.g., Dixon, 1995; Salthouse, 1990). Put simply, the riddle is that despite the many cognitive losses accompanying aging, many normal older adults are still able to perform complex cognitive tasks competently. These tasks include those performed in everyday professional or leisure pursuits involving reading, writing, conversations, storytelling, decision making, problem solving, advice giving, debating, mentoring, comparison shopping, knowledge updating, and memory. Overall cognitive decline is a function of normal, ineluctable neurological and sensory decrements. The performance of complex cognitive skills is predicated on the adequate (if not optimal) functioning of fundamental components or mechanisms, especially those that undergo decline with aging. Given this scenario, by what mechanism(s) can maintenance of complex, everyday cognitive skills occur? Because a comprehensive understanding of cognitive development in adulthood must include explanations for the rules of cognitive aging, as well as for the exceptions, the implications for theoretical advances in cognitive aging are potentially profound (Dixon & Hertzog, 1996).

In one form or another, scholars have attempted to define and understand this perplexing but intriguing riddle. The following list presents selected efforts to understand the riddle and the implications that can be drawn from it.

Individual Differences in Change. Schaie (1990, 1996) explored the extent to which intellectual loss can be later, less uniform, and less universal than expected, given stereotypes or global loss models. He argued that, despite a pattern of overall longitudinal decline, substantial individual differences in rate and magnitude of loss are observed.

Gains in Alternative Processes. Is it possible that there are processes for which the natural direction of cognitive aging is improvement? According to research in implicit theories and beliefs about aging and actual performance, such growth-linked processes could include wisdom (e.g., Heckhausen, Dixon, & Baltes, 1989). To date, however, research in wisdom performance has not resulted in uniformly optimistic results regarding aging.

Lacunae in Studies of Practical Cognition. One possibility is that cognitive aging researchers have traditionally focused on laboratory tasks that, although sound experimentally or psychometrically, may inadequately represent or measure processes or performances more relevant to everyday professional or leisure performance. Therefore, an argument could be made that the predominate results from traditional cognitive aging research may underestimate the actual degree of cognitive adaptation to everyday life displayed by normal and exceptional older adults. For this reason, research in applied or practical cognitive aging has flourished in recent years (e.g., Hertzog & Dunlosky, 1996; Park, 1992; Willis & Dubin, 1990), although the results of this research do not yet support a strong discrepancy between practical and laboratory tasks (e.g., Kausler, 1991).

Role of Practice and Training. Several researchers (e.g., Charness, 1989; Ericsson & Charness, 1994; Salthouse, 1987) have focused attention on the extent to which expertise (including continued practice, application, and upgrading) in particular domains may be associated with maintenance or continued gains rather than losses. In this sense, performance in domains of expertise may not reveal the same pattern of aging-related losses typically observed in more domain-general, standardized psychometric, or laboratory-based cognitive tasks. This field continues to be a promising avenue of research in cognitive aging (Ericsson & Smith, 1991).

Compensatory Mechanisms. The possibility of compensating for declining skills via several identifiable mechanisms, such that overall competence is maintained, has been examined (e.g., Bäckman & Dixon, 1992; Dixon & Bäckman, 1995). Prominent compensatory mechanisms include substitution (performing a task via alternate pathways, components, or mechanisms), accommodation (adjusting or devaluing blocked goals, reducing criteria of success, rearranging priorities), remediation (investing more time and effort in performing the declining skill), or assimilation (modifying the environment or expectations of others) (Brandtstädter & Wentura, 1995; Charness & Bosman, 1995; Dixon & Bäckman, 1995; Marsiske, Lang, Baltes, & Baltes, 1995; Salthouse, 1987, 1995). In a variety of research areas—including social and cognitive aging—such compensatory mechanisms have been investigated and applied.

Summary

The theoretical significance of collaborative cognition is that it provides a window through which many of the stated issues can be explored. In particular, some specific explanations of the apparent discrepancies between everyday competence and laboratory performance on basic mechanisms can be addressed. As an illustration, consider the following scenario: Given that there are individual differences in rate and timing of cognitive decline, some individuals of a given older cohort may have relatively preserved basic cognitive mechanisms and skills, whereas others may have experienced more precipitous decline. In addition, older individuals may have experienced more or less decline in different dimensions of cognition. In the normal range of cognitive aging, one means through which aging Individual X's performance in particular cognitively demanding tasks may be improved or maintained could be the recruitment of other individuals whose skills are relatively preserved or complementary to those of Individual X.

The recruitment of a collaborator is analogous to the use of external memory aids. An important difference, of course, is that the collaborator may contribute actively, strategically, productively, and fallibly in a continuing, dynamic, online fashion. The collaborative situation can be viewed as interacting human external aids, with all the potential benefits and complications accompanying that status. Elsewhere, we have argued that the previous scenario is by no means rare and it may in fact involve both issues of expertise and compensation (Dixon, 1992, 1996). We return to these issues later in this chapter. We turn now to practical reasons for the recent interest in collaborative cognition among researchers in cognitive aging.

Practical Issues

The theoretically puzzling discrepancy between lab and life for some older adults has immediate practical implications in the study of cognitive aging. Let us assume momentarily that there are exceptions to the rule of cognitive decline with aging, and that these exceptions can be organized coherently under categories such as those listed earlier. Some scholars have therefore surmised that, although abilities (as measured by standardized tests and tasks) generally decline with aging, competencies in selected everyday skills may be more resilient. Theories of cognitive aging may be adjusted to reflect this qualification. In addition, views of cognitive aging in everyday life may also be adjusted so as to reflect the theoretically based potential for maintenance of skills, at least in select domains. Moreover, the role that collaboration may play in promoting such cognitive maintenance or resilience should be addressed. That is, as a mechanism for overcoming or mitigating aging-related losses in everyday professional or leisure pursuits, collaboration may be of substantial practical utility.

Collaborative cognition occurs frequently in everyday situations. Examples include (a) groups of friends or family collectively attempting to reconstruct stories from their shared past; (b) vulnerable or dificient individuals enlisting the help of a friend or spouse in remembering special anniversaries, appointments, tasks, duties, or parking places; (c) colleagues in business, science, engineering, sports, or law attempting collectively to analyze or solve thorny problems related to success in the profession; (d) travelers consulting strangers in a unknown region or city to resolve a way-finding or map-reading dilemma; and (e) students, parents, or teachers accomplishing learning projects together in tutorial or peer educational settings (Dixon, 1992).

If collaboration occurs frequently in everyday life—as most observers suggest—and if it can be shown to be associated with more effective performance of selected skills—then its practical utility may be established or at least investigated (Greeno & Moore, 1993; Vygotsky, 1978). Note, however, that by practical utility one does not necessarily imply optimal utility. That is, a criterion for evaluating the practical utility of collaborative cognition in mitigating individual-level cognitive aging decline does not necessarily have to be that it completely overcomes cognitive deficits or that it is a process that produces optimal performance. Such issues of evaluating the actual products and processes of collaborative cognition vis-à-vis the expected or predicted levels based on estimates of optimal group performance are more pertinent in some areas of psychology (e.g., educational) than in cognitive aging (Dixon, 1996).

COLLABORATIVE MEMORY AND AGING: ACCURACY VERSUS DISTORTION

In a review of collaborative memory and aging, Dixon (1996) identified a set of principal research issues and objectives. These issues and objectives were derived from convergent and divergent research agendas of collaborative cognition (in general) and cognitive aging. They focused, however, on the unique theoretical and practical application to collaborative cognition and aging. We select and summarize several points relevant to the present chapter.

First, in determining the accuracy or productivity of collaborative performance, it is insufficient to compare groups or individuals exclusively in terms of a single quantity representing the amount of recalled materials. In cognitive aging, there is a tradition of including a variety of memory performance indicators, including accurate recall, errors or distortions, elaborations (i.e., statements consistent with, but not actually in, the original information), macrostatements (i.e., summary or thematic statements), and metastatements (i.e., comments regarding memory performance or processes). Such performance indicators may have substantial theoretical and practical utility for understanding memory and aging.

Second, in determining the productivity of a collaborative performance, it is useful to examine the processes represented in the actual collaboration. Several indicators of strategic, communicative, and even affective processes occurring during collaboration have been explored. We refer to two classes of variables, product and process variables. Third, an initial descriptive research question concerns the extent to which younger and older adults can and do use collaborators to perform complex cognitive tasks. A focus here is on descriptive comparisons between the products and processes used by different constellations of groups varying in age.

Fourth, more theoretical research questions concern such issues as whether collaborative or interactive expertise may develop with long-term associations, as can be typical of aging. Does long-term experience at collaboration lead to more skillful collaborative processes and, possibly, better collaborative products (Engeström, 1992)? If so, it is possible that such collaborative expertise may affect comparisons among the variety of group constellations and ages. A related theoretical question concerns the extent to which evidence might be observed for compensation in older adult collaborating groups. Specifically, given that there are inevitable individual-level aging-related cognitive declines, under what conditions and through what processes could collaborating older adults compensate for such decrements? The probability for such compensation may increase for older collaborative experts (Dixon & Gould, 1996).

These issues and research questions are relatively unique to the context of cognitive aging. Furthermore, they are not typically identified or pursued in neighboring domains of collaborative or interactive cognition. Therefore, only limited research has been conducted bearing on these issues and questions. In the following section, we summarize some of our own recent efforts to examine these issues.

Initial Studies Comparing Accuracy and Distortion

In a series of studies, we have examined collaborative memory for narratives. Most research conducted on memory for narratives has been executed at the individual level of analysis. Only recently has the case of interacting, collaborating individuals been programmatically considered. There is an informative tradition of research in neighboring areas, including collaborative recall of news events, personal or shared stories, forensic situations, and autobiographical events (e.g., Clark & Stephenson, 1989; Middleton & Edwards, 1990; Resnick et al., 1991). We combine interests from the individual-level tradition, lessons learned from previous research in the group-level condition, with questions and issues derived from cognitive aging. Our recent work has been reviewed elsewhere (e.g., Dixon, 1996; Dixon & Gould, 1996). Our present goal is to summarize our findings pertaining to accuracy and distortion in collaborating groups of younger and older adults.

In comparing unacquainted groups of younger and older adults, the general finding has been that the quantity of accurate recall increases across group size for both cohorts. In one study, we found that, for both younger and older adults, tetrads (groups of four) recalled more accurate story information than did dyads (groups of two) and individuals (working alone; Dixon & Gould, in press). In examining the patterns of recall, we also found that the groups accurately identified and recalled the main ideas and themes of the story. In addition, the recalled story information was well-structured, as indicated by the ratio of main ideas to details.

As we have alluded (and presented more fully elsewhere; Dixon, 1996), in our view it is important to examine more than just quantity of items recalled. Therefore, in this research we also examined such non-recall productions as macrostatements, errors, and elaborations. Whereas macrostatements must be considered as productive, errors are of course considered as distortions. Overall, there were very few macrostatements and errors produced, especially as compared to the number of correctly recalled propositions. In terms of trends, however, the older groups produced more macrostatements and fewer errors than did the younger groups. Both trends are consistent with some results at the individual level of functioning. Whereas the former may reflect some tendency for older adults to generate more thematic than detailed statements, the latter may reflect a group-level caution in responsiveness.

We analyzed the elaborations separately. In this study (Gould, Trevithick, & Dixon, 1991), we found that there were actually two different categories of elaborations. *Denotative elaborations* are statements that are based on information contained in the story or from world knowledge relevant to the content of the story (e.g., inferences). *Annotative elaborations* are those statements that are based on personal evaluations, interpretations, or experiences regarding some aspect or character in the story. Obviously, the former are more closely related to accurate recall. Should the latter be considered distortions? We found that the annotative elaborations were indeed further from the content of the original text, but that they were (a) used to possibly enhance or vivify the retelling of the story, (b) not so distant that they could be considered evidence of off-target verbosity, and (c) used relatively sparingly. In fact, we found that the number of denotative elaborations increased across group size for both younger and older groups. In contrast, the number of annotative elaborations was relatively low and increased across group size only for older adults. This latter increase could be considered distortion, if the criterion was only accurate recall of list items. As we observed, however, many of the older adults viewed the task differently; they viewed it as an opportunity to tell an interesting story, as well as recall a stimulus narrative. In this sense, then, annotative elaborations may indeed be considered productive (Gould et al., 1991).

Role of Collaborative Expertise

We have also begun to examine the potential role of collaborative expertise, focusing on one variety of naturally occurring expert collaborative groups. Specifically, married couples frequently work together in solving many practical and complex cognitive problems, including those that bear a structural resemblance to story retelling. Long-term (over 40 years) married couples are naturally older adults. How well would they perform collaborative cognitive tasks, as compared to younger married couples, and older unacquainted groups?

Our earliest studies showed that older married couples produced accurate story recall at a rate higher than that of older and younger unacquainted dyads; older couples' rates were essentially equivalent to those of younger married couples (Dixon & Gould, in press). As age-equivalent performance in complex cognitive tasks is rare in the cognitive aging literature, we interpreted this as one (among other) pieces of evidence supporting the notion that collaborative expertise may be involved (Dixon, 1996). Furthermore, no evidence of substantial or increased memory errors was observed.

In a later study, we replicated and extended these results (Gagnon, 1995). Overall, all positive recall products (i.e., propositional recall, macrostatements, inferences) were relatively high for older married couples whereas all negative recall products (i.e., errors) were quite low. In addition, the level of production for each of these measures was, as compared to unacquainted younger and older adults and younger married couples, predictable from a collaborative expertise model.

Finally, in another study we examined the communication processes that occur during collaborative recall conversations (Gould, Kurzman, & Dixon, 1994). The goal was to explore possible dynamic explanations for the success of collaborative expert older couples. We identified a mechanism that could be interpreted as supporting the contention that older couples sought to maximize the accuracy and completeness of their collaborative performance while minimizing their errors and distortions. Specifically, older couples, unlike younger and older unacquainted dyads and younger couples, increased their interactive strategic efforts to further their performance throughout the collaborative conversations (Gould et al., 1994).

Summary

This brief review has demonstrated that there is evidence that, in some circumstances, collaborative cognition can result in equivalent (or even increased) accurate recall rates and correspondingly lower error rates. This may be of special interest because the target group was one that had, as individuals, experienced memory decline. Despite the memory impairment, in an everyday setting, older interactive expert adults were able to compensate for individual deficits. There are several amplifications and qualifications that could be mentioned (see Dixon, 1996, for further information). We turn now, however, from the questions of accuracy and distortions in actual cognitive performance to the issue of beliefs about collaborative effectiveness. To our knowledge, this topic has not previously been explored.

BELIEFS ABOUT COLLABORATIVE ACCURACY AND DISTORTION

Beliefs and Cognitive Aging: An Overview

Increasingly since the 1970s, scholars have been examining a variety of aspects of metacognition, and the extent to which they can affect how one behaves or performs in particular cognitively demanding situations or even how one develops cognitively across the life span (Metcalfe & Shimamura, 1994). Relevant research has been guided by several general questions, three of which are especially pertinent in this chapter. First, can cognitive performance and cognitive development be better understood by reference to what one knows or believes about cognitive abilities, cognitive skills, specific cognitive tasks, current online performance, or life-span cognitive development? Second, can individual differences in performance (e.g., developmental gains in childhood, developmental losses in adulthood, organic impairments) be better understood by reference to one or more of these aspects of knowledge and beliefs? A third question pertains to whether it is possible and productive to differentiate among aspects of knowledge, awareness, beliefs, and affect concerning cognition. These issues have been discussed extensively in literatures such as general metacognition (e.g., Metcalfe & Shimamura, 1994), neuropsychology (e.g., Prigatano & Schacter, 1991; Wilson & Watson, 1996), child development (e.g., Cavanaugh & Perlmutter, 1982), and adult development and aging (e.g., Hertzog & Dixon, 1994; Light, 1991).

In the latter area—and especially cognitive aging—the role of beliefs about cognitive skills, cognitive abilities, and cognitive aging have been shown to be of considerable importance. Specifically, beliefs may function to determine whether an older adult engages in cognitive activity, the extent and breadth of such engagement, the effort invested in performing well, the attribution made for successful performance, and the accommodation made for unsuccessful performance (e.g., Hertzog & Dixon, 1994). As examined in the metacognition and aging literature, the term *beliefs* refers to several interlinked processes. These include self-theories and schemata, implicit beliefs, sense of control, self-efficacy, and so forth (e.g., Berry & West, 1993; Cavanaugh, 1996; Hertzog & Dixon, 1994). Thus, an older person who has acquired a belief that memory declines with aging may interpret (if not confirm) that belief through personal experiences of memory failures and distortions in everyday life. These failures may be of no greater magnitude or frequency than those of younger adults (or than the older adult experienced when younger). Nevertheless, such beliefs may result in reduced expectations for personal performance in everyday memory-demanding situations, and subsequently lower probabilities of marshaling and investing significant cognitive and personal resources in memory performance. On the one hand, such modifications of goals serve a useful compensatory function for conditions involving impairment, injury, or decline (Bäckman & Dixon, 1992; Dixon & Bäckman, 1995). On the other hand, such beliefs may foreclose the alternative, namely, that further investment of effort or even training could result in maintained levels of memory performance.

Beliefs about cognitive aging—in general and one's own—may thus contribute to the extent and quality of everyday cognitive performance, social

engagement and interactions, and even cognitive and social development. To
this point, researchers have investigated these metacognitive questions only at
the individual level of analysis. Consistent with our interest in exploring
cognitive performance at the dyadic level of analysis, we have recently
collected data pertaining to beliefs about collaborative cognition.

Beliefs about Collaborative Cognition

We explored this issue in the context of a larger study of collaborative
cognition in younger and older married couples and unacquainted dyads
(Gagnon, 1995). The three fundamental research questions we pursued in the
exploratory work on beliefs follow. First, how would the age and
collaborative condition groups (stranger vs. spouse) compare with regard to
beliefs about general memory performance for individuals and dyads?
Second, how would the age and collaborative condition groups compare on
self-efficacy beliefs about performance on specific memory tasks? Third, how
would older and younger adults respond to questions about collaborative
effectiveness across forms of collaboration (e.g., with spouse, friend, stranger,
alone)? The first two questions represent straightforward applications of the
conventional metacognitive concern with beliefs about own (in this case,
collaborative) performance. The third question, on the other hand, is designed
to reflect implicit theories about collaborative effectiveness and the possibility
that younger and older adults may possess different views.

   General Memory Beliefs. In order to examine how collaborators viewed
their collaborative memory abilities in general, we adapted a single-item
question from the Memory Functioning Questionnaire (MFQ; Gilewski,
Zelinski, & Schaie, 1990), which has been shown to relate to memory self-
efficacy beliefs in younger and older adults (Dixon, Hultsch, & Hertzog, 1988;
Hertzog, Hultsch, & Dixon, 1989). Whereas the original item queries the
participant's beliefs about their own memory functioning, the adapted item
focused on memory functioning when either working with their spouse or
working with a stranger. Responses are collected on a 7-point Likert-type
scale, with higher numbers associated with higher beliefs in memory
functioning. Higher memory beliefs are thought to reflect higher memory self-
efficacy and confidence. The participants (younger and older adults, spouses
and strangers) responded to both the original item (as individuals) and the
adapted item (when working in a collaborative dyad).
   The most interesting result of our analyses is presented in Fig. 5.1. The
interaction involved the three major factors of the analysis: (a) adult age, or
whether the participant was younger or older; (b) collaborative condition, or

whether one was recruited and tested as a married couple or as a unacquainted dyad; and (c) recall condition, or whether the level of analysis for the task was at the individual or dyadic level. Notably, younger and older married couples rated their general memory performance as a couple to be greater than their individual-level memory performance. Indeed, the intriguing tendency for older individuals was that their ratings of individual- and couple-level memory beliefs were quite discrepant. Another interesting observation is that in the dyad recall condition there was a greater difference between older spouse versus stranger dyads than there was for younger spouse versus stranger dyads. In fact, older adults participating as stranger dyads rated their dyadic memory performance as essentially equivalent to older adult individual-level memory performance. The results suggest that the implicit theory of collaborative memory may be that experienced collaboration can result in better memory performance than when working alone. In addition, the belief is apparently that collaboration is more effective when one is working with a spouse than when one is working with a stranger. This latter belief is especially evident for older adults. All of the older adults in the couple condition were long-term married couples, so their beliefs about memory functioning may reflect an endorsement of collaboration with a long-term collaborator. Such a belief is consistent with performance-based research suggesting that indeed for older adults interactive expertise may be associated with relatively higher levels of memory performance (Dixon, 1996). These beliefs, however, were only moderately correlated with actual memory performance in the present study (Gagnon, 1995). This is a common finding in the metamemory and individual aging literature, reflecting both psychological processes (e.g., knowledge vs. self-efficacy beliefs) and methodological constraints (i.e., lack of domain-specific matching).

Task-Specific Memory Self-Efficacy Beliefs. We explored task-specific memory self-efficacy at both the individual and dyad levels. Because the memory performance measures used in the larger study featured indicators of story memory and working memory, we emphasized memory self-efficacy in everyday examples of these two tasks. We adapted a method described by Berry, West, and Dennehy (1989) in which participants are presented with a brief description of an everyday memory problem and initially queried whether they believe they could accomplish it. For example, the story item was, "If I heard a 1-page story about an event in a fictional person's life, I could remember 10% of the story word for word." Participants respond with a "yes" or "no." If they select "yes," they are asked to indicate their level of confidence according to a scale of 0% to 100%. They then move on to the next item, which raises the expected performance bar to 40%, a bar that is raised in successive steps to 60%, 75%, and 100%. That is, the items present

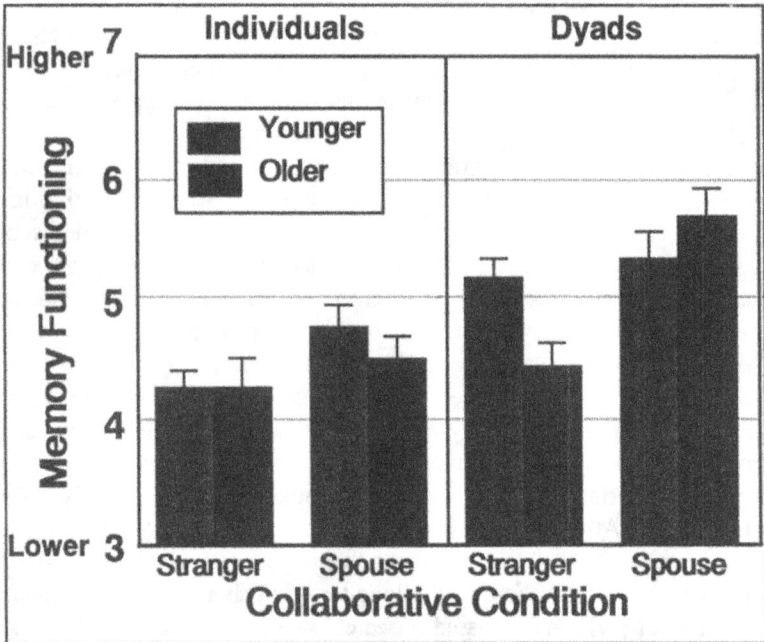

Fig. 5.1. General memory ratings for individual, dyad, and couple performance

successively more difficult memory tasks. Several variables are of interest, including the number of "yes" responses and the pattern of confidence ratings across increasing difficulty.

The pertinent result for the story memory belief item was represented in a three-way interaction among age, recall condition (individual vs. dyad), and confidence rating (in two levels). In general, for the two initial difficulty levels, older adults gave similar confidence ratings whether they were working with a partner or not (although their confidence was generally low, about 35% for both situations). In contrast, younger adults gave higher confidence ratings to working with a partner (about 70%) than to working alone (about 55%). Note that the overall confidence levels associated with a "yes" response to the two easiest difficulty levels were quite different for younger and older adults.

The analogous second item concerned an everyday working memory problem: "If I purchased 12 hardware items, 5 minutes later I could list 2 of the items from most expensive to least expensive without referring to the receipt." This easiest difficulty level was followed by four further levels, raising the difficulty bar, respectively, to 5, 8, 10, and all 12 items. Overall, participants gave higher confidence ratings to dyadic performance than to individual performance. For illustrative purposes, we present the full set of means in Fig. 5.2. This was not a significant interaction, but it does reveal some potentially interesting avenues for further research on task-specific collaborative memory self-efficacy beliefs. For example, consider this: Focusing on the dyad data, it appears that the drop-off in confidence is similar for spouse and stranger dyads, although younger dyads reduce confidence levels more slowly than do older dyads. Recall that in the earlier general memory belief item, older spouses rated their collaborative memories much higher than did older stranger dyads, and even marginally higher than did younger collaborating couples. Why did quite different results appear for a task-specific memory belief item? Research at the individual level on change in memory beliefs (e.g., McDonald-Miszczak, Hertzog, & Hultsch, 1995) and measurement of memory beliefs (e.g., Berry et al., 1989; Dixon et al., 1988; Hertzog & Dixon, 1994) and effects of experiential factors (e.g., West, Dennehy-Basile, & Norris, 1996) may hold the solution to this puzzle. For example, could one's general beliefs about collaborative effectiveness be largely a function of implicit theories whereas one's beliefs about specific tasks are more influenced by particular instances of success (or failure)? Could there be actual task differences in the expectations about collaborative memory accuracy and distortion? For example, collaboration, especially with expert collaborative teams, may be viewed as a general means to cognitive success in everyday life, but it does not necessarily apply to every cognitive task one might encounter. Further research may help to clarify these intriguing questions.

Beliefs About Forms of Collaboration. Finally, we asked two sets of questions concerning participants' comparative beliefs about collaborative memory effectiveness. In the first set, we asked participants to rank-order the effectiveness (regarding memory performance) of the following recall conditions: working alone, working with a spouse, working with a friend (same gender), working with a friend (other gender), working with a stranger (same gender) and working with a stranger (other gender).

The resulting rank orders are presented in Fig. 5.3. Note first that the rank orders for both age groups are identical. For both younger and older adults, collaborating with a spouse was believed to be the most effective mechanism of memory performance. Following this, in order, the participants believed that memory performance would be more effective when collaborating with friends (same gender), collaborating with friends (other gender), working alone, collaborating with stranger (same gender), and collaborating with stranger (other gender). Interestingly, collaborating with strangers was viewed as potentially less effective than working alone. Furthermore, an intriguing gender-specificity was implied: Namely, except for working with a spouse, the

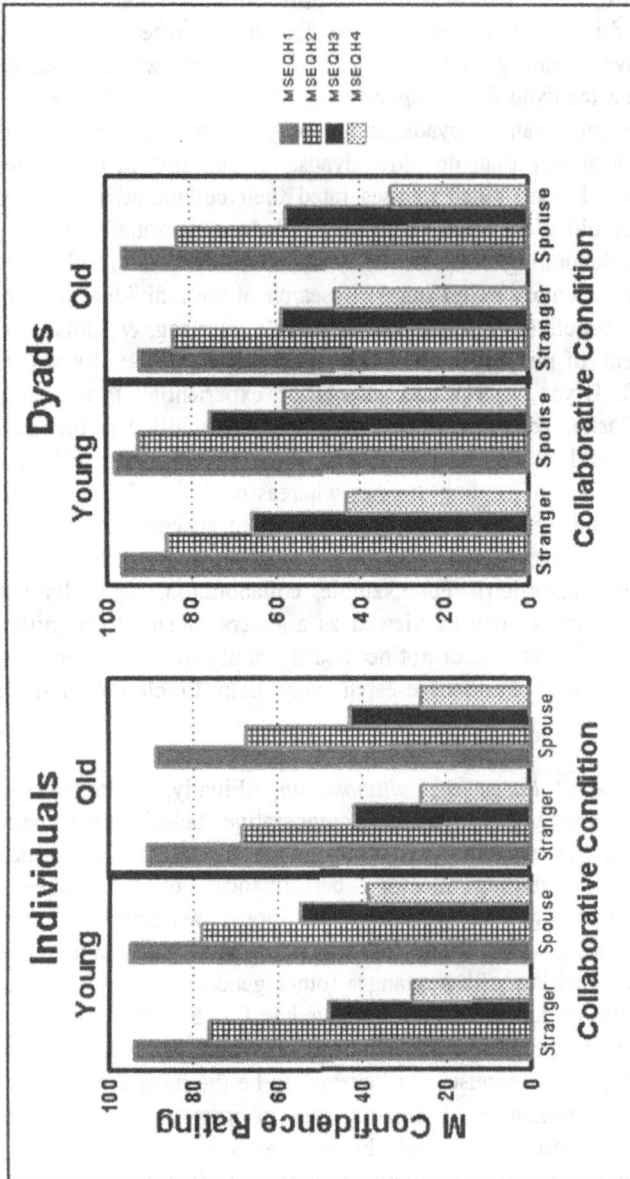

Fig. 5.2. Task-specific (working memory) confidence ratings across four levels of difficulty.

participants believed that working with a member of the same gender was more effective than working with a member of the other gender.

Although the rank orders were the same for both age groups, there may be a subtle difference in the belief systems represented. Closer examination of the profile of means across the six categories separately for younger and older adults suggests a potentially interesting difference. The younger adults' profile is consistent with the interpretation that the six categories reflect two levels of collaborative effectiveness. Specifically, the first level of believed greater effectiveness contains three forms of collaboration, namely, with a spouse or with a friend (same and other gender). The level of believed lesser effectiveness contains the collaborative forms of working alone or with a stranger (same or other gender). In contrast, the pattern of beliefs associated with older adults is consistent with an interpretation that there are three levels of collaborative effectiveness. According to older adults, working with a spouse is the most effective form of collaboration. Following this, working with a friend (same or other gender) or alone constitute the next level of believed collaborative effectiveness. The level of believed least collaborative effectiveness contains only working with a stranger (same or other gender). Thus, younger and older adults may produce the same rank order regarding beliefs of collaborative effectiveness, but in fact have an underlying belief system structure that is substantially different.

What reasons would adults have for ranking collaborative effectiveness as they do? We sought to explore this issue in a second set of open-ended questions. Following the rank-order item, we asked each individual to comment on the advantages and disadvantages of each of the six forms of collaboration. A team of reliable coders then sorted and counted their responses. Six general categories of responses pertaining to the advantages and six corresponding categories pertaining to the disadvantages were generated. The six categories of advantages were:

- *External memory source*, or the notion that the individuals in the collaborating group may act as external aids or references for one another,
- *Differentiation of expertise*, or the idea that alternative or complementary perspectives, knowledge, and skills may be contributed by collaborating individuals,
- *Interpersonal understanding*, or the possibility that knowing a partner's strengths and weaknesses may promote performance,
- *Communication strategies*, or referring to the beneficial effects of collaborating partners developing interactive strategies, cross-cuing, investing more effort, and focusing on the task,
- *Personal or social advantages*, or the notion that the social atmosphere is better whether working alone or together,

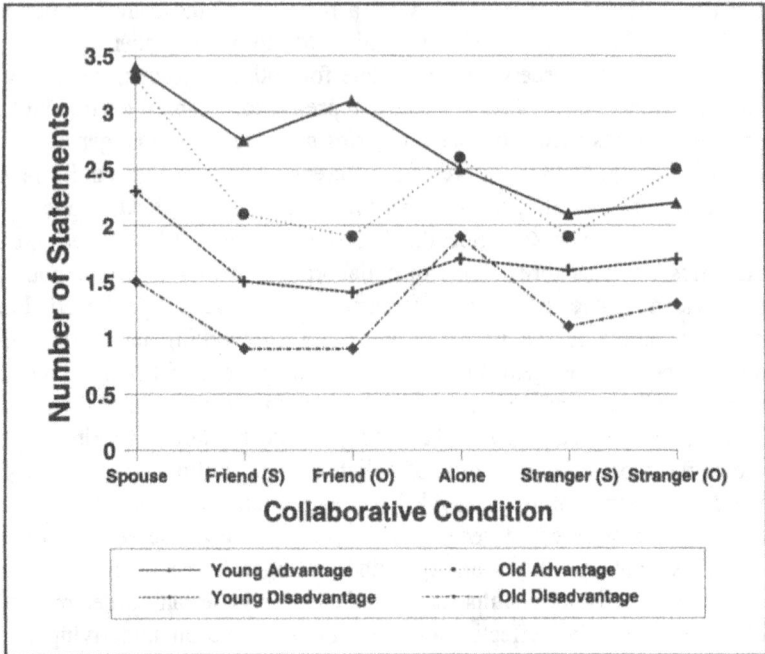

Fig. 5.3. Rank-ordered beliefs about collaborative performance.

- *Task and process-related advantages*, or the proposition that there are inherent advantages to the task or the process of collaborating (or working alone).

The six corresponding categories of disadvantages were:

- *Failure as an external memory source*, or noting the possibility that the collaborative partner could be incorrect or loafing or that an individual working alone is lacking a collaborative partner,
- *Lack of differentiation*, or the possibility that the skills and perspectives of collaborating partners are redundant and noncomplementary, or that one partner may dominate the other,
- *Lack of interpersonal understanding*, or the notion that lack of familiarity or knowledge about a collaborating partner could be a limiting factor in performance, if not detrimental to it,
- *Communication and individual memory systems breakdown*, or the idea that (a) in the collaborative situation, communicative difficulties or interruptions may diminish combined productivity and (b) in the individual situation, inhibitions or distractions may not be compensated by a partner,

- *Personal or social disadvantages*, such as the presence of conflict, discomfort, or social distractions,
- *Task and process disadvantages*, in which inherent task- or process-related characteristics operate to diminish recall performance in either the collaborative or individual situation.

A category for no advantages or disadvantages was also included, but used quite infrequently.

A summary of these data is presented in Fig. 5.4. Overall, more comments concerning advantages than disadvantages were produced by the participants. In addition, younger adults produced more statements pertaining to advantages and disadvantages than did older adults. An ANOVA on these data revealed a significant three-way interaction, as portrayed in the figure. Among the interesting trends in this interaction are (a) the notable high and equivalent number of advantages for working with a spouse produced by younger and older adults, (b) the relatively high number of comments pertaining to disadvantages of working alone, and (c) the upturn in disadvantages for working with a stranger (other gender) as compared to stranger (same gender).

For older adults, no category of advantages or disadvantages received as much attention as did working with a spouse. What did the older adults actually say about collaborating with spouses? Did their beliefs about the advantages of such collaboration match the theory we have been elaborating? Next, we present some examples of the astute comments regarding the advantages of spousal communication in collaborative cognition. We have modified the comments slightly in the interest of readability, but the content has not been changed.

Older Woman: For spouses who have been married as long as I have, you know how the other person's mind works and what will trigger memory in them. If you're having difficulty remembering something you can give them a hint that will help them remember what you're thinking of, a cue word that brings out the answer you're looking for . . . With a spouse, because you can understand one another you can rely on them for your weaknesses and vice versa.

Older Woman: I think the main advantage is that you can fill in each other's gaps . . . And also you can use your spouse as a memory board to remind you about doing things . . .

Older Woman: I find that we remember different things so we sort of complement each other fairly well. I remember numbers and telephone numbers, addresses, and people's names, whereas he remembers more important things, such as knowing where we've been and where we're going . . . together we jog each other's memory.

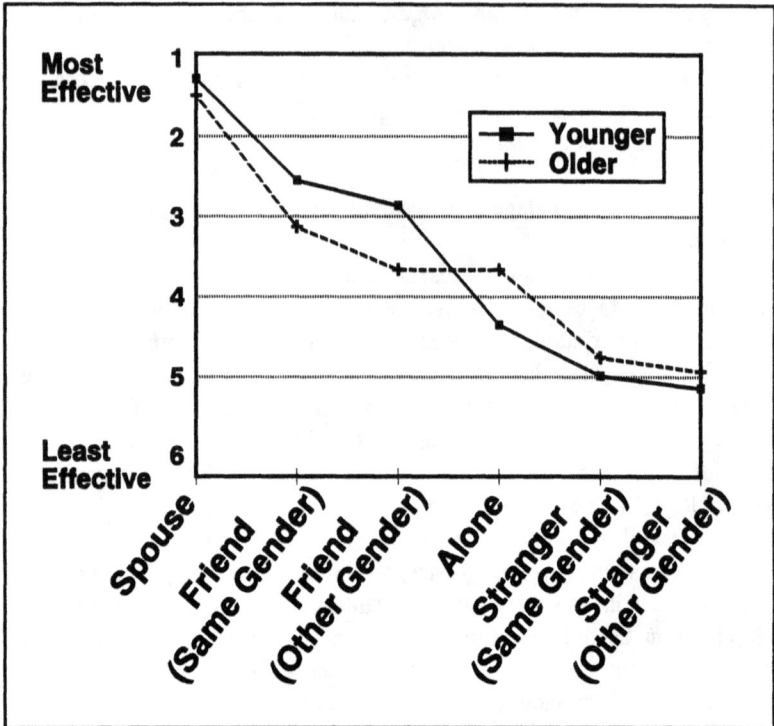

Fig. 5.4. Number of statements produced regarding advantages or disadvantages of six collaborative conditions.

Older Woman: We have different kinds of memory and one fills in where the other fails. Obviously, our memories are not failing at the same rate . . . and different things have impressed us . . . so one will remember . . . Between us, we can come up with a pretty good memory of what we've experienced.

Older Man: I think when you apply two brains to a problem you're bound to [do better]. Two heads are better than one . . . [but] too many cooks can spoil the broth . . . [but] the more people who are putting their heads together to work on a problem the better chance you have of solving it.

Older Man: I think that I would be almost lost without my wife. We complement each other very much; we do something or see something and we start recounting it to our spouse and she fills in so much of what I didn't recall or didn't appreciate . . . Recall or memory are so much enhanced because you love your spouse.

Older Man: If one of us makes a mistake the other can correct that mistake. And so we are less apt to make a mistake that would carry on, we're more apt to correct it at the time.

Overall, the theme of these comments is that working with a spouse presents some distinct advantages over collaborating with others or working alone. The complementarity and familiarity achieved over many years of everyday collaboration can lead to a heightened sense of collaborative memory self-efficacy—a belief that accuracy and comprehensiveness are enhanced and errors and distortions are minimized, if not corrected. The enthusiasm that older adults expressed in their comments is reflected not only in the content (as illustrated in the quotations) but in the fact that this query brought forth the lengthiest responses. Equally interesting, perhaps, is the fact that several studies of collaborative performance by older married couples have revealed some evidence supportive of these optimistic beliefs.

CONCLUSION

Collaborative activity is a common fact of life for adults of all ages. An apparent presumption of collaboration is that, at least to some point, having more than one person working on a task may lead to better (more accurate, more complete, faster, error-free) products than when one person works alone. An implicit belief in the aphorism, "two heads are better than one," is present (Hill, 1982). The extent to which collaboration is actually associated with benefits or losses has been studied in a variety of literatures. Recently, researchers in cognitive science, applied cognitive psychology, social cognition, and cognitive development and aging have explored selected aspects of the processes and products of collaboration. To be sure, the results have not been entirely consistent—nor favorable to the aphorism. In cognitive aging, however, some emerging evidence suggests that selected indicators of positive performance may be improved, and selected indicators of negative performance may be diminished, with collaboration. This differentiation may be especially true for collaborating units that may be characterized as interactive experts.

What about the aphorism itself—and the implicit belief it may reflect? New exploratory research on beliefs about collaborative performance and aging was summarized. For older adults, knowledge and beliefs about cognition—known as metacognition—are thought to be associated with factors that promote or diminish a sense of mastery, confidence, effort, control, perseverance, causal attributions, strategic behaviors, and so forth. Although collaborative cognition and aging has been studied, virtually no previous research has considered such metacognitive issues in a collaborative setting.

Overall, we found that beliefs about collaboration and aging are relatively representative of the research in this area. The general sense is that collaboration is effective in promoting accuracy and in diminishing distortion. But there are interesting qualifications and subtleties. First, collaboration is not viewed as a royal road to accurate and comprehensive memory performance. The beliefs were relatively well-rounded, with both advantages and disadvantages mentioned. Nevertheless, in the open format questions, advantages of collaboration were mentioned significantly more frequently than were disadvantages. In addition, for only one collaborative condition were the number of advantages matched by the number of disadvantages—and that was working alone. Second, there are some distinctions made between forms—or the units—of collaboration. Overall, interactive experts are believed to be more efficient and productive than are interactive friends and strangers. For both younger and older adults—and especially the latter—this was especially true for working with a spouse. Interestingly, working alone is believed to be potentially as (or more) effective than collaborating with strangers. Participants identify reasonable advantages and disadvantages of different constellations of interaction. The continuum they generate is consistent with a belief system that values experience and familiarity in collaborative settings.

Obviously, beliefs may vary when one is faced with specific everyday problems. Whereas strangers may not be viewed as the optimal form of collaboration when one is asked to remember a story or a shopping list, if one is lost in an unfamiliar city, consulting a friendly stranger at a corner shop may indeed be a viable option. Beliefs about collaborative memory accuracy and distortion could, in future research, be explored further for both their practical implications and their theoretical importance.

ACKNOWLEDGMENTS

The first author acknowledges grant support from the Natural Sciences and Engineering Research Council of Canada and from the National Institute on Aging (AG 08235).

REFERENCES

Bäckman, L., & Dixon, R. A. (1992). Psychological compensation: A theoretical framework. *Psychological Bulletin, 112*, 259–283.
Baltes, P. B. (1987). Theoretical propositions of life-span developmental psychology: On the dynamics between growth and decline. *Developmental Psychology, 23*, 611–626.

Baltes, P. B., & Staudinger, U. M. (Eds.). (1996). *Interactive minds: Life-span perspectives on the social foundation of cognition.* New York: Cambridge University Press.

Berry, J. M., & West, R. L. (1993). Cognitive self-efficacy in relation to personal mastery and goal setting across the life span. *International Journal of Behavioral Development, 16,* 251–379.

Berry, J. M., West, R. L., & Dennehy, D. M. (1989). Reliability and validity of the Metamemory Self-efficacy Questionnaire (MSEQ). *Developmental Psychology, 25,* 701–713.

Brandtstädter, J., & Wentura, D. (1995). Adjustment to shifting possibility frontiers in later life: Complementary adaptive modes. In R. A. Dixon & L. Bäckman (Eds.), *Compensating for psychological deficits and declines: Managing losses and promoting gains* (pp. 83–106). Mahwah, NJ: Lawrence Erlbaum Associates.

Cavanaugh, J. C. (1996). Memory self-efficacy as a moderator of memory change. In F. Blanchard-Fields & T. M. Hess (Eds.), *Perspectives on cognitive change in adulthood and aging* (pp. 488–507). New York: McGraw-Hill.

Cavanaugh, J. C., & Perlmutter, M. (1982). Metamemory: A critical examination. *Child Development, 53,* 11–28.

Charness, N. (1989). Age and expertise: Responding to Talland's challenge. In L. W. Poon, D. C. Rubin, & B. A. Wilson (Eds.), *Everyday cognition in adulthood and late life* (pp. 437–456). New York: Cambridge University Press.

Charness, N., & Bosman, E. (1995). Compensation through environmental modification. In R. A. Dixon & L. Bäckman (Eds.), *Compensating for psychological deficits and declines: Managing losses and promoting gains* (pp. 147–168). Mahwah, NJ: Lawrence Erlbaum Associates.

Clark, N. K., & Stephenson, G. M. (1989). Group remembering. In P. B. Paulus (Ed.), *Psychology of group influence* (pp. 357–391). Hillsdale, NJ: Lawrence Erlbaum Associates.

Craik, F. I. M., & Jennings, J. M. (1992). Human memory. In F. I. M. Craik & T. A. Salthouse (Eds.), *The handbook of aging and cognition* (pp. 51–110). Hillsdale, NJ: Lawrence Erlbaum Associates.

Dixon, R. A. (1992). Contextual approaches to adult intellectual development. In R. J. Sternberg & C. A. Berg (Eds.), *Intellectual development* (pp. 350–380). New York: Cambridge University Press.

Dixon, R. A. (1995). Promoting competence through compensation. In L. Bond, S. Cutler, & A. Grams (Eds.), *Promoting successful and productive aging* (pp. 220–238). Newbury Park, CA: Sage.

Dixon, R. A. (1996). Collaborative memory and aging. In D. J. Herrmann, M. K. Johnson, C. L. McEvoy, C. Hertzog, & P. Hertel (Eds.), *Basic and applied memory: Theory in context* (pp. 359–383). Mahwah, NJ: Lawrence Erlbaum Associates.

Dixon, R. A., & Bäckman, L. (1995). Concepts of compensation: Integrated, differentiated, and Janus-faced. In R. A. Dixon & L. Bäckman (Eds.), *Compensating for psychological deficits and declines: Managing losses and promoting gains* (pp. 3–19). Mahwah, NJ: Lawrence Erlbaum Associates.

Dixon, R. A., & Gould, O. N. (1996). Adults telling and retelling stories collaboratively. In P. B. Baltes & U. M. Staudinger (Eds.), *Interactive minds: Life-span perspectives on the social foundation of cognition* (pp. 221–241). New York: Cambridge University Press.

Dixon, R. A., & Gould, O. N. (in press). Younger and older adults collaborating on retelling everyday stories. *Applied Developmental Science.*

Dixon, R. A., & Hertzog, C. (1996). Theoretical issues in cognition and aging. In T. M. Hess & F. Blanchard-Fields (Eds.), *Perspectives on cognitive changes in adulthood and aging* (pp. 25–65). New York: McGraw-Hill.

Dixon, R. A., Hultsch, D. F., & Hertzog, C. (1988). The Metamemory in Adulthood (MIA) questionnaire. *Psychopharmacology Bulletin, 24,* 671–688.

Engeström, Y. (1992). Interactive expertise: Studies in distributed working intelligence. *Research Bulletin, 83* (Department of Education, University of Helsinki).

Ericsson, K. A., & Charness, N. (1994). Expert performance: Its structure and acquisition. *American Psychologist, 49,* 725–747.

Ericsson, K. A., & Smith, J. (Eds.). (1991). *Toward a general theory of expertise: Prospects and limits.* Cambridge, England: Cambridge University Press.

Gagnon, L. M. (1995). *Collaborative remembering: Are there age-related differences in working with a stranger or with a spouse?* Unpublished master's thesis, University of Victoria, Canada.

Galegher, J., Kraut, R. E., & Egido, C. (Eds.). (1990). *Intellectual teamwork: Social and technological foundations of cooperative work.* Hillsdale, NJ: Lawrence Erlbaum Associates.

Gilewski, M. J., Zelinski, E. M., & Schaie, K. W. (1990). The Memory Functioning Questionnaire for assessment of memory complaints in adulthood and old age. *Psychology and Aging, 5,* 482–490.

Gould, O. N., Kurzman, D., & Dixon, R. A. (1994). Communication during prose recall conversations by young and old dyads. *Discourse Processes, 17,* 149–165.

Gould, O. N., Trevithick, L., & Dixon, R. A. (1991). Adult age differences in elaborations produced during prose recall. *Psychology and Aging, 6,* 93–99.

Greeno, J. G., & Moore, J. L. (1993). Situativity and symbols: Response to Vera and Simon. *Cognitive Science, 17,* 49–59.

Heckhausen, J., Dixon, R. A., & Baltes, P. B. (1989). Gains and losses in development throughout adulthood as perceived by different adult age groups. *Developmental Psychology, 25,* 109–121.

Hertzog, C., & Dixon, R. A. (1994). Metacognitive development in adulthood and old age. In J. Metcalfe & A. P. Shimamura (Eds.), *Metacognition: Knowing about knowing* (pp. 227–251). Cambridge, MA: MIT Press.

Hertzog, C., & Dunlosky, J. (1996). The aging of practical memory: An overview. In D. J. Herrmann, M. K. Johnson, C. L. McEvoy, C. Hertzog, & P. Hertel (Eds.), *Basic and applied memory: Theory in context* (pp. 337–358). Mahwah, NJ: Lawrence Erlbaum Associates.

Hertzog, C., Hultsch, D. F., & Dixon, R. A. (1989). Evidence for the convergent validity of two self-report metamemory questionnaires. *Developmental Psychology, 25,* 687–700.

Hill, G. W. (1982). Group versus individual performance: Are N + 1 heads better than one? *Psychological Bulletin, 91,* 517–539.

Kausler, D. H. (1991). *Experimental psychology, cognition, and human aging* (2nd ed.). New York: Springer.

Light, L. L. (1991). Memory and aging: Four hypotheses in search of data. *Annual Review of Psychology, 42,* 333–376.

Lindenberger, U., & Baltes, P. B. (1994). Sensory functioning and intelligence in old age. *Psychology and Aging, 9,* 339–355.

Marsiske, M., Lang, F. R., Baltes, P. B., & Baltes, M. M. (1995). Selective optimization with compensation: Life-span perspectives on successful human development. In R. A. Dixon & L. Bäckman (Eds.), *Compensating for psychological deficits and declines: Managing losses and promoting gains* (pp. 35–79). Mahwah, NJ: Lawrence Erlbaum Associates.

McDonald–Miszczak, L., Hertzog, C., & Hultsch, D. F. (1995). Stability and accuracy of metamemory in adulthood and aging: A longitudinal analysis. *Psychology and Aging, 10,* 553–564.

Metcalfe, J., & Shimamura, A. P. (Eds.). (1994). *Metacognition: Knowing about knowing.* Cambridge, MA: MIT Press.

Middleton, D., & Edwards, D. (Eds.). (1990). *Collective remembering.* Newbury Park, CA: Sage.

Park, D. C. (1992). Applied cognitive aging research. In F. I. M. Craik & T. A. Salthouse (Eds.), *The handbook of aging and cognition* (pp. 449–493). Hillsdale, NJ: Lawrence Erlbaum Associates.

Paulus, P. B. (Ed.). (1989). *Psychology of group influence.* Hillsdale, NJ: Lawrence Erlbaum Associates.

Prigatano, G. P., & Schacter, D. L. (Eds.). (1991). *Awareness of deficit after brain injury: Clinical and theoretical perspectives.* New York: Oxford University Press.

Resnick, L. B., Levine, J. M., & Teasley, S. D. (Eds.). (1991). *Perspectives on socially shared cognition.* Washington, DC: American Psychological Association.

Salthouse, T. A. (1987). Age, experience, and compensation. In C. Schooler & K. W. Schaie (Eds.), *Cognitive functioning and social structure over the life course* (pp. 142–157). Norwood, NJ: Ablex.

Salthouse, T. A. (1990). Cognitive competence and expertise. In J. E. Birren & K. W. Schaie (Eds.), *Handbook of the psychology of aging* (3rd ed., pp. 310–319). San Diego: Academic Press.

Salthouse, T. A. (1991). *Theoretical perspectives on cognitive aging.* Hillsdale, NJ: Lawrence Erlbaum Associates.

Salthouse, T. A. (1994). The nature of the influence of speed on adult age differences in cognition. *Developmental Psychology, 30,* 240–259.

Salthouse, T. A. (1995). Refining the concept of compensation. In R. A. Dixon & L. Bäckman (Eds.), *Compensating for psychological deficits and declines:*

Managing losses and promoting gains (pp. 21–34). Mahwah, NJ: Lawrence Erlbaum Associates.

Schaie, K. W. (1990). Intellectual development in adulthood. In J. E. Birren & K. W. Schaie (Eds.), *Handbook of the psychology of aging* (3rd ed., pp. 291–309). San Diego, CA: Academic Press.

Schaie, K. W. (1996). *Intellectual development in adulthood: The Seattle Longitudinal Study.* Cambridge, England: Cambridge University Press.

Steiner, I. D. (1972). *Group process and productivity.* New York: Academic Press.

Vygotsky, L. S. (1978). *Mind in society: The development of higher psychological processes.* Cambridge, MA: Harvard University Press.

West, R. L., Dennehy-Basile, D., & Norris, M. P. (1996). Memory self-evaluation: The effects of age and experience. *Aging, Neuropsychology, and Cognition, 3,* 67–83.

Wilson, B. A., & Watson, P. C. (1996). A practical framework for understanding compensatory behaviour in people with organic memory impairment. *Memory, 4,* 456–486.

Willis, S. L., & Dubin, S. S. (Eds.). (1990). *Maintaining professional competence.* San Francisco, CA: Jossey-Bass.

6

Sociocultural and Practical Influences on Spatial Memory

Mary Gauvain
University of California, Riverside

Spatial memory and distortions of spatial memory are discussed in relation to two contextual influences: practical activity and culture. Three types of spatial distortions in memory are described: distortions of distance, spatial relations, and direction. The ways in which practical activity and culture may help understand these distortions is discussed. Research on spatial memory conducted in Western and non-Western communities and with children and adults is used to illustrate how practical activity and culture influence spatial memory and may contribute to certain patterns of distortions of these memories.

Imagine living in a vast desert and having to search for food and shelter, scarce resources in this setting. When you come across places that provide nourishment or safe haven, you will want to remember where they are located. You may write down this information in narrative form or draw a map or perhaps create some type of mnemonic, such as a story, to help you remember. Now imagine that the desert you live in is a cold one, the Arctic. In addition to remembering useful places, you also need to know the seasonal conditions that affect travel. In the spring and summer, travel occurs over land and water. In the winter, the very long, dark winter, travel occurs over ice and snow-covered land. Furthermore, the shape of the land is always changing. Ice fields break off, snow melts. How might living in such a setting affect spatial memory as well as people's ability to move around in the environment? What ways have people who live in this type of environment devised to describe and remember information about the space? And, finally, how might consideration of this type of spatial memory help us understand certain distortions of spatial memory?

To address these questions, this chapter adopts a sociocultural approach to spatial memory. I argue that better understanding of the linkages between spatial memory and the sociocultural context in which this knowledge develops and is used is important for examining both spatial memory and its distortions. The chapter begins with a description of some of the more common distortions of spatial memory. In general, these distortions are explained in two ways. One type of explanation focuses on internal reasons, mainly processing limitations or biases. The other type of explanation emphasizes external influences, especially the role that past experience plays in what we learn and remember about a space. Although the chapter touches on both of these explanations, it is primarily concerned with tracing how past experiences may influence spatial memory and perhaps explain some of the patterns of distortion often contained in these memories. To do this, I examine the relation between spatial memory and two contextual aspects of past experience, namely the role of practical or goal-directed activity and the influence of culture on the development and organization of spatial memory. Illustrations from research in Western and non-Western cultures and with children and adults will be used to demonstrate ways in which practical activity and culture influence spatial memory.

In this chapter, three key concepts of a sociocultural approach to cognition and cognitive development are applied to the study of spatial cognition. First, human spatial thinking is largely influenced by culture. Much of what we remember about the environment reflects knowledge that is important to and valued by our culture. Second, culture influences the types of activities we conduct in space and, as a result, provides both opportunities for and constraints on what we can learn about space. Third, because spatial thinking is both complex and essential to human functioning, cultures have, over the course of history, devised ways of supporting the development and maintenance of spatial memory. Cultures have created tools (or artifacts) for representing spatial information, such as maps, and for communicating spatial memory, such as conventional forms of describing space. Cultures have also created social and behavioral practices or routines that direct action in space, such as navigational practices. These tools and practices mediate human spatial activity (Cole, 1996). As such, they influence how and what we learn about the environment in the course of our travels as well as how we organize and store spatial information for later use.

Considering spatial thinking in relation to culture and practical experience is consistent with activity theory (Leont'ev, 1981; Vygotsky, 1978; Zinchenko, 1981). One of the important premises of activity theory is that human behavior and thinking occur in meaningful contexts as people conduct purposeful, goal-directed actions in which physical and social mechanisms (or tools) of a culture facilitate and mediate the origin and conduct of the activity.

Before we examine how practical activity and cultural context help people acquire and organize spatial memory, I return to the example that opened the chapter to introduce a discussion of distortions of spatial memory.

DISTORTIONS OF SPATIAL MEMORY

In order to describe and remember important places, the native peoples of the Arctic, the Inuit, drew maps. These traditional maps were drawn on the snow, on paper, and sometimes on antlers or walrus tusks. However, unlike survey maps of large land areas that contain fairly accurate information about the distances between locations, the maps of the Inuits were only accurate about the relative locations and directions of important places. In other words, the scale of the drawings was often way off. These maps impressed nonnative travelers to the region at the turn of the century (Boas, 1884–85). These visitors found that the maps included much detail about the region and often covered areas as large as 500 miles. Like more familiar schematic maps (e.g. of subway routes; Bartram & Smith, 1984), spatial relations are preserved but distances are distorted.

Distortion of distance is one frequent type of distortion of spatial memory. People also distort information about spatial relations and direction or orientation. In general, these distortions reflect patterned ways in which people select and organize spatial information for memory. Some of these distortions simplify or regularize spatial information, whereas others reflect tendencies to group or categorize spatial information in certain ways. In the main, these distortions represent efforts to manage the large amount of spatial input we encounter in daily life. We need to select, from all the spatial information that is available to us, information that is important and useful, and then we need to remember it in a form that will be helpful later.

Distortions of Distance

Distortion of distance in spatial memory is fairly commonplace. In general, the longer the distance, the less accurate the estimate (Anooshian & Kromer, 1986). However, we also tend to overestimate the distance of shorter routes, especially when they are spatially complex. Both adults and children overestimate distance when a barrier is placed between objects (Kosslyn, Pick, & Fariello, 1974). Basically, spatial clutter, such as many turns or landmarks, can lead to overestimation (Byrne, 1979; Sadalla & Magel, 1980; Thorndyke, 1981). The additional demands on spatial processing in more complex settings apparently leads to overestimation. It seems that perceived distance matters more than metric distance in distance estimation.

Some distortions of distance reflect a combination of the nature of the setting and the type of information that is important to remember. Consider the maps of the Inuits. In these maps, great distances are collapsed and viewed only in relative terms. In this way, a large portion of the environment can be remembered. Furthermore, the changing conditions of the landscape affect how accurately distance can be represented.

Does the distortion of distance that appears in maps such as these indicate that spatial memory is also distorted? This is a difficult question to answer, but some evidence suggests that this may not be so. Thorndyke (1981) showed that errors in distance estimation resulting from map use can be due to the added processing required when using maps that contain lots of spatial complexity, like the number of spatial relations portrayed or the actual distance, and not to the spatial memory per se. Errors did not appear when people were tested for their memory of the map overall, but they did appear when people were asked to make judgments on the basis of information derived from the map. Thus, distance errors do not necessarily mean that the person's spatial memory is inaccurate.

Distortions of Spatial Relations

Spatial relations can also be distorted in memory. This has been demonstrated in research by asking people the relative position of geographic locations. When Stevens and Coupe (1978) asked adults in the United States where two cities, Reno, Nevada and San Diego, California, are in relation to one another, respondents typically erred by stating that Reno is northeast of San Diego, when the correct direction is northwest. Why do adults make this error?

It seems that the spatial memory for these two cities is encoded as a subunit of information in the superordinate relations of the states of Nevada and California. Most of Nevada is to the east of California. However, because of the shape and curvature of the states, some of the northern cities of Nevada fall west of some of the southern cities of California. Thus, when people are asked to make relational inferences about these subunits and the information is stored in terms of the more superordinate groupings to which they have been assigned, errors can result.

This type of heuristic or strategy helps simplify spatial tasks and reduce the amount of specialized spatial information that needs to be stored (Tversky, 1981). Research indicates that spatial relations are remembered in ways that involve hierarchical relations, as in the Reno–San Diego example (Chase & Chi, 1980) or in ways that align spatial relations based on other types of spatial inferences. For example, Moar (1979) showed that when people think of relations of land areas to one another, the terms *up* and *down* are seen as corresponding with North and South and *right* and *left* as corresponding with East and West. These alignments can lead to relational errors also. Thus, distortions of relative locations result from grouping spatial information in relation to larger units or from alignment with a more general or conventional frame of reference, such as that depicted on large-scale geographic maps.

Distortions of Direction

Another common distortion in spatial memory involves directionality. Movement in large-scale space often requires us to integrate information collected over a period of time and that may not be visually available at the same time. This means that we need to go beyond the information provided in the immediate visual array to infer where out-of-sight locations are. When direction estimates require complex inferences, for instance the identification of a site after taking many turns or a reversal of direction along a familiar route, distortion frequently occurs. Children in particular have difficulty in drawing accurate directional inferences under such conditions (Anooshian & Nelson, 1985, cited in Anooshian & Siegel, 1985).

One reason that directional inferences are difficult may be because of the tendency for people to normalize and regularize angles toward 90° (Byrne, 1979). When Byrne had adults draw the angles of a road from memory, all types of angles were drawn more like the right angle than they actually were. This may be a consequence of a more general cognitive bias to regularize information in alignment with prototypic angles and shapes. In fact, as early as 3 months of age infants appear to have spatial memories that reflect prototypical geometric information. Bomba and Siqueland (1983) showed infants a series of dot patterns that resembled but did not duplicate regular geometric shapes. When 3- and 4-month-olds were then shown the prototypic forms, the infants habituated to them sooner. That is, they acted as if they had seen them before even though they had only seen distorted versions of them. This suggests that the infants had either abstracted the prototypic form from the less regular versions or had actually encoded the less regular versions in more prototypic form at the outset when viewing the less regular versions.

A tendency to regularize spatial information in relation to prototypic angles and shapes would lead to distortion in directional estimates. Such distortions need not impede travel except in certain conditions. In moving through space, adjustments can be readily made, especially if the actual direction is not too far off from the remembered version. Grosser directional distortions may be less easily remedied, however. This may help explain why some short cuts work and some do not.

SPATIAL DISTORTIONS AND CONTEXT

It appears that distortions of spatial memory reflect certain internal tendencies or biases like simplification, regularization, and organization. However, they also appear to reflect external influences, like past experience and, in particular, the context in which these memories are acquired and used. For instance, the accuracy of distance estimations reflects how familiar people are with the route being estimated (Blades, 1990). Inferences about spatial relations may be based on relational groupings that people have learned (Evans & Pezdek, 1980). Directional distortions can result from the type of spatial orientation with which people are experienced (Levinson, 1996).

In order to examine further the influence of past experience on spatial memory, I concentrate on two important aspects of past experience: culture and practical experience. The next section explores the ways in which practical experience may influence the development and organization of spatial memory. This information sets the stage for the following section that integrates what we know about the practical aspects of spatial memory with the larger cultural frame in which spatial thinking and memory occur.

PRACTICAL ACTIVITY AND SPATIAL THINKING

Spatial knowledge is acquired through experience. To understand the organization, development, and use of spatial knowledge we need to consider the experience that led to the knowledge, including the structure of the activity or task—in particular the task goal and materials—and the actor's involvement in the task. To do this, studies have examined how the amount and the type of experience in an environment influence the development and organization of spatial memory.

Amount of Experience and Spatial Memory

One factor that has been studied extensively in research on spatial memory is the role that experience in a setting plays in the acquisition and organization of spatial skill and knowledge (Acredolo, 1982). Hardly surprising is the consistent result that increased familiarity due to experience in an environment enhances memory for the space (Acredolo, Pick, & Olson, 1975; Evans, Marrero, & Butler, 1981; Herman, Kail, & Siegel, 1979) and facilitates spatial orientation (Gärling, Lindberg, & Mäntylä, 1983). The use of particular features in previous activities helps determine whether these features are used to conduct subsequent activities in the space, especially if similar or related goals are operative. For instance, the use of natural topographic features as landmarks in spatial memory is related to previous experience (e.g., hiking) in natural environments (Heft, 1979).

Both children and adults gain much information about space as they conduct activities and move around in the environment. However, amount of experience alone does not explain spatial learning and memory. Other considerations, like type of experience in a setting, are also important to consider.

Type of Experience and Spatial Memory

Does more active exploration of a space, that is, actual movement through a space, influence spatial learning differently from more passive exploration? In a study by Cornell and Hay (1984), 5- and 8-year-old children viewed a route in one of three ways: as a slide presentation, on videotape, or by walking along the route with a guide. Each child viewed the route only once and was then asked to retrace the route in both forward and reverse directions. There was little difference in performance in the slide or videotape conditions, but there were many fewer errors made by children in the walking condition. Other research reports similar results. Cohen and Weatherford (1981) conducted an experiment in which children viewed a model town from its periphery or were able to walk through it. Again, active learning resulted in more accurate spatial memory than more passive experience. In a more ecologically based study, Hart (1979) found that children's environmental knowledge was directly related to their activity range during play.

These and other findings (Appleyard, 1975; Feldman & Acredolo, 1979; Gale, Golledge, Pellegrino, & Doherty, 1990; Poag, Cohen, & Weatherford, 1983) suggest that spatial memory is facilitated by the experience of actually moving around in the environment. Movement may provide the type of visual information useful for extracting and integrating spatial locations and relations in an area. This is not to say that vision is the sole source of spatial information. We know from research with blind children and adults that other nonvisual cues, such as sound, texture, smell, and the consequences of one's own movement, can be used to learn about and guide effective action in the environment (Warren, 1984). The important point is that active exploration of the environment is conducive to learning about and remembering spatial information. Yet, focusing on type of movement does not tell the entire story either. We must also consider the connection between movement and the goal of the activity.

Activity Goals and Spatial Memory

Despite substantial support for the idea that active exploration influences spatial learning more than passive exploration, some studies have found no difference in spatial memory as a result of more active exploration (Herman, 1980; Herman & Siegel, 1978; Heth & Cornell, 1985). However, these results may be explained by noting that movement is most effective for acquiring spatial knowledge when it is related to the goal or purpose of the activity. Thus, movement per se may not be as vital as the match between the goal of the activity and the movement used to attain the goal.

To demonstrate this, Gauvain and Rogoff (1986) had children explore a novel area, with one group of children instructed to remember the best route through the space and the other group instructed to remember the layout or configuration of the space. Children given instructions to study the layout remembered layout-relevant information, whereas route-focused children recalled much less about the presence or location of places in the space that were not on the route. This result is interesting in light of the fact that a common view of spatial representations and their development is the idea that route-based representations precede more survey or configurational representations (Siegel & White, 1975). The data do not dispute this claim in that the children with configurational knowledge also possessed route knowledge and the children with route knowledge did not display survey knowledge. However, whether or not the children's spatial memory contained either of these types of information was due to the instructional goal that directed the children's exploration of the space and, consequently, what was remembered.

In sum, research suggests that memory for space is influenced by the goal of the activity. Spatial memory may, therefore, be best understood on tasks where there is a relation between the actions performed in the space and the overall goal of the activity.

PRACTICAL ACTIVITY AND SPATIAL MEMORY

To examine this connection further, I consider how the everyday activities of adults and children—activities defined by their practical, goal-directed actions—influence the development, organization, and use of spatial memory. My illustrations focus on how children's social experience with adults can influence their spatial understanding and how adults' experience in the workplace can influence their knowledge and use of space. Both of these represent important daily experiences of these groups.

Role of Social Experience with Adults in Children's Learning About and Memory for Space

Research conducted by the Munroes in Kenya (Munroe & Munroe, 1971; Munroe, Munroe, & Brasher, 1985) found a relation between the distance children played from their village and spatial skill. Boys who were involved in spatial activities that were directed by adults, such as herding, running errands to neighboring villages, and weeding crops in the field, performed better on several spatial tasks than children who also traveled away from home but engaged primarily in nonadult defined activities, that is, free play. For boys at least, it appears that adult-directed–child-conducted activity in the environment facilitates the development of spatial skill. (Explanations for these effects in boys but not girls are unclear; however, it is important to note that parents in most cultures allow boys, relative to girls, greater activity range and involvement in activities that require travel away from home. This, along with other experiential factors like gender-typed play, may contribute to differential skill by boys and girls on certain spatial tasks.)

The Munroes' observations are consistent with those from laboratory-based research. Cohen and Cohen (1985) found that children had better spatial memory after they engaged in an adult-defined, goal-directed activity. Although these results appear to contradict other findings (e.g., Poag et al., 1983) that show that adult-controlled spatial experience may interfere with the development of children's spatial knowledge, closer examination of the role adults play in children's spatial learning is needed. It seems that children benefit in terms of spatial learning from participating in social activities that are organized for them by adults. This point is consistent with Vygotsky's (1978) notion of the zone of proximal development in which more experienced cultural members are considered central agents in socializing children to the type of activities and cognitive practices that are valued and passed on by the community. It is also similar to research that has shown that adults aid children in learning about space and how to use it effectively. For instance, Radziszewska and Rogoff (1988) demonstrated that children's ability to understand and use a map of a village to plan errands is enhanced following collaboration with adults.

In research by both the Munroes (Munroe & Munroe, 1971; Munroe, Munroe, & Brasher, 1985) and the Cohens (Cohen & Cohen, 1985), the assistance provided by adults pertained to the overall goal of the spatial activity. This assistance did not supplant the children's active control of actions to attain this goal. In fact, it may have helped the children in framing their actions in relation to particular spatial features. This, in turn, may have facilitated learning as children maintained responsibility for directing their own use and exploration of the environment in the framework of a superordinate, spatially based goal. This interpretation is consistent with another finding by Poag et al. (1983) that opportunity for children to move through and view space under their own control led to greater spatial understanding. It is the integration of means and goal, or action and intention, and its relation to child versus adult control that appear to affect spatial learning in these contexts. Perhaps in terms of the zone of proximal development, adult assistance in developing spatial understanding in young children may be more beneficial when it provides a goal and leaves the means of exploration to the child. This type of active mental involvement between an adult and a child provides quite different developmental opportunities for spatial cognition than child-directed free play that may or may not entail activities directed toward spatial learning. Learning about a space during free play may be incidental to the goals of the play and therefore less well remembered.

Influence of Adults' Experience in the Workplace on Spatial Memory

Adults' daily activities at work are goal-directed and the nature of these goals contributes to spatial memory. For instance, Scribner, Gauvain, and Fahrmeier (1984) demonstrated that workers in a milk processing plant relied on their extensive knowledge of the plant to shape their work assignment so that it was more adapted to human needs. Dairy workers were observed as they filled store orders and loaded them on delivery trucks. The warehouse was very large and workers, apparently realizing this condition, filled the orders in a sequence reflecting the proximity of items in the warehouse and not according to the sequence presented on the order forms. This saved the workers as much as 5 miles of walking per shift.

Research conducted by Rand (1968) comparing the route maps and survey maps drawn by taxi drivers and student pilots from the same city indicated that the taxi drivers were unable to coordinate the routes into a map-like organization, whereas none of the pilots had such difficulty. Despite deficiencies in their survey maps, the taxi drivers were expert in organizing the relations between places in the course of carrying out their jobs, such as reversing routes, interrupting and continuing routes, combining routes in novel ways, and overcoming detours—all of which imply an understanding of configurational spatial relations. However, the convention of representing large-scale space from an overview perspective was apparently enhanced for the pilots, who were afforded such a view in their jobs. Although pilots and taxi drivers may gravitate to their occupations because of inherent differences in spatial abilities, it is also true that expert spatial knowledge can result from specific training and experience. Specialists trained to use contour maps were better at remembering contour features from maps than nonexperts (Gilhoody, Wood, Kinnear, & Green, 1988).

In everyday life, adults and children are often called on to describe spatial networks and locations in the form of directions to other people. Individuals differ in their ability at organizing and presenting useful directional information. However, performance may also reflect the practical experiences a person has had in a setting. Gauvain and Klaue (1989) examined this by investigating how individuals with differing job experiences in the same setting organize directional information for practical use. We hypothesized that employees with jobs that required extensive attention to and experience with the physical features of the setting would provide more spatial information in their directions than employees whose jobs primarily pertained to other features of the setting.

Twenty-two employees of the New York City Public Library participated. Their average length of employment was 12.3 years (sd = 11.6 years, range: 3 mos. to 40 yrs.), and half worked as reference librarians and half worked as security guards. Participants were approached individually at their work site and asked to provide directions to seven locations in the library. Directions were audiotaped. Because permission was granted prior to data collection, it was possible to ascertain the first set of directions before the participant was informed that the study was being conducted. Four of the seven requests for directions asked for information linking two locations on the same floor (horizontal directions) and the other three involved getting from one location to another across floors (vertical directions). The first set of directions was always a vertical request and involved a route that had no fewer than three and no greater than five decision points on it. After providing the directions, participants were interviewed about their experience moving around the library during their workday and how often they provided directions and tours for patrons.

Directions were coded for spatial deixis, which included the provision of directional information (e.g. left, right); landmark information (e.g. the archway, the Map Division); floor information (e.g. the ground floor); trajectory information (e.g. up, down); and distance information (e.g. halfway down the hall). Responses to the first request for directions were analyzed separately from the remaining six because the latter occurred after they were informed that this was a research project. To examine the quality of the directions, the position of the subject and the location of the target site indicated in the first request for directions were plotted onto a floor map of the library. The number of spatial decision points along the route was determined, and then the number of these decision points that was both anticipated and resolved in the directions was calculated. The resulting percentage was used to index the quality of the directions in terms of their usefulness for guiding practical action.

The security guards and the reference librarians did not differ in their length of employment, their daily amount of walking, or in how often they provided directions or tours for patrons. Despite these similarities, type of employment did distinguish how the participants organized spatial information in their directions. Directions provided by the guards included more spatial terms, both in the initial and later directions, than those provided by librarians. Guards also provided better quality directions than librarians in that they anticipated and resolved a greater proportion of decision points along the routes. Using regression analysis, the best predictor of the quality of directions was type of job. Length of employment added to the prediction, but did not predict quality of directions independent of job status.

It is important to stress that the spatial knowledge of the participants was not studied separately from the practice of giving directions. Thus, their spatial skills, other than those associated with giving directions in this setting, are unknown. Presumably, both guards and librarians possessed a similar working knowledge of the space. After all, both groups managed to work there without any apparent difficulty in getting around. However, given this, it is interesting to find a discrepancy in the nature and quality of spatial information these two groups of individuals provided in the form of directions to patrons. This discrepancy, which could be called a distortion on the librarians' part (their directions were incomplete and sometimes did not even lead to the destination), could be due to the fact that security guards are more likely to deal with lost or frustrated patrons on the job. This experience may have sharpened their direction-giving skills.

In sum, experience at work can provide adults with the opportunity to develop spatial skill. Relevant experiences include practice in particular ways of solving spatial problems, opportunities for certain types of vantage points or perspectives, and increased awareness of certain features in the environment. For both children and adults, prior experience in a setting, defined by practical activity, is an important part of a spatial problem solving context. For children, everyday experience with adults helps them organize exploration and memory of large-scale space. For adults, everyday experience helps refine and direct their spatial skills and expertise. Thus, consideration of a person's practical experiences in a setting may be critical for understanding the development and organization of spatial memory. This raises the question of what determines practical activity and, consequently, the spatial knowledge that is likely to develop. To help answer this I turn my discussion to a consideration of sociocultural influences on everyday spatial activity.

SOCIOCULTURAL INFLUENCES ON EVERYDAY SPATIAL ACTIVITY

Everyday spatial activity reflects the sociocultural context in which the activity is performed. Culture defines the goals that are important to achieve, as well as the activities people engage in to realize these goals. This suggests that cultural differences in spatial memory and its distortions cannot be understood without careful examination of the ecocultural context in which these memories are developed and used.

How might culture influence the development and organization of spatial memory? In Berry's (1966, 1976) ecocultural framework, the development and organization of spatial skill depends on cultural and ecological factors. Berry predicted that participation in activities like hunting and gathering would require people to develop more spatial competence than participation in agricultural activities. He was able to support this prediction in 17 societies that differed along ecological and cultural dimensions associated with such food-accumulation practices. Developmental research consistent with this view has shown that certain spatial concepts develop more rapidly in nomadic and hunting and gathering societies, like that of the Australian Aborigines and Inuit, than in more sedentary communities, such as the Baoulé of Ivory Coast (Dasen, 1975). Although the spatial skills Berry and Dasen used to test this hypothesis did not involved solving problems in large-scale space (e.g., they used the embedded figures test and judgments of horizontality of a liquid when its container is tilted), these results support the general contention that cultural practices may influence spatial memory. Other research, also conducted with Australian Aborigines but focused on more everyday spatial experience (spatial location skills), had similar findings. Aboriginal children reared in the desert were better at spatial location than Euro-Australian children reared in the city (Kearins, 1981).

Beyond ecocultural considerations, how else might culture influence the development and organization of spatial memory? Culture may influence spatial memory by providing mechanisms that support exploration and memory of space. For instance, when we describe a space or solve a problem in large-scale space, we often employ communicative conventions, such as route descriptions, material or symbolic tools, such as maps, and traditional practices for conducting activities in space, such as navigational routines. All of these reflect the sociocultural frame in which spatial thinking occurs and they help us accomplish activities in space by mediating the conduct and content of our activity. Additionally, competence at using these cultural means to support spatial activity is an important developmental achievement that has critical consequences for the development and organization of spatial memory.

Communicative Conventions and Spatial Memory

A central developmental task is the acquisition of skills for organizing knowledge and communicating it in understandable ways to others (Shatz, 1983). These skills not only help people organize their knowledge for effective use, they also allow people to share their knowledge with one another and thereby connect members of a community to each other. In fact, a prerequisite for participation in many of the sociocultural processes essential for intellectual growth may be the development of skill in the conventional forms of organizing and communicating knowledge.

Research on the development of spatial thinking illustrates the role of communicative conventions in the development and organization of this type of knowledge. Spencer and Darvizeh (1983) found route descriptions provided by British and Iranian preschoolers to differ. Descriptions provided by Iranian 3-year-olds living in Britain included more vivid and fuller accounts of the sites along a route but less directional information than those provided by British children. This difference suggests that as early as 3 years of age, children are displaying some of the values of their cultural community with respect to presentation of spatial information to others. These variations (or distortions) of spatial memory reflect cultural values and practices.

In everyday life, adults and children are often called on to describe spatial networks and locations in order to communicate a layout or to give directions. When adults describe spatial networks, they tend to employ relatively structured narratives that resemble route directions. These contain information about the temporal and spatial contiguity of areas in the space (Linde & Labov, 1975). This form of presentation, a mental tour, helps listeners understand the space via an imagined walk through it. It is more accessible to listeners than a simple listing of areas in a space, which may not contain sufficient spatial information to connect different areas, or an overview perspective, which conveys survey or configurational information about space but no movement or route information.

To examine the developmental course of this communicative convention, Gauvain and Rogoff (1989) had 6- and 9-year-old children explore a novel environment guided by instructions to study either the layout or the route and were later asked to describe the space. Few age differences appeared in the children's memory of the space. However, the descriptions provided by the older children resembled those of adults (Linde & Labov, 1975) regardless of whether these children received instructions to study the layout or the route. Younger children only provided route-like (mental tour) descriptions when they were previously instructed to attend to the route. When they were instructed to attend to the layout, younger children's descriptions were nonspatial in character and tended to contain a list of places without reference to spatial relations.

It appears that with development, children become increasingly skilled at using pragmatic conventions, such as a mental tour, for organizing and communicating spatial knowledge. Whether conventions such as this are universal in appearance or form is unknown. Certainly the experiences they rely on are universal. Children throughout the world have increasing opportunity with development to navigate through and use large-scale space. Greater skill in using this convention may reflect increasing practice with age in following spatial directions, in self-guided wayfinding, and in receiving feedback from others when providing spatial descriptions. Communicative conventions such as this may play an important role in conveying spatial information and listeners may respond to their use in meaningful ways and even expect and rely on them when spatial information is provided.

Such conventions may also contain standard ways that cultures have devised to deal with spatial information. A certain level of distance, directional or relational accuracy may be expected. Too much or too little detail on any of these counts may lead to dissatisfaction by the listener and perhaps an evaluation of inadequacy. Although I know of no data to support this supposition, it is an interesting direction of inquiry. That is, how in the course of everyday discourse that includes spatial information do people respond to information that includes spatial detail or distortions? I suspect that, in the main, some distortions of spatial information may be expected and overlooked, for example, metric precision, whereas others may be considered problematic, for example, directional omissions. In this way, cultural ways of communicating about space may mediate both the production and evaluation of distortions of spatial memory.

Although research indicates that ways of speaking about space are influenced by cultural conventions, the more intriguing question is whether these conventional forms influence the process of thinking about space. This is a difficult question to answer, but some suggestive evidence exists. Levinson (1996) studied spatial thinking among the Guugu Yimithirr, an Aboriginal community in eastern Australia. The language of these people does not rely on relativistic terms, like left, right, up, down, for describing spatial information. Rather, it encodes spatial information in absolute position in accord with cardinal directions, such as north, south, east, and west. In a series of studies involving dead reckoning (pointing to out-of-sight locations) in the desert and reproducing the arrangements of the objects on table tops in adjacent rooms, Levinson found that Guugu Yimithirr speakers identify and reconstruct spatial information according to the absolute rather than the relative positioning of objects. Thus, even when they were not speaking, they behaved in ways consistent with their communicative conventions for describing space.

For example, community members were asked to arrange familiar objects on a table in a room exactly as they had been arranged on a table in a nearby room that was oriented differently from the testing room (it was across the hall). If you or I were to do this we would probably place the cup to the left of the book and the pencil above the cup, and so forth in the same way as the objects had been arranged in the original presentation. Guugu Yimithirr participants did not do this. They arranged the items in their cardinal positions, that is, the cup was placed to the north because it had been northward previously, and so on. Note that this is the opposite of the placements that we made in our relativistic solution. (This contrast calls into question the notion of the same way. What does *the same way* mean? In this case, the same way has no objective meaning separate from the person performing the task.) The rapidity and precision with which the participants provided absolute spatial information on this and other tasks led Levinson to conclude that their spatial encoding reflected an orientation consistent with the linguistic form.

The fact that these observations were made among a people who have long been known to possess extraordinary spatial skill (Davidson, 1979) is noteworthy. The existence of superior spatial skill and the need for such skill in the harsh environs inhabited by Aboriginal peoples of Australia for the last 40,000 years begs the question of how communicative systems and cognitive systems coordinate over time and place. To be sure, an individual's sense of direction may also influence performance on such tasks. However, directional orientation is not automatic. It relies on attention, effort, and repeated experience (Kozlowski & Bryant, 1977). I add to this that spatial orientation may also be aided by the availability in a culture of cognitive tools or conventions that foster certain types of spatial memory, and may result in unique patterns of distortion of these memories.

MAPS AND SPATIAL MEMORY

One spatial memory tool that has received much attention is mapping. Maps are common tools for representing spatial information and they appear in most cultures and across history. For instance, Mesoamerican códices (ancient books) from the Precolumbian Period contain hieroglyphs that relate the migrations of early Indians in the region (Weaver, 1972).

Research on the development of map-reading skills indicates that even preschoolers can acquire some integrated knowledge about the relative positions of locations from a map and that this knowledge can aid subsequent navigation (Uttal & Wellman, 1989). Despite the early appearance of rudimentary map-reading skills, even school-age children are not expert map users. In fact, full competence in map reading may not be acquired until adolescence (Presson, 1987), depending on the type of map and cultural opportunities available for developing these skills (Gauvain, 1993). Maps such as those representing the locations of secret and important places that are carved by the Ngatatjara people of the Australian desert on weapons, rocks, and the human body (Gould, 1969) and those devised by electrical engineers to track circuits may be inaccessible to most adolescents and adults in our culture. Whereas the former may be understood by some or all mature members in the group of origin, the latter may be understood by only those Westerners interested and experienced in electrical circuitry. Thus, success or failure on a mapping task not only reflects spatial or representational skills, it also reflects skill and practice with a system of representation, a tool available in a particular cultural context.

When we examine the maps drawn by the Inuits it is evident that living in a setting with vastly changing conditions in terms of the proximity and accessibility of regions can lead to the development by the culture of representational forms or tools, in this case a type of map, that reflects the unique demands of the setting and the needs of the people. As such, it is an adaptive and culturally organized response to a problem of spatial memory. If we focus on only one dimension of the map, like topographical accuracy, to index spatial memory, we may overlook the important role that culturally organized activities and goals, and the tools devised to support these, play in the formation and organization of memory for space. Can one conclude on the basis of maps such as these that spatial memory is also distorted? Behavioral observations certainly suggest that distortions in representations such as these do not imply similar distortions in memory. The Inuit are successful travelers and hunters and have been so for centuries. Likewise, users of more familiar schematic maps are able to travel effectively while using them.

Thus, rather than raising questions about whether the spatial memory of the Inuit is distorted, this illustration directs our attention elsewhere, toward the types of representational tools that are developed and used by cultures to help people remember spatial information. Conventional map forms may lead to distortions of spatial memory, such as certain ways of grouping areas together on schematic maps. But these distortions may not, in general, interfere with moving about or conducting activities in space. In fact, as in the case of the

Inuit, the existence of maps may enhance spatial activity by providing support for spatial memory that would otherwise not be as easily available.

Traditional Navigational Practices and Spatial Memory

A third way in which culture may exert influence on spatial memory is via traditional navigational practices. In well-known research on this topic, both Gladwin (1971) and Hutchins (1983) described the traditional navigational practices of Puluwat seafarers, an indigenous group in Micronesia. These navigators do not employ modern instruments to organize their travel. Rather they learn a set of principles and use these to derive information that guides their navigation. Some of this information is directly observed, such as wave patterns, and other parts are inferred, such as the star compass. The star compass is an abstract mental reference system of 32 star paths that defines the courses among islands in terms of an abstract sidereal compass (Hutchins, 1983). The huge memorization task this involves is eased by the use of myths as mnemonics (Hage, 1978). The remarkable skill of traditional Puluwat navigators relies on knowing many star paths that define courses among islands. Like our knowledge of familiar local space, star paths are not fixed map routes or action sequences but a reservoir of possible action plans for solving navigational problems (see Gärling & Evans, 1991). Locomotion, either real or imagined, provides information about landmarks and actual or potential routes, as well as cues to update and adjust spatial orientation and route finding.

Despite the impressive accomplishments involved in developing and using this traditional navigational procedure, the spatial information it contains is distorted in an interesting way. Although the Puluwat system of navigation is well suited to a host of navigational events that the islanders are likely to encounter, it contains several internal inconsistencies. Gladwin (1971) speculated that because the islanders' goal of navigating was met, no further adjustments to the system were needed. In contrast to the Puluwats, participants from cultures that value organizing information into general, rule-based frameworks would more than likely consider this system distorted. But such an interpretation is flawed in that it ignores the connection between human thinking and the culturally organized goals through which thinking is operationalized.

Cultural values contain tacit understandings about what is an appropriate goal or what a good performance should look like (Goodnow, 1990). Certain features of intellectual performance, such as generalization, completeness of problem solutions, and conventional interpretations of tasks and task solutions, reflect the goals and values of a culture (Goodnow, 1976). For instance, the propensity among thinkers in Western communities to generalize information may hinge on cultural values that regard a search for universals or principles across events as important and worthy of pursuit (Cole, 1996).

The fact that the Puluwats do not extend their navigational system and thereby eliminate its inconsistencies does not mean that they are incapable of the reasoning that would be required to do so. Nor does this example imply that participants in Western cultures generalize and those in other cultures do not. Far too little is known about such goal structures to warrant any such interpretation. The main point is that navigational practices are rooted in cultural values and beliefs. Such values and beliefs take form in specific activities, primarily through the goals that organize action and the means that are used to support action. This may result in patterned ways of remembering, and even distorting, spatial knowledge.

CONCLUSION

What we remember about a large-scale space is what is useful and important to remember. It is true that we remember information consistent with our expectations (Brewer & Treyens, 1981), and we sometimes remember information that we find strange or interesting. But in the main, spatial knowledge is pragmatic. It is influenced by practical concerns that arise from and are embedded in everyday activities. And these activities are largely defined by the culture in which they occur. This suggests that in order to understand spatial knowledge we must attend to the activities and cultural practices through which individuals become exposed to and learn about large-scale space.

A sociocultural perspective may be useful for addressing questions about spatial memory and its distortions. I have tried to show that spatial memory depends on the activity that organizes an individual's experience in a space and reflects the cultural tools and practices that individuals use in the course of learning about and using large-scale space. One direction of future study is the investigation of how material and social resources are related to the ways in which we understand large-scale space, and how this information may result in apparent distortions of spatial memory. However, in order to advance a sociocultural view of spatial memory, researchers will have to attend to how people conduct activities in large-scale space and examine how opportunities and constraints provided by culture influence spatial memory and its distortions. Such research may foster examination of spatial memory as it is integrated with human activity, and thereby provide a more comprehensive understanding of human spatial cognition than is currently available.

ACKNOWLEDGMENT

Much thanks are due to Lee Munroe and Kathy Pezdek for their helpful comments during the writing of this chapter.

REFERENCES

Acredolo, L. P. (1982). The familiarity factor in spatial research. In R. Cohen (Ed.), *New directions for child development: Children's conceptions of spatial relationships* (pp. 19–31). San Francisco: Jossey-Bass.

Acredolo, L. P., Pick, H. L., & Olson, M. G. (1975). The role of self-produced movement and visual tracking in infant spatial orientation. *Journal of Experimental Child Psychology, 38*, 312–327.

Anooshian, L. J., & Kromer, M. K. (1986). Children's spatial knowledge of their school campus. *Developmental Psychology, 22*, 854–860.

Anooshian, L. J., & Siegel, A. W. (1985). From cognitive to procedural mapping. In C. J. Brainerd, & M. Pressley (Eds.), *Basic processes in memory development* (pp. 47–101). New York: Springer-Verlag.

Appleyard, D. (1975). *Planning a pluralistic city: Conflicting realities in Ciudad Guayana.* Cambridge, MA: MIT Press.

Bartram, D., & Smith, P. (1984). Everyday memory for everyday places. In J. E. Harris & P. E. Morris (Eds.), *Everyday memory, actions and absentmindedness* (pp. 35–62). London: Academic Press.

Berry, J. W. (1966). Temne and Eskimo perceptual skills. *International Journal of Psychology, 4*, 119–128.

Berry, J. W. (1976). *Human ecology and cognitive style: Comparative studies in cultural and psychological adaptation.* New York: Sage/Halsted/Wiley.

Blades, M. (1990). The reliability of data collected from sketch maps. *Journal of Environmental Psychology, 10*, 327–339.

Boas, F. (1884-85). The central Eskimo. In *Sixth annual report of the Bureau of American Ethnology.* Washington, DC: Smithsonian Institution.

Bomba, P. C., & Siqueland, E. R. (1983). The nature and structure of infant form categories. *Journal of Experimental Child Psychology, 35*, 294–328.

Brewer, W. F., & Treyens, J. C. (1981). Role of schemata in memory for places. *Cognitive Psychology, 13*, 117–129.

Byrne, R. (1979). Memory for urban geography. *Quarterly Journal of Experimental Psychology, 31*, 147–154.

Chase, W. G., & Chi, M. T. H. (1980). Cognitive skill: Implications for spatial skill in large-scale environments. In J. Harvey (Ed.), *Cognition, social behavior, and the environment* (pp. 111–136). Hillsdale, NJ: Lawrence Erlbaum Associates.

Cohen, S., & Cohen, R. (1985). The role of activity in spatial cognition. In R. Cohen (Ed.), *The development of spatial cognition* (pp. 199–223). Hillsdale, NJ: Lawrence Erlbaum Associates.

Cohen, R., & Weatherford, D., (1981). The effect of barriers on spatial representations. *Child Development, 52,* 1087–1090.

Cole, M. (1996). *Cultural psychology: A once and future discipline.* Cambridge, MA: Harvard University Press.

Cornell, E. H., & Hay, D. H. (1984). Children's acquisition of a route via different media. *Environment and Behavior, 16,* 627–641.

Dasen, P. R. (1975). Concrete operational development in three cultures. *Journal of Cross-Cultural Psychology, 7,* 75–85.

Davidson, G. R. (1979). An ethnographic psychology of aboriginal cognition. *Oceania, 49,* 270–294.

Evans, G. W., Marrero, D. G., & Butler, P. A. (1981). Environmental learning and cognitive mapping. *Environment and Behavior, 13,* 83–104.

Evans, G. H., & Pezdek, K. (1980). Cognitive mapping: Knowledge of real world distance and location information. *Journal of Experimental Psychology: Human Learning and Memory, 6,* 13–24.

Feldman, A., & Acredolo, L. P. (1979). The effect of active vs. passive exploration on memory for spatial location in children. *Child Development, 50,* 698–704.

Gale, N., Golledge, R. G., Pellegrino, J. W., & Doherty, S. (1990). The acquisition and integration of route knowledge in an unfamiliar neighborhood. *Journal of Experimental Psychology, 10,* 3–25.

Gärling, T., & Evans, G. W. (1991). *Environment, cognition, and action: An integrated approach.* New York: Oxford University Press.

Gärling, T., Lindberg, E., & Mäntylä, T. (1983). Orientation in buildings: Effects of familiarity, visual access, and orientation aids. *Journal of Applied Psychology, 68,* 177–185.

Gauvain, M. (1993). The development of spatial thinking in everyday activity. *Developmental Review, 13,* 92–121.

Gauvain, M., & Klaue, K. (1989, June). *Influence of experience in an environment on the organization of directional information.* Paper presented at the meetings of The Jean Piaget Society, Philadelphia.

Gauvain, M., & Rogoff, B. (1986). Influence of the goal on children's exploration and memory of large-scale space. *Developmental Psychology, 22,* 72–77.

Gauvain, M., & Rogoff, B. (1989). Ways of speaking about space: The development of children's skill at communicating spatial knowledge. *Cognitive Development, 4,* 295–307.

Gilhoody, K. J., Wood, M., Kinnear, P. R., & Green, C. (1988). Skill in map reading and memory for maps. *Quarterly Journal of Experimental Psychology, 40,* 87–107.

Gladwin, T. (1971). *East is a big bird.* Cambridge, MA: Harvard University Press.

Goodnow, J. J. (1976). The nature of intelligent behavior: Questions raised by cross-cultural studies. In L. B. Resnick (Ed.), *The nature of intelligence* (pp. 169–188). Hillsdale, NJ: Lawrence Erlbaum Associates.

Goodnow, J. J. (1990). The socialization of cognition. In J. W. Stigler, R. A. Shweder, & G. Herdt (Eds.), *Cultural psychology* (pp. 259–286). New York: Cambridge University Press.

Gould, R. A. (1969). *Yiwara: Foragers of the Australian desert.* New York: Scribners.

Hage, P. (1978). Speculations on Puluwatese mnemonic structure. *Oceania, 49,* 81–95.

Hart, R. A. (1979). *Children's experience of place: A developmental study.* New York: Irvington.

Heft, H. (1979). The role of environmental features in route learning: Two exploratory studies of way finding. *Environmental Psychology and Nonverbal Behavior, 3,* 751–759.

Herman, J. F. (1980). Children's cognitive maps of large-scale spaces: Effects of exploration, directions, and repeated experience. *Journal of Experimental Child Psychology, 29,* 126–143.

Herman, J. F., Kail, R. V., & Siegel, A. W. (1979). Cognitive maps of a college campus: A new look at freshman orientation. *Bulletin of the Psychonomic Society, 13,* 183–186.

Herman, J. F., & Siegel, A. W. (1978). The development of cognitive mapping of the large-scale environment. *Journal of Experimental Child Psychology, 26,* 389–406.

Heth, C. D., & Cornell, E. H. (1985). Three experiences affecting spatial discrimination learning by ambulatory children. *Journal of Experimental Child Psychology, 29,* 246–264.

Hutchins, E. (1983). Understanding Micronesian navigation. In D. Gentner & A. Stevens (Eds.), *Mental models* (pp. 191–225). Hillsdale, N J: Lawrence Erlbaum Associates.

Kearins, J. M. (1981). Visual spatial memory in Australian aboriginal children of desert regions. *Cognitive Psychology, 13,* 434–460.

Kosslyn, S. M., Pick, H., & Fariello, G. (1974). Cognitive maps in children and men. *Child Development, 45,* 707–716.

Kozlowski, L. T., & Bryant, K. J. (1977). Sense of direction, spatial orientation, and cognitive maps. *Journal of Experimental Psychology: Human Perception and Performance, 3,* 590–598.

Leont'ev, A. N. (1981). The problem of activity in psychology. In J. V. Wertsch (Ed.), *The concept of activity in Soviet psychology* (pp. 37–61). Armonk, NY: Sharpe.

Levinson, S. C. (1996). Frames of reference and Molyneux's question: Crosslinguistic evidence. In P. Bloom, M. A. Peterson, L. Nadel, & M. F. Garrett (Eds.), *Language and space* (pp. 109–169). Cambridge, MA: MIT Press.

Linde, C., & Labov, W. (1975). Spatial networks as a site for the study of language and thought. *Language, 51,* 924–939.

Moar, I. (1979). *The internal geometry of cognitive maps.* Unpublished doctoral dissertation, Cambridge University, Cambridge, England.

Munroe, R. L., & Munroe, R. H. (1971). Effect of environmental experience on spatial ability in an East African society. *The Journal of Social Psychology, 83,* 15–22.

Munroe, R. H., Munroe, R. L., & Brasher, A. (1985). Precursors of spatial ability: A longitudinal study among the Logoli of Kenya. *The Journal of Social Psychology, 125,* 23–33.

Poag, C., Cohen, R., & Weatherford, D. L. (1983). Spatial representations of young children: The role of self- versus other-directed movement and viewing. *Journal of Experimental Child Psychology, 35,* 172–179.

Presson, C. C. (1987). The development of spatial cognition: Secondary uses of spatial information. In N. Eisenberg (Ed.), *Contemporary topics in developmental psychology* (pp. 77–112). New York: Wiley.

Radziszewska, B., & Rogoff, B. (1988). Influence of adult and peer collaborators on children's planning skills. *Developmental Psychology, 24,* 840–848.

Rand, G. (1968). Pre-Copernican views of the city. *Architectural Forum, 131,* 76–81.

Sadalla, E. K., & Magel, S. G. (1980). The perception of traversed distance. *Environment and Behavior, 12,* 167–182.

Scribner, S., Gauvain, M., & Fahrmeier, E. (1984). Use of spatial knowledge in the organization of work. *The Quarterly Newsletter of the Laboratory of Comparative Human Cognition, 6,* 32–34.

Shatz, M. (1983). Communication. In P. Mussen (Series Ed.), J. H. Flavell, & E. M. Markman (Vol. Eds.), *Handbook of child psychology: Vol. 3. Cognitive development* (4th ed., pp. 841–890). New York: Wiley.

Siegel, A. W., & White, S. (1975). The development of spatial representations of large-scale environments. In H. W. Reese (Ed.), *Advances in child development and behavior* (Vol. 10, pp. 9–55). New York: Academic Press.

Spencer, C., & Darvizeh, Z. (1983). Young children's place descriptions, maps and route-finding: A comparison of nursery school children in Iran and Britain. *International Journal of Early Childhood, 15,* 26–31.

Stevens, A., & Coupe, P. (1978). Distortions in judged spatial relations. *Cognitive Psychology, 10,* 422–437.

Thorndyke, P. (1981). Distance estimation from cognitive maps. *Cognitive Psychology, 13,* 526–550.

Tversky, B. (1981). Distortions in memory for maps. *Cognitive Psychology, 13,* 407–433.

Uttal, D. H., & Wellman, H. M. (1989). Young children's representations of spatial information acquired from maps. *Developmental Psychology, 25,* 128–138.

Vygotsky, L. S. (1978). *Mind in society.* Cambridge, MA: Harvard University Press.

Warren, D. H. (1984). *Blindness and early childhood development* (2nd ed.). New York: American Foundation for the Blind.

Weaver, M. P. (1972). *The Aztecs, Maya, and their predecessors.* New York: Seminar Press.

Zinchenko, P. I. (1981). Involuntary memory and the goal-directed nature of activity in Soviet psychology. In J. V. Wertsch (Ed.), *The concept of activity in Soviet psychology* (pp. 300–340). Armonk, New York: Sharpe.

7

Retention of Procedural and Declarative Information from the Colorado Drivers' Manual

Mary Beth Jensen
Alice F. Healy
University of Colorado

Two naturalistic memory experiments tested a procedural reinstatement hypothesis, according to which long-term retention is better for procedural information (motoric, perceptual, or cognitive operations) than for declarative information (facts or knowledge). The experiments examined retention of information from a drivers' manual. The declarative questions (e.g., height from ground of fastening license plates) differed from the procedural questions (e.g., distance from curb when parking) in the extent to which they involved driving procedures although they had identical numerical answers. The advantage for procedural questions was evident for recall tests but not for recognition tests, suggesting that procedural reinstatement is most crucial for retrieval of information.

Recent studies have demonstrated a distinct advantage for remembering procedural information (motoric, perceptual, or cognitive operations) relative to declarative information (facts or knowledge; see Anderson, 1983, for a discussion of this distinction). In contrast to studies of verbal learning in which information is lost rapidly even over very short retention intervals (e.g., Peterson & Peterson, 1959), studies of target detection (e.g., Healy, Fendrich,

& Proctor, 1990), mental arithmetic (e.g., Fendrich, Healy, & Bourne, 1993), and data entry (e.g., Fendrich, Healy, & Bourne, 1991) skills have shown remarkably good long-term retention with little or no loss evident for intervals as long as 15 months. This superior long-term retention of these skills was explained in terms of a procedural reinstatement hypothesis (Healy et al., 1992), according to which the durability of memory depends critically on the extent to which the procedures used during learning are reinstated during testing. This hypothesis follows from earlier arguments concerning the importance of mental procedures to memory (see Kolers & Roediger, 1984). It is also consistent with the principle of transfer appropriate processing (see Morris, Bransford, & Franks, 1977) and the encoding specificity principle (see Tulving & Thomson, 1973).

The power of procedural reinstatement for durable retention is perhaps best illustrated in a study of the complex task of tank gunnery (Marmie & Healy, 1995). This task is predominantly procedural but involves multiple skills, including both discrete and continuous motor responses and both physical and cognitive components. Despite the complexity of the task, the procedural reinstatement hypothesis predicts very good long-term retention, whereas other theoretical frameworks (see, e.g., Adams, 1987; Driskell, Willis, & Copper, 1992; Fisk & Hodge, 1992) predict that long-term retention will be poor for this task. In fact, in agreement with the procedural reinstatement hypothesis, it was found that retention of this task was extremely good, with virtually no forgetting and even some improvement evident across retention intervals up to 22 months in length.

An experiment on digit data entry (Fendrich, Gesi, Healy, & Bourne, 1995) also illustrates the importance of procedural reinstatement for long-term memory. Subjects were shown sequences of digits on a computer screen. In one condition, the subjects simply read each sequence. In a second condition, they typed each sequence with the numeric keypad. In a third condition, they typed each sequence with the horizontal number row. After a 1-week retention interval, subjects typed old and new digit sequences with either the number row or the keypad. After typing each sequence, the subjects made a recognition judgment. It was found that the recognition scores were highest for the sequences typed with the same key configuration at test as used at study. When old sequences were typed with a different key configuration at study and at test (i.e., the number row at study and the numeric keypad at test or the numeric keypad at study and the number row at test), the recognition scores were no better than when the old sequences were simply read at study. Typing the sequence at study only improved recognition scores if the sequences were typed in the same way on the retention test.

A related line of support for the procedural reinstatement hypothesis came from studies of the generation effect, which is the finding that memory is enhanced for items that are produced by subjects rather than simply read by them (see, e.g., Slamecka & Graf, 1978). For example, subjects are better able to recall a list of answers to simple multiplication problems if the problems are given to the subjects without the answers during study (generate condition, e.g., $6 \times 8 = ?$), so that the subjects are required to generate the answers themselves, than if the problems are given to the subjects along with the answers during study (read condition, e.g., $6 \times 8 = 48$), so that the subjects are required only to read the answers (see, e.g., Gardiner & Rowley, 1984). Crutcher and Healy (1989) showed that this generation effect occurred because the subjects were more likely to use the mental arithmetic operations, which are the relevant cognitive procedures, in the generate condition than in the read condition. Subjects who read the answers at study but were required to perform the arithmetic operations because they had to verify the answers (verify condition) showed similar recall levels to those in the generate condition, whereas subjects who had to generate the answers but were not required to perform the arithmetic operations themselves because they were instructed to use a calculator (calculate condition) showed similar recall levels to those in the read condition. McNamara and Healy (1995) showed further that the generation effect required that subjects perform the same procedures at test as they used at study. In experiments in which subjects were given arithmetic problems at study, a generation effect was found only for subjects who used an operand retrieval strategy at test, whereby they recalled the arithmetic problem operands shown during study (e.g., 6×8) and used them as retrieval cues for the list of answers (e.g., 48). These subjects used the same procedures—the arithmetic operations—at test as they used at study.

Additional support for the procedural reinstatement hypothesis was provided from a naturalistic study (Wittman & Healy, 1995) of students' memory for their course schedules. This study showed that spatial information about where a class was held was retained better by undergraduate university students than the item and temporal information about who taught the course, what the course title was, and when the class met. It was argued that the spatial information could be more easily linked with procedures, such as those involved in walking to the class. That is, at the time of test the subjects could more easily reinstate the initial mental procedures that were used in acquiring the spatial information; they could mentally retrace their steps. Indeed, in a follow-up study in which subjects learned fictitious course schedules, King (1992; see also Healy, King, & Sinclair, 1997) showed that the superiority for spatial information recall was restricted to subjects who had previous procedural experience with the college campus. However, the types of information being compared in these studies of memory for course schedules differed along many dimensions as well as that relevant to the distinction between declarative and procedural information. A better test of the procedural reinstatement hypothesis would compare memory for two types of information that differ only in the extent to which they are linked with procedures.

Toward this end, the present study includes two naturalistic experiments that seek to confirm the superiority of procedural over declarative memory using information from the *Colorado Drivers' Manual*. Two types of questions were selected. Procedural questions had to do with the actual operation and driving of a vehicle, whereas declarative questions had to do with ancillary facts. The two types of questions were paired, both questions in a pair having the identical numerical answers, so that the to-be-remembered information was the same for the two types. They differed only in the extent to which driving procedures were relevant.

EXPERIMENT 1

Two forms of a multiple-choice recognition test were used, with three pairs of questions on each form. On each form the same numerical answer choices were given to the two questions in a pair. The forms differed in the specific set of choices used for each question pair (e.g., for the pair with the correct answer 30, the set was either 15, 30, 45, 60 or 10, 20, 30, 40).

Method

Subjects. Sixty-four undergraduates from the University of Colorado, Boulder, participated for course credit. None had also participated in a previous pilot experiment on this topic (see Jensen, 1994).

Apparatus and Materials. This experiment was conducted using paper and pencil. The questions were compiled using the State of Colorado (1979, 1990, 1992) *Colorado Drivers' Manual*. Questions were based on information that was found in all three versions of the manual and were structured so as to use as many of the original words or sentences found in the manual as possible.

There were six questions asked, three declarative and three procedural. The mean length of the declarative questions was 18.67 words, whereas the mean length of the procedural questions was 14.67 words. Although the declarative questions were longer on average than the procedural questions, the answer to each question was identical in length. In any event, the additional length of the declarative questions could only serve to improve memory performance for the declarative questions so would work against finding a memory advantage for the procedural questions. The questions were selected from a larger set used in a pilot experiment (see Jensen, 1994). An independent set of 17 subjects from the same pool used in the present experiment rated (on a 6-point scale) that the procedural questions (M = 4.1) more than the declarative questions (M = 2.9) "involved procedures used for operating a vehicle or driving," $F(1,16)$ = 8.4, p = .01.

Each question had four numerical answer choices. Each declarative question was paired with a procedural one that had the same answer and the same answer choices. Thus, there were three answer sets, each of which appeared twice in the list of questions. The questions were in a random order.

Two forms of the test were made. The questions were identical on the two forms, but the set of answer choices differed. See Table 7.1 for all three pairs of questions and answer choices in the two forms.

A set of demographic questions was constructed to determine whether a given subject was a Colorado driver who had previously passed the Colorado drivers' license written examination.

Procedure and Design.   Each subject was given a questionnaire that contained the multiple-choice recognition test followed by the demographic questions. There was one between-subjects independent variable (test form) and one within-subjects independent variable (type of question). The dependent variable was the percentage of correct responses.

Results

Overall accuracy was quite low (56.8% correct) but clearly above the 25% guessing level. A two-way mixed analysis of variance (ANOVA) on the percentage of correct responses for all 64 subjects revealed no significant main effect of question type, although the procedural questions showed higher scores than the declarative (see Table 7.2). There was, however, a main effect of test form, $F(1,62)$ = 5.5, p = .021. Overall the mean for Form 1 (M = 62.5%) was higher than that for Form 2 (M = 51.0%). There was also an interaction of form by question type, $F(1,62)$ = 4.3, p = .04. Form 1 showed an advantage for procedural relative to declarative questions; in contrast, Form 2 revealed procedural questions at a slight disadvantage relative to declarative questions (see Table 7.2). It is difficult to account for this unexpected interaction. However, a detailed analysis of the answers to one of the questions helps clarify this finding. The first procedural question involved the speed limit in a residence district. This speed limit is ordinarily not posted; rather the exceptions are posted. Furthermore, this same speed limit regulation does not apply to driving in all states. These postings of the exceptions or the different regulations in other states seem to have influenced the subjects' responses

TABLE 7.1

Complete Set of Questions and Answer Choices from the Two Forms of the
Test Used in Experiment 1 (* Indicates Correct Answer)

1. *Declarative question*: If you are moving into Colorado, you must obtain
your new license plates within _____ days after becoming a resident.
   Procedural question: Colorado speed limit in any residence district is
_____ mph.

Form 1   Form 2
 a) 15   a) 10
*b) 30   b) 20
 c) 45   *c) 30
 d) 60   d) 40

2. *Declarative question*: Driving under the influence (DUI) is presumed by
blood alcohol content of _____ parts in 10,000.
   Procedural question: Under normal conditions a good rule of thumb is to
follow no closer than one car length for every _____ mph of speed.

Form 1   Form 2
 a) 4   a) 5
 b) 6   *b) 10
 c) 8   c) 15
*d) 10   d) 20

3. *Declarative question*: License plates must be fastened horizontally in a
manner to prevent swinging at a height of at least _____ inches from the
ground.
   Procedural question: Where parking is permitted, your vehicle must be
within _____ inches of the curb.

Form 1   Form 2
*a) 12   a) 6
 b) 18   *b) 12
 c) 24   c) 18
 d) 30   d) 24

Note. The same questions were used in Experiment 2 except that they were
presented in a fill-in-the-blank recall format without the answer choices.

TABLE 7.2

Percentage of Correct Responses on the Declarative and Procedural Questions in Experiment 1 (Recognition Test) and Experiment 2 (Recall Test)

Type of Test	Declarative	Procedural
Recognition Test		
Experiment 1 (*n* = 64)	54.2	59.4
Form 1 (*n* = 32)	55.2	69.8
Form 2 (*n* = 32)	53.1	49.0
Recall Test		
Experiment 2 (*n* = 75)	31.6	39.6

because when asked for the answer to that question without being given alternatives in Experiment 2 (see the description of this experiment that follows), 45 of the 75 subjects gave the answer 25; only 12 of the 75 subjects responded with the correct answer of 30. In Experiment 1, the choices for Form 2 included one answer close to 25 (i.e., 20), which was selected by 17 of the 32 subjects given that form; only 12 of the 32 subjects selected the correct answer 30. In contrast, the closest answer to 25 on Form 1 was the correct answer 30, which was selected by 22 of the 32 subjects; the next closest answer was 15, which was selected by 8 of the 32 subjects. This pattern of results suggests that the significant interaction of form by question type reflects the relationship between the alternatives given on each form and the subjects' best estimate of the answer.

Of the 64 subjects, 40 were Colorado drivers who had passed the Colorado drivers' license written examination. These are the subjects who clearly had been exposed to the information contained in the *Colorado Drivers' Manual* (because the written examination is based on that information) and had had the relevant driving experience. The results for these subjects are summarized in Table 7.3, along with the results for the remaining 24 subjects. (These 24 subjects included 23 who had a drivers license from another state and 1 who had no current license but had some driving experience.)   Although the procedural questions showed higher scores than the declarative for the Colorado drivers, an ANOVA restricted to only these subjects also yielded no significant effect of question type.

TABLE 7.3

Percentage of Correct Responses on the Declarative and Procedural Questions as a Function of Driving Category in Experiment 1 (Recognition Test) and Experiment 2 (Recall Test)

Type of Test

	Declarative	_Procedural_
Recognition Test (Experiment 1)		
Colorado Drivers ($n = 40$)	55.8	63.3
Others ($n = 24$)	51.4	52.8
Recall Test (Experiment 2)		
Colorado Drivers ($n = 46$)	31.9	45.7
Others ($n = 29$)	31.0	29.9

EXPERIMENT 2

The purpose of Experiment 2 was to determine whether a recall procedure would yield more definitive results than did the recognition procedure used in Experiment 1 because the pattern of results in Experiment 1 was found to depend on the specific set of answer choices given and no answer choices are given in a recall test. Also, the reinstatement of driving procedures might be more helpful for the retrieval of information, and it is generally believed that recall, but not recognition, involves answer retrieval (or generation; see, e.g., Kintsch, 1970).

Method

Subjects. Seventy-five subjects from the same population as used in Experiment 1 participated in this experiment. None of them had participated in either the previous experiment or the pilot experiment (see Jensen, 1994).

Apparatus and Materials. The same test questions were used as in Experiment 1. However, the test was designed as a recall test (or fill in the blank), rather than a multiple-choice recognition test.

Procedure and Design. Subjects were asked to fill in the blank for each question as best as they could, giving numerical answers. There was only one within-subjects independent variable (type of question). Otherwise the procedure and design were the same as in Experiment 1.

Results

Overall accuracy was lower in this experiment (35.6%) than in Experiment 1 (54.8%), as in many previous comparisons of recall and recognition (see, e.g., Kintsch, 1970). A one-way repeated measures ANOVA on the percentage of correct responses revealed a marginally significant advantage for procedural over declarative questions, $F(1,74) = 3.3$, $p = .068$ (see Table 7.2).

There were 46 Colorado drivers out of the 75 subjects. The results for these subjects are summarized in Table 7.3, along with the results for the remaining 29 subjects. (These 29 subjects included 25 who had a drivers license from another state, 3 who reported having a Colorado license but never taking the Colorado license written examination, and 1 who reported having a Colorado license but also reported an average of 0 hours per week driving at present.) There was a significant advantage for procedural questions relative to declarative questions according to a one-way repeated measures ANOVA restricted to the subjects who were Colorado drivers, $F(1,45) = 6.0$, $p = .018$. Because the other subjects, who were not Colorado drivers but who did have some driving experience, actually showed a slight trend in the opposite direction (see Table 7.3), this procedural advantage for the Colorado drivers is clearly due to their experience with driving in Colorado and their knowledge of the Colorado driving regulations.

GENERAL DISCUSSION

Experiment 1 revealed that the set of alternative answers affected the number of correct responses and modulated the difference between declarative and procedural questions. This finding has important implications for test construction. The actual number choices in a test can be manipulated to make the test easier or more difficult.

Experiment 2, which involved a recall test, demonstrated a significant advantage for procedural relative to declarative questions for those subjects who had been exposed to the relevant information (i.e., the driving regulations specified in the *Colorado Drivers' Manual*) and who had had the relevant experience driving in Colorado (but not for other subjects). Because the advantage was not evident for both forms in Experiment 1, which involved a recognition test, it is hypothesized that the availability of procedures aids the process of answer retrieval (which is assumed to be required on a recall test but not on a recognition test; see, e.g., Kintsch, 1970). For example, when retrieving the answer "12 inches," subjects may be helped by thinking about operating a vehicle for the procedural question about the distance from the curb when parking (see Table 7.1). Such help is less likely for the matched declarative question about the height from the ground at which to fasten license plates, which is less closely linked to operating a vehicle. Although both drivers and nondrivers frequently see how far away parked cars are from the curb and how far away license plates are from the ground, drivers (but not nondrivers) can relate the information about parking the cars, but not that about the license plates, to the actual cognitive, perceptual, and motoric procedures they frequently engage in while operating a motor vehicle. This study thus lends support to the procedural reinstatement hypothesis proposed by Healy et al. (1992).

The procedural reinstatement principle has important direct practical implications for education and training because it implies that to enhance long-term retention, instructional techniques should relate to-be-learned information to procedures that can be reinstated at the time of test. For example, students who must learn a set of telephone numbers could improve their memory performance by going through the motoric procedures of entering the numbers on the phone keypad both at the time of studying the numbers and at the subsequent memory test (see, e.g., Fendrich et al., 1995). This principle also has more indirect but equally important implications concerning the prevention of memory distortions. Because retrieval of specific facts is best when those facts are linked to procedures used at study and subsequently reinstated, memory distortions may be minimized by requiring individuals at the time of memory retrieval to reinstate as closely as possible the procedures associated with the specific facts during acquisition. For example, individuals who are eye witnesses to a crime could improve their memory performance by going through the motoric and cognitive procedures that they were using at the time of the prior incident.

ACKNOWLEDGMENTS

This research was supported in part by Army Research Institute Contracts MDA903-93K-0010 and DASW01-96K-0010 to the University of Colorado (Alice F. Healy, Principal Investigator). We are indebted to Immanuel Barshi, Lyle Bourne, Margaret Intons-Peterson, Danielle McNamara, and Vivian Schneider for helpful discussions about this research and comments on an earlier version of this chapter.

REFERENCES

Adams, J. A. (1987). Historical review and appraisal of research on the learning, retention, and transfer of human motor skills. *Psychological Bulletin, 101,* 41–74.

Anderson, J. R. (1983). *The architecture of cognition.* Cambridge, MA: Harvard University Press.

Crutcher, R. J., & Healy, A. F. (1989). Cognitive operations and the generation effect. *Journal of Experimental Psychology: Learning, Memory, and Cognition, 15,* 669–675.

Driskell, J. E., Willis, R. P., & Copper, C. (1992). Effect of overlearning on retention. *Journal of Applied Psychology, 77,* 615–622.

Fendrich, D. W., Gesi, A. T., Healy, A. F., & Bourne, L. E., Jr. (1995). The contribution of procedural reinstatement to implicit and explicit memory effects in a motor task. In A. F. Healy & L. E. Bourne, Jr. (Eds.), *Learning and memory of knowledge and skills: Durability and specificity* (pp. 66–94). Thousand Oaks, CA: Sage.

Fendrich, D. W., Healy, A. F., & Bourne, L. E., Jr. (1991). Long-term repetition effects for motoric and perceptual procedures. *Journal of Experimental Psychology: Learning, Memory, and Cognition, 17,* 137–151.

Fendrich, D. W., Healy, A. F., & Bourne, L. E., Jr. (1993). Mental arithmetic: Training and retention of multiplication skill. In C. Izawa (Ed.), *Cognitive psychology applied* (pp. 111–133). Hillsdale, New Jersey: Lawrence Erlbaum Associates.

Fisk, A. D., & Hodge, K. A. (1992). Retention of trained performance in consistent mapping search after extended delays. *Human Factors, 34,* 147–164.

Gardiner, J. M., & Rowley, J. M. C. (1984). A generation effect with numbers rather than words. *Memory & Cognition, 12,* 443–445.

Healy, A. F., Fendrich, D. W., Crutcher, R. J., Wittman, W. T., Gesi, A. T., Ericsson, K. A., & Bourne, L. E., Jr. (1992). The long-term retention of skills. In A. F. Healy, S. M. Kosslyn, & R. M. Shiffrin (Eds.), *From learning processes to cognitive processes: Essays in honor of William K. Estes* (Vol. 2, pp. 87–118). Hillsdale, NJ: Lawrence Erlbaum Associates.

Healy, A. F., Fendrich, D. W., & Proctor, J. D. (1990). Acquisition and retention of a letter-detection skill. *Journal of Experimental Psychology: Learning, Memory, and Cognition, 16,* 270–281.

Healy, A. F., King, C. L., & Sinclair, G. P. (1997). Maintenance of knowledge about temporal, spatial, and item information: Memory for course schedules and word lists. In D. G. Payne & F. G. Conrad (Eds.), *Intersections in basic and applied memory research* (pp. 215–230). Mahwah, NJ: Lawrence Erlbaum Associates.

Jensen, M. B. (1994). *Retention of procedural vs. declarative information in the Colorado Drivers' Manual.* Unpublished senior honor's thesis, University of Colorado, Boulder.

King, C. L. (1992). *Familiarity effects on the retention of spatial, temporal, and item information in course schedules.* Unpublished doctoral dissertation, Colorado State University, Fort Collins.

Kintsch, W. (1970), Models for free recall and recognition. In D. A. Norman (Ed.), *Models of human memory.* New York: Academic Press.

Kolers, P. A., & Roediger, H. L. (1984). Procedures of mind. *Journal of Verbal Learning and Verbal Behavior, 23,* 425–449.

Marmie, W. R., & Healy, A. F. (1995). The long-term retention of a complex skill. In A. F. Healy & L. E. Bourne, Jr. (Eds.), *Learning and memory of knowledge and skills: Durability and specificity* (pp. 30–65). Thousand Oaks, CA: Sage.

McNamara, D. S., & Healy, A. F. (1995). A procedural explanation of the generation effect: The use of an operand retrieval strategy for multiplication and addition problems. *Journal of Memory and Language, 34,* 399–416.

Morris, C. D., Bransford, J. D., & Franks, J. J. (1977). Levels of processing versus transfer appropriate processing. *Journal of Verbal Learning and Verbal Behavior, 16,* 519–533.

Peterson, L. R., & Peterson, M. J. (1959). Short-term retention of individual verbal items. *Journal of Experimental Psychology, 58,* 193–198.

Slamecka, N. J., & Graf, P. (1978). The generation effect: Delineation of a phenomenon. *Journal of Experimental Psychology: Human Learning and Memory, 4,* 592–604.

State of Colorado (1979). *Colorado drivers' manual and supplemental motorcycle drivers' manual.* (DR-PUB 37, Revised 1979). Denver, CO: Colorado Department of Transportation.

State of Colorado (1990). *Colorado drivers' manual and supplemental motorcycle drivers' manual.* (DRP 2337, Revised 1990). Denver, CO: Colorado Department of Transportation.

State of Colorado (1992). *Colorado drivers' manual and supplemental motorcycle drivers' manual.* (DRP 2337, Revised 07/92). Denver, CO: Colorado Department of Transportation.

Tulving, E., & Thomson, D. M. (1973). Encoding specificity and retrieval processes in episodic memory. *Psychological Review, 80,* 352–373.

Wittman, W. T., & Healy, A. F. (1995). A long-term retention advantage for spatial information learned naturally and in the laboratory. In A. F. Healy & L. E. Bourne, Jr. (Eds.), *Learning and memory of knowledge and skills: Durability and specificity* (pp. 170–205). Thousand Oaks, CA: Sage.

8

Curriculum on Medical and Other Ignorance: Shifting Paradigms on Learning and Discovery

Marlys Hearst Witte
Ann Kerwin
Charles L. Witte
The University of Arizona College of Medicine

The background for the development of the University of Arizona's innovative Curriculum on Medical and Other Ignorance (CMI) is described along with the nature of the philosophical and pedagogical paradigm shift from epistemology and knowledge to n-epistemology and ignorance. The relation of the ignorance explosion to the information explosion and links to chaos and failure theory are examined. The curriculum encourages the student-learner to explore the multifaceted domains of ignorance in medicine, sciences, and other fields, provides tools for questioning, and a variety of educational formats including research experiences, seminars, rounds, and reports. Evaluation feedback and program impact are summarized.

The greatest single achievement of science in this most scientific productive of centuries is the discovery that we are profoundly ignorant. We know very little about nature and we understand even less. I wish there were some formal courses in medical school on medical ignorance, textbooks as well although they would have to be very heavy volumes.

—Lewis Thomas (physician-essayist, 1982, p. xliii)

Why ignorance, and particularly medical ignorance, as the starting point for examining shifting paradigms of learning and discovery? Thomas' (1982) novel idea struck a responsive chord. For example, regarding acquired immunodeficiency syndrome (AIDS), after more than 15 years of fundamental discoveries at the molecular level, promises of successive clinical drug trials (currently, the costly protease inhibitor cocktails), sound cautionaries in prophylaxis, and great expenditures of money, time, and effort, there has been little dent in the burgeoning global pandemic and the prospect of effective vaccine development remains elusive. Perhaps an admission of ignorance or insertion of blank pages in the section in medical textbooks on solid organ cancers such as of the brain and pancreas might more accurately reflect how little can be done practically to arrest tumor growth; at the same time the gap might also stimulate young minds to pursue new paths of investigation. Even artificial hearts and organ transplants, the miracles of modern surgery, attest to the fundamental ignorance of cardiac function, heart disease, other organ dysfunction, and their progression, so that only at the most advanced stages or in desperation are these highly technological operations offered for rejuvenated life. Indeed, surgery itself as a discipline with its reliance on operations is the ultimate biologic exercise in ignorance—removing organs and mutilating the body. As legendary surgeon John Hunter summed up several centuries ago: "It (operation) is like an armed savage who attempts to get that by force which a civilized man would get by strategem" (cited by Kobler, 1960, p. 108). Although an operation is often the best treatment currently available for many ailments, it is at the same time a stark testimonial to a basic lack of understanding (*viz.* ignorance) of the underlying disease process and inability to arrest its progression by natural means. Whereas the surgeon resorts to barbarism by slashing, the radiotherapist attempts to vaporize the intruder (usually cancer) by high energy gamma rays (burning).

In this setting, we reasoned that courses on medical ignorance, lectures, exercises, and ultimately a textbook, would not only be a fitting prescription for ailing medical education but also a potent stimulus for new ideas and fundamental research. As the CMI evolved, the power and reach of the ignorance paradigm has been progressively revealed.

Shifting Philosophical Paradigms: From Epistemology to N-Epistemology (Kerwin, 1993)

For the past 3 millennia, philosophers in Western epistemic lore have been fascinated, even obsessed, by ever more elusive conditions of knowledge about which they have debated passionately, brilliantly, and inconclusively. This tradition—firmly, even insidiously, embedded in Western languages, concepts, frameworks, and values—decrees that knowledge and ignorance are polar opposites. Knowledge is glory and ignorance or nonknowledge the enemy. Ignorance obstructs; knowledge liberates. Ignorance threatens; knowledge protects. The antithesis of knowledge and its rival, ignorance, seems a bug in our ambitious schemes to know—and thus to control—a universe too vast, complex, and inhuman for human comprehension and mastery. Thus, we have learned to fear ignorance, to avoid and purge it, if knowledge is to triumph and humans to advance.

In the real world, however, knowledge and ignorance are not irreconcilable polarities. Learning is not a fight to the death between epistemic blacks and whites. In fact, knowing and not knowing are inextricably intertwined and symbiotic. It takes knowledge to acknowledge ignorance, and it takes acknowledgment to inquire and face what we do not know. Thus, fallibility, incompleteness and infinite revisability characterize the best of hypotheses and the whole of learning. As James (1971) reminded the intelligentsia of his day:

> Think how many new conceptions have arisen in our own generation, how many new problems have been formulated that were never thought of before, and then cast an eye on the brevity of science's career . . . Is it credible that such a mushroom of knowledge, such a growth overnight as this, can represent more than the minutest glimpse of what the universe will really prove to be when adequately understood? No! Our science is a drop, our ignorance a sea. Whatever else is certain, this at least is certain,—that the world of our present natural knowledge is enveloped in a larger world of some sort of whose residual properties we can at present frame no positive idea. (pp. 82–83)

In other words, ignorance is neither a void nor lack. Rather, it is a plenum: full and fertile. Not only can ignorance not be avoided, but it would be foolish to try. Learning itself depends on ignorance. Every time we learn, discover, create, or invent, we do so in the domain—and by the grace—of ignorance. Learning is a continuing encounter and inexhaustible alliance with ignorance. It requires understanding, sometimes a great deal, to be aware of what we do not know. The more we understand something, the better we realize how little we know about it, and how much more we have to learn. As 17th century mathematician Pascal observed, "Knowledge is like a sphere, the greater its volume, the larger its contact with the unknown" (see Witte & Witte, 1995, p. 511). That is why true experts acknowledge more ignorance than those less versed—more questions, more unknowns to be sought; they pursue more unanswered questions, suggestive hypotheses, and pregnant puzzles. As they head for the terra incognita, they are prepared for disorder, confusion, failure, surprise, frustration, revelation, for risk, for questions that multiply and fertilize, and answers that biodegrade quickly. As Nobelist in Medicine Jacob (1988) described his life's work:

The game was that of continually inventing a possible world, or a piece of a possible world, and then of comparing it with the real world . . . A race without end . . . What mattered more than the answers were the questions . . , the answer led to new questions . . . For me, this world of questions and the provisional, this chase after an answer that was always put off to the next day, all that was euphoric. I lived in the future . . . I had turned my anxiety into my profession. (pp. 8–9)

Seen in this light, ignorance is dynamic: Its topography shifts with inquiry, it is interdisciplinary. It is learner's land and discover's space. There are at least six lands within the domain of ignorance (Kerwin, 1993):

- All the things we know we don't know (known unknowns).
- All the things we don't know we don't know (unknown unknowns).
- All the things we think we know but don't (error).
- All the things we don't know we know (tacit knowing, subception, intuition).
- The taboo (forbidden knowledge; Shattuck, 1996).
- Denial.

Each of these lands is explored in the CMI.

Paradigm Shift on the Information Superhighway: The Off Ramp to the Age of Ignorance

Society at large is confronting a profound paradigm shift as the information explosion gradually transforms into a knowledge culture (corporations are now recruiting CKOs or chief knowledge officers) but stops short of wisdom. The current transformation remains limited by the insight and vision of the computer gurus controlling it: William Gates' virtual reality with everything at his fingertips or media mogul Ted Turner's infotainment offer of W^3 (whatever, wherever, and whenever you want it) but without surprises. But others warn that the information superhighway is hurtling us to a cyberfuture of information haves and have nots, of cybermoguls and cyberslaves. Management expert Drucker (1992a) advised, "Be data literate. Know what to know . . ." [Rather than the] " . . . greater speed and greater memories, the challenges increasingly will be not technical but to convert data into usable information that is actually being used" (Tenner, 1996, p. 346). People are seeking more socialization; by stifling competition, Microsoft is producing a counterrevolution; and technology has a way of biting back. Media philosopher Postman (1995, pp. 10-11) expressed fear of a society of information junkies overloaded with "information which they don't know what to do with, have no sense of what is relevant and what is irrelevant," and pointed out that the 19th century was a culture of information scarcity that was addressed by photography and telegraphy and now a new, never experienced problem has developed—"information glut, information meaninglessness, information incoherence . . . Children starving in Somalia . . . crime rampant in the streets in New York . . . none of that has anything to do with inadequate information." Further, Meyers (1995, p. 358) suggested that the major environmental problems in the world are less a consequence of ignorance than of "ignore*a*nce," meaning we choose to ignore problems. We choose not to study them, and when we have the information, we choose to turn our backs on it. And most environmental hazards are not surprises at all. We have just not identified them as problems and started asking questions about them. Drucker (1992b) advised: "plan for uncertainty; [the] vague new world [will] require us to plan for what we don't know. Unless a business plans on the basis of what they already know for what they think the future is and they can create this future, they will be unable to compete" (p. A12).

In the world of computer design, for example, an article in *Inside Tucson Business* (1995) entitled "Ignorance Is Bliss to the World of Computer Design," argued that:

> Market ignorance, not market information, is the dominant driver of technological innovation . . . Today's customers are so demanding precisely because they don't know an awful lot, and they don't really want to know it. They don't want to read the books, they want to be able to call an expert and have him take care of the problem. (p. 9)

In his insightful tome on *Scientific Literacy and the Myth of the Scientific Method,* chemist Bauer (1992) maintained that all knowledge from the most subjective and unreliable to the most reliable and objective passes progressively through a knowledge filter (Fig. 8.1). There are "all different degrees of probabilities and certainties that are changing always with time as we go from word of mouth to what's in the textbooks" (p. 45). And in the June 11, 1993 (p. A10, reference section) issue of the *Wall Street Journal,* economist Stein welcomed the coming "age of ignorance."

From Success and Order in the World of Knowledge to Failure and Chaos in the World of Ignorance (Witte, 1991)

In his text *Ignorance and Uncertainty: Emerging Paradigms,* psychologist Smithson (1989) examined disciplines as diverse as physics, mathematics, sociology, and psychology to illustrate how complexity and fuzzy are

SUBJECTIVE
UNREL|IABLE

ALL HUMAN TRAITS

CONVENTIONAL WISDOM · CONSERVATISM · HUNCHES · SLOPPINESS · WILD IDEAS · UNDERGRADUATE EDUCATION · WISDOM · IMAGINATION · IGNORANCE · INSPIRATION · PIG-HEADEDNESS · COMPETENCE · JEALOUSY · DEDICATION · INCOMPETENCE · ANARCHY · GRADUATE TRAINING · LAZINESS · AMBITION · CARE · PERSISTENCE · GREED

← NONSENSE
← STUPIDITY
← PSEUDO-SCIENCE

"WHAT WILL THEY THINK?"
PROPOSAL REVIEWING
GRANT FUNDING

BRIGHT IDEAS · SILLY IDEAS · LUCK · RUTHLESSNESS · CUTTING CORNERS · QUICK & DIRTY EXPERIMENTS · GENEROSITY · TRIAL & ERROR · HUNCHES · INGENUITY · IDIOSYNCRACY · STUBBORNESS · MIXED MOTIVES · CONFLICTS OF INTEREST

FRONTIER
SCIENCE

← BIAS
← ERROR
← DISHONESTY

"CAN THIS GET PUBLISHED?"
REPLICATE & CLEAN UP
SEMINARS & PREPRINTS
EDITORS & REFEREES

RESEARCH PAPERS · MOSTLY NOT OBVIOUSLY WRONG · PUTATIVE SCIENCE · ABSTRACTS · MIGHT BE RIGHT

PRIMARY
LITERATURE

← MISTAKES
← UNINTERESTING STUFF
← FRAUD

TESTING & USE BY OTHERS
MODIFICATION & EXTENSION
CITATION OF USEFUL WORK

REVIEW ARTICLES · MONOGRAPHS · MOSTLY RELIABLE

SECONDARY
LITERATURE

← MISTAKES
← OBSOLESCENCE

TIME
USE BY OTHERS
CONCORDANCE WITH OTHER FIELDS

MOSTLY VERY RELIABLE

TEXTBOOK
SCIENCE

← INADEQUACIES

TIME
USE BY OTHERS
CONNECTIONS AMONG SCIENCES

WORK WELL

TEXTBOOKS
OF THE FUTURE

TIME

RELIABLE
↓
OBJECTIVE

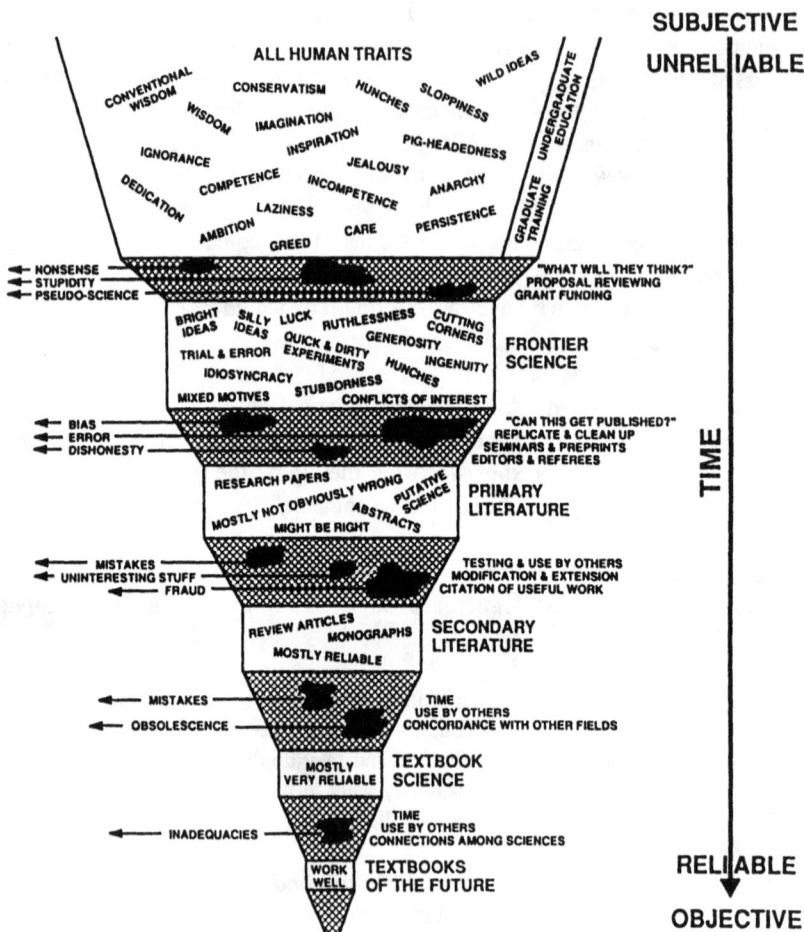

Fig. 8.1. The knowledge filter. In stages, deficiencies are eliminated by virtue of the social institutions that science has evolved, peer review in particular. (Reprinted with permission from Bauer, 1992).

permeating themes. This world of ignorance, albeit frightening, is exciting, surprising, and full of endless possibilities, questions, lingering doubts, black holes, ambiguity, unknowns and the unknowable, with the recurring counterpoint of failure and chaos (Witte, 1991). Fascination with failure and its interplay with success threads through many recent writings. In the past decade and largely since the insider trading scandals on Wall Street, business schools and colleges of engineering have introduced courses such as "Failure 101" to analyze and rethink what happens when a great idea goes down in flames or a brilliant strategy fails (Blum, 1990; Johnson, 1989). Wurman (1989), in his provocative book *Information Anxiety*, examines sequentially the Tacoma Narrows bridge that collapsed, Clarence Darrow's living legend of lost courtroom cases that forced the rethinking of constitutional safeguards, Columbus' wrong turn on the way to the East Indies that discovered America, Newton's and Einstein's failures in elementary math courses, and Goodyear's messed up experiments that stumbled on vulcanized rubber. Game players, whether chess masters or football stars, know that it is great to win but learning is greatest after losing and then analyzing the reasons for the loss. Physicians traditionally have "Mortality and Morbidity" conferences (M&Ms; the equivalent of failure rounds) to pinpoint what went wrong in caring for patients who sustain unexpected complications or death and to discuss how to avoid undesirable outcomes. Whereas greater knowledge of the known sometimes can improve outcomes, more often such crucial knowledge remains to be discovered. Mulconrey (1992, p. A12) told us that Thomas Edison "designed failure into the system" because he learned and invented from the thousand approaches that did not work. Increasingly, critics of medical practice are examining the dynamics of mistakes in clinical decision-making so that performance and innovation can be enhanced (Wu, Folkman, McPhee, & Lo, 1991).

In *Chaos: The Making of a New Science*, Gleick (1987) eloquently described the discovery of the revolutionary chaos theory by a physicist who wiled away countless hours watching meandering streams and gathering clouds. Whether a butterfly flapping its wings in Rio de Janeiro and creating a tornado in Texas, the dynamics of the AIDS epidemic, turbulent blood flow in an arterial aneurysm, epilepsy, panic attacks, or cardiac arrhythmias, these complex chaotic phenomena disobey the simple linear laws once thought to govern them. Similarly, a terrorist's bomb exploding in a remote communication network could culminate in nuclear war, or a blip in the stock market plunge faraway nations into financial ruin. The human body, even in health but more so in disease, is full of movement, oscillation, branching, trafficking, feedback mechanisms, and complex rhythms that are not understood (Cotton, 1991; Gleick, 1987), and even this field of chaos is itself undergoing upheaval (Regaldo, 1995). Recent nonlinear dynamics research suggests that the emphasis on controlling chaos may be misplaced. Chaos itself may be desirable. In other words, health, youth, and non-disease represent an ongoing chaotic disequilibrium poised for rapid response and adaptation; aging is a condition of increasing stability where arrhythmias and other life-threatening and degenerative disorders are more likely because the capacity to promptly and continuously adjust is muted. Ironically, prochaos manipulations may thereby be useful treatment for a variety of diseases. And for successful corporations, management guru Peters (1987) advised not just facing but instead "thriving on chaos" because those companies that recognize chaos, appreciate uncertainty, and take the necessary risks, will be the ones that make it into the next century. Other experts encourage more "negative thinking" (Smith, 1994), even "skepticemia" (Skrabanek & McCormick, 1989), and greater experimentation with new types of self-organization, deconstruction, and cognitive dissonance.

Paradigm Shift in Pedagogy: From Answers to Questions and From Knowledge to Learning

> Our students should be freed from the stupefying excesses of fact engorgement, which threatens to convert them into floppy disks encoded for our present ignorance. (L. Smith, 1990, p. B1)

As medical educators, we must prepare physicians for the 21st century. Yet medical students spend much of the basic science years memorizing the knowledge of the day and largely repeating correct answers to questions generated by the teachers. No one knows with certainty what the next century will bring, nor what opportunities and challenges await future medical practitioners. Much of the knowledge memorized today will be outdated; current procedures will be surpassed; some heresies will become dogma; and some orthodoxy will be overthrown. As Ravitch (1987) remarked, "Textbooks of several generations ago were as large as the textbooks of today; they just contained different misinformation" (p. 126). At a premium, then, is not so much what medical students today know as how conscientiously and well they are able to learn, largely independently, and continuously, over the course of a lifetime. In order to function in the complex, ambiguous, and uncertain terrain of medical diagnosis and treatment, students must be able to question skillfully and effectively; they must identify known unknowns; seek unknown unknowns; question pat answers; and devise new approaches or resources. Such focused expertise in learning—specifically in the identification, exploration, and utilization of medical ignorance—is neither a standard nor central feature of most medical curricula. In order to help students become life-long learners and to function optimally in the vast and daunting arena of medical ignorance, we inaugurated in 1984 the CMI in the Department of Surgery and Medical Student Research Program at University of Arizona (Witte, Kerwin, & Witte, 1991; Witte, Witte, M. H., & Kerwin, 1994; Witte, Kerwin, & Witte, 1988; Witte, Kerwin, & Witte, 1989; Witte, Witte, & Kerwin, 1994).

The core content—the what—of this curriculum is the terrain of ignorance. In any discipline or for any individual, these unanswered questions are also the *terra incognita* for all future learning and discovery. Accordingly, a specific topic or a whole discipline can be explored by charting the map of its lands of ignorance (*vide infra*) from a global or personal perspective.

How does one teach ignorance, that is, acquire the skills and attitudes to recognize and deal with it? Small children are boundless in asking probing questions about the world around them. Yet by the second grade, most get the message not to ask questions. Intermediate schools, universities, and medical colleges too often reinforce this negative message. On the other hand, CMI demands and reinforces the questioning process. To facilitate the uncorking of questions, we first solicit as many as possible from the student regarding a series of specific medical topics, for example, AIDS, cancer, or organ transplants. Once long-suppressed inhibitions about asking questions are released, a dialogue begins using the classification of three generic types of questions—fundamental questions, for example, about basic biology (Type I), clinical or practical management questions about a specific patient or medical problem (Type II), and those that go beyond the patient and relate to societal, economic, legal, and ethical issues (Type III). Then with each topic and each patient, the student formulates questions of each type (I, II, and III) to avoid fixing solely on a particular subcategory and to encourage questions of far-reaching variety. Considerable pedagogical references exist on questioning but most focus on teacher questions—and how to get teachers to ask students better, more demanding, higher order questions. In contrast, the CMI expects the student to ask the questions, the patient to ask the questions, the physician, the professor, the Nobel laureate to ask and pursue their own questions even if no answer is currently available. These questions are not easily classified into low order and high order by form or complexity. For example, among the most profound questions of this century was the seemingly simplistic or low-order question of Einstein, namely, "What time is it?" by which he meant, "What time is it really?" Ultimately, it turned out to be earthshaking, culminating in the theory of general relativity.

In summary, the what and how of the CMI are questions and questioning. As physicians work in this uncertain terrain, most become accustomed to it. Yet there have been few formal ways to discuss, teach, transmit, and gain respect for this uncertain domain. Indeed, physicians who admit or emphasize ignorance may lose respect, be shunned by their peers or, worse yet, suffer the fate of a modern-day Socrates.

Syllabus of the Curriculum on Medical (and All Other) Ignorance

As Thomas' (1982) suggested curricular reform embodies and Pascal's (Witte, & Witte, 1995, p. 511) "enlarging sphere of knowledge" envisions, the more we know, the more we need to recognize what we do not know. To be overconfident, smug, and arrogant in having limited knowledge is to be immature, unwise, and unknowledgeable about the world and existent poorly understood diseases. How then does one take the foregoing ideas and themes and amalgamate them into a bona fide curriculum? First, we prepared a guidebook—a curricula syllabus for students, physicians, teachers, visiting professors, and other participants (Witte, M. H. et al., 1989, 1996). To disabuse students of misguided impressions that good physicians know or can even access most of medicine's problems, is a prime reason for CMI to counterbalance the illusion of universities as knowledge factories.

CMI's goals in a nutshell (Table 8.1) are to gain an understanding of the shifting domains of ignorance, uncertainty, and the unknown; to improve skills such as questioning, communicating, and collaborating to recognize and deal productively with ignorance, uncertainty, and the unknown; and then to reinforce positive attitudes and values of curiosity, optimism, humility, self-confidence, and skepticism. Begun with full-time research experiences (basic molecular and cell biology as well as clinical and field research), the Summer Institute on Medical Ignorance (SIMI) involves about 20% to 25% of our medical students and since 1987 also incorporates high school students from underrepresented minority populations along with K through 12 science teachers, comprising approximately 75 summer students in all. The program is symbolized by a question mark: students begin with questions at the start of their projects and end with a new set of questions at summer's close. The basic and clinical research experiences are a full-time hands-on, brain-on immersion in ignorance. Biweekly participatory seminars involve faculty members from The University of Arizona and visiting professors, who present their own probing questions on what they do not know, how it has stimulated productivity, and what they have learned from sick patients through questioning.

Thus, the first medical school accredited course on Ignorance focuses on various clinical topics, such as AIDS, schizophrenia, breast cancer, pain, liver cirrhosis. Each student selects and specializes on a single subject, uncovering first what is known and then delving into what is not known and ultimately amalgamating the material into an oral and written final ignorance report. They also are assigned a patient with a particular disorder, examine the decision-making processes in diagnosis and treatment, and identify the logical progression of questions already raised, others that should have been or could have been asked, and what biologic aspects remain to be discovered. The central focus on unanswered questions, that is, on what is not, rather than what is known, requires effort and thought. Thus, for example, to compose a sophisticated report on what is not known about breast cancer first requires formulating and organizing a host of straightforward questions about what is currently accepted, critically evaluating this body of facts, and then asking what is not known about breast cancer (e.g., in terms of intricate workings of

TABLE 8.1

Goals and Activities of the Curriculum on Medical and Other Ignorance

Curriculum Goals	Activities
Gain understanding of the shifting domains of ignorance, uncertainty, and the unknown: philosophical and psychological foundations and approaches to learning, questioning, and creating knowledge; history and development of selected ideas and methods in basic and clinical medical science; mastery by in-depth multidimensional exploration of selected timely medical topics.	Summer Institute on Medical Ignorance Full-time basic and clinical research Seminars and Clinics on Medical Ignorance Freshman Colloquium on Introduction to Medical and Other Ignorance Questions and Questioning Exercises Creative Thinking Exercises
Improve skills to recognize and deal productively with ignorance, uncertainty, and the unknown: questioning critically and creatively focusing on raising, listening to, analyzing, prioritizing, and answering questions from different points of view; communicating clearly in different media with various audiences; collaborating effectively with different people and other resources.	Final Oral and Written Reports on Selected Topics in Medical Ignorance Weekly Ignorance Logs Ignorance Field Trips Pondering Rounds Failure Rounds Ignorance Ward and Grand Rounds Ignorance Conferences Visiting Professors of Medical Ignorance La Residencia del Incógnito
Reinforce positive attitudes and values of curiosity, optimism, humility, self-confidence, and skepticism.	

the cancer cell, earlier and better diagnosis, genetic implications, and less destructive treatment)? As for AIDS, even the establishment has begun to admit and articulate many uncertainties about pathogenesis and treatment of this condition. During the first decade of the AIDS epidemic, there was unbridled optimism and few words about not knowing, not understanding, or being baffled. To fill this gap, we organized two symposia (Vienna in 1987 and Tokyo in 1989), under the auspices of the International Society of Lymphology, focusing on AIDS, Kaposi sarcoma, the lymphatic system, and medical ignorance (Witte, 1988; Witte & Shirai, 1990). In 1991, we featured AIDS as a topic addressed from the ignorance perspective by international experts in the field during the first International Conference on Medical Ignorance (Figure 8.2). It was not until 1993, however, that *Science* magazine, where many landmark articles are published, featured a full cover and extensive exploration on "Unanswered Questions" in AIDS. In this symposium, AIDS experts explored the many unresolved known unknowns, including some previously erroneously claimed to be well understood (*Science*, 1993).

In other exercises, Visiting Professors of Medical Ignorance, that is, distinguished ignorami even of Nobel laureate caliber, each renowned for their outstanding expertise in a specific research area, offer two seminars. The first is a traditional knowledge seminar highlighting the speaker's sophistication. This presentation typically encompasses many slides in a large auditorium setting. Then the distinguished guest strolls over to *La Residencia del Incógnito* (the House of Ignorance), where books and papers are discouraged, and talks about what he/she does not know about the same subject. The latter discourse is characteristically much livelier with greater audience participation and interchange, with questions stimulated by ongoing investigations. The contrast between lecturing on what is known and exposing what is not known and the personal reaction of the visiting professor and that of the students to enlightened ignorance generates a very different kind of give-and-take interactive experience. The seminars also include a wide variety of other engaging Ignorance Exercises.

The Ignorance map (Figure 8.2), a large question mark with indistinct borders and abundant empty space, is provided to the students to chart the lands of ignorance (*vide supra*) pertaining to a given topic (or patient). Mapping gives a physical reality to the unknown, and documents student progress in exploring its content and dimensions and mining its resources.

The Ignorance Log (Figure 8.3) is another centerpiece. In a newly launched accredited University of Arizona undergraduate Freshman Colloquium, catalogued under Arts and Sciences 195 as "Introduction to Medical and Other Ignorance," participating college students submit weekly logs of an increasing number of personal daily questions along with their approach to finding the answers. Typically, they fill the whole back of the page with seemingly endless questions. Often these questions relate to personal reflections or anxieties about university life, social relationships, and career aspirations; others concern medical topics or even cosmic musings. These logs are particularly useful for documenting the progress of a student's questions. It is

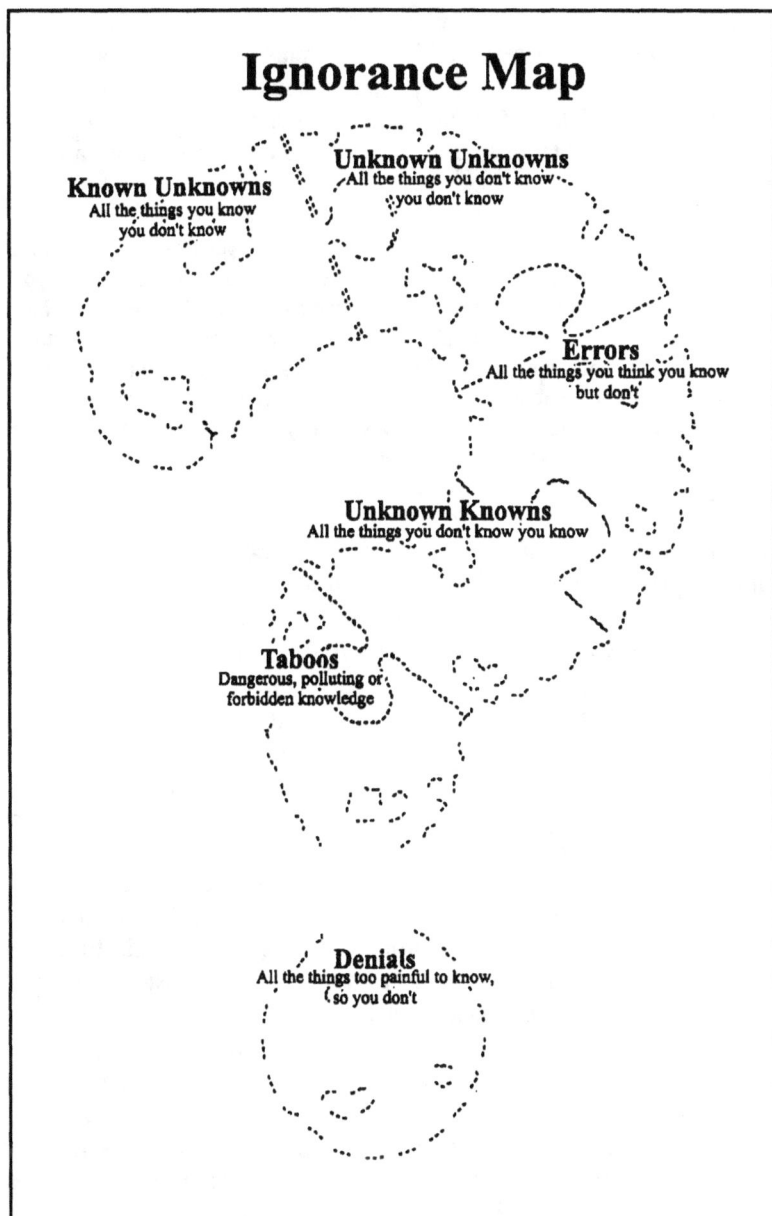

Ignorance Map

Known Unknowns
All the things you know
you don't know

Unknown Unknowns
All the things you don't know
you don't know

Errors
All the things you think you know
but don't

Unknown Knowns
All the things you don't know you know

Taboos
Dangerous, polluting or
forbidden knowledge

Denials
All the things too painful to know,
so you don't

Fig. 8.2. Ignorance map.

noteworthy that Nobel laureate in Physics Feynman (1988) kept a daily diary of scientific questions that resembled these ignorance logs.

In a Creative Thinking Exercise, "Grow Your Own Organ" (Witte et al., 1989, 1996) the students analyze a sensational press release about a fictitious scientific breakthrough:

> A 3-month old baby girl dying from a rare metabolic liver disease received the gift of a new liver from her mother. Sources revealed that 2 months ago, a golf ball-sized portion of her mother's liver was removed and subsequently "grown up" in tissue culture to a normal infant size in preparation for the historic operation. Last night, the infant's failing liver was subtotally removed and the "made to order" new one implanted in its place. University of Arizona surgeons and basic scientists predict that this approach may be used to produce a whole variety of new "grow your own" organs eliminating the need for donors and harmful anti-rejection drugs. Anybody need an extra leg? (p. 40, syllabus)

When this science fiction newspaper story was concocted 12 years ago, we did not anticipate that cloning of sheep and monkeys was so close at hand. CMI students explain what the press release means, what basic biologic questions are raised, and other questions related to clinical practice and to ethical or moral considerations (Types I—III questions). These questions are addressed including how some can be approached and answered, how others are ongoing dilemmas that permeate medicine, and how still others can be used as themes for teaching embryology or transplantation biology or even medical ethics. It is emphasized that advances in medicine increasingly appear first in newspaper accounts or on the Internet, with the public learning about new information and misinformation often even before physicians. Indeed, in a few years of the fictitious "Grow Your Own Organ" exercise, a sensational tabloid headlined, "You Can Regrow Lost Arms and Legs," and a mainstream press blared, "Fatty Tissue Transfer is Implant Possibility" for breast enlargement by transferring fatty tissue from another body site as a grow your own expander. Indeed, the rapid advances and clinical applications of partial liver, bone marrow, and stem cell transplantation, improved organ preservation, and now the cloning of whole mammals from the DNA of differentiated adult cells have made this once far-fetched science fiction almost a reality. Students are encouraged to search for other contemporary news items that can serve as exercises in ignorance.

"Pondering Rounds" are also a monthly feature. Students, faculty, and staff assemble to discuss their daydreams and preoccupations; what they are contemplating during quiet periods or lectures. Often these ponderings include astronomical considerations, personal worries, biologic or medical phenomena, and political, domestic, or metaphysical concerns. During the summer (SIMI),

Sample Ignorance Log   Week of _____

Name:_____

Questions considered and new ones raised?

Activities and progress?

New ideas and approaches?

Areas of knowledge and ignorance
uncovered (your own and others)?

New resources to consider?

General comments?

Fill the other side of the page with questions.

Fig. 8.3. Sample Ignorance Log

more than 75 research students at different educational levels verbally each
communicate their ponders of the month in less than 1 minute. Examples
include: "Why do medical personnel sterilely scrub the site of lethal injection
of condemned prisoners? Is there a rational basis for alternative medicine?
How sexually active are octogenarians in nursing homes? And simply, where

will my life take me?" Failure Rounds, usually featured at the midpoint of the summer research program, focuses on the errors and disappointments experienced by the students and their mentors and how to admit, analyze, correct, and circumvent them.

Ignorance Ward Rounds was surprisingly difficult at first for medical students and houseofficers (resident physicians) because of a longstanding reluctance to admit to unanswered questions. Closer scrutiny revealed that they were actually more afraid to be tested on the questions raised. Once assured that answers were not the point of the exercise, questions poured forth illustrating how inhibiting the hospital teaching environment has become for questions and yet how critical the process is for learning, relearning, and unlearning. The exercise is designed to bring the unanswered questions—like suppressed memories—into the open for greater scrutiny. In Ignorance Ward Rounds, a complex patient (include history, physical examination, laboratory findings, and clinical courses) is presented, and then a plethora of questions are elicited from the audience, including the most knowledgeable senior faculty, seasoned practitioners, and department heads. Comparison of faculty-generated questions to those of resident physicians and medical students reveals that many so-called stupid, naive questions that students and resident physicians have suppressed are also uppermost on the minds of experienced professors. This realization is not only a comforting thought but also a starting point for breaking down barriers between teacher and student—all learners—so that medicine's limitations and unknowns can be frankly and productively examined.

A variety of conferences, symposia, workshops, and seminars have also been organized locally, nationally, and internationally around the theme of medical and other ignorance and targeted to diverse audiences (see Appendix for detailed listing). As already mentioned, the 1991 International Conference on Ignorance (Fig. 8.4) generated worldwide participation and interest, and the specific topics featured at that forum, namely, AIDS, breast cancer, organ transplantation, and medical practice parameters (algorithms) remain hot areas of ignorance. Critical-Creative Thinking Workshops for teachers, primarily in conjunction with the annual summer International Conference on Critical Thinking at Sonoma State University in Northern California, have encompassed diverse fields that range from music, history, and political science to business, civil engineering, and biomedicine at multiple educational levels. Indeed, any elementary, high school, undergraduate, or graduate college class is ripe for such innovation. At our university, for example, an undergraduate Honors Seminar in Material Sciences Engineering covers what material science engineering is all about. As surgical faculty, we are less informed than most engineering undergraduates, yet we are able to raise student awareness of ignorance in their field and facilitate their questioning by

Schedule of Events

Thursday, November 14th

Morning

8:00	Registration: UMC DuVal Auditorium
9:00	Welcome, Manuel Pacheco, UA President
9:10	Keynote: "Courses on Medical Ignorance and Textbooks, Too," Lewis Thomas
9:40	"CMI and the Topography of Medical Ignorance," M.H. Witte and A. Kerwin
10:00	"Tribulations of Clinical Trials," H.O. Conn
10:30	Questioning Free-For-All
11:00	Ignorance Ward Rounds

Afternoon

12:15	Luncheon
1:45	"Germ Theory of Medical Ignorance," D. Rohatyn
2:15	"Medical Practice Parameters, Malpractice and Innovation," Panel: D. Cloud, W. Mangold, G. Henderson, M.H. Witte, and C.L. Witte
3:00	"Ergogenic Aids for Athletes: Fact or Fancy?" E. Percy
3:30	"Future of DNA Fingerprinting and the Human Genome Project," Panel: J. Sninsky, R. Erickson, H. Bernstein, H.E. Hoyme, and K. Iserson
4:30	Questioning Free-For-All

Friday, November 15th

Morning

8:15	Welcome: James Dalen, UA Dean of Medicine
8:30	Keynote: "What Doctors Don't Know They Know About Clinical Science," Alvan Feinstein
9:15	"Treatment of Breast Cancer: Progress or Illusion?"

	Panel: C.L. Witte, M. Granberry, I. Ariel and H.M. Shapiro
10:15	Questioning-Free-For-All
10:30	"The Problem of Problems," R. Root-Bernstein
11:00	Ignorance Ward Rounds
11:45	Summer Institute on Medical Ignorance, Medical Student Research Program, NIH-Minority Research High School Apprentice and Science Teacher Program, and La Residencia del Incognitó. Tour: M. Witte, G. Ramirez, W. Williams, M. Granberry, and UA medical students

Afternoon

12:15	Luncheon
1:45	"Do We Know the Nature, Cause, and Treatment of AIDS and Kaposi Sarcoma?" Panel: R. Root-Bernstein, Z. McGee, A.A. Gottlieb, M. Witte
2:30	"Can We Teach Critical Thinking About the Unknown?" G. Nosich
3:00	"Departmental Ignorance Grand Rounds: Frontiers in Radiology," P. Capp, D. Patton, W. Williams and Radiology Faculty and Residents
3:30	"Terra Incognita of Transplantation Biology and Artificial Organs," J. Copeland, B. Jarrell, J. Marchalonis, K. Iserson, and C. Zukoski
4:30	Questioning Free-For-All

Saturday, November 16th

Morning

9-11:00 Medical Ignorance Round-Up and Wrap-Up

Much has been made of the need to put the product of medical research into the bag of the practitioner... Hardly ever mentioned, however, is a need equally important for the doctor: that of adapting his attitude and work to the mass of non-knowledge... to uncertainties... The medical profession must disabuse itself and others of the idea that there is anything improper or calamitous about admitting ignorance... so that solutions can be achieved by considered study rather than by frantic edict.

Franz Inglefinger,
late editor of the
New England Journal of Medicine

MED·I·CAL IG·NO·RANCE:
"what we know we don't know, what we don't know we don't know, and what we think we know but don't."

And just maybe a new set of courses dealing systematically with ignorance and science might take hold. The scientist might discover in it a new and subversive technique for catching the attention of students driven by curiosity, delighted and surprised to learn that science is... an 'endless frontier.' The humanists for their part might take considerable satisfaction in watching their scientific colleagues confess openly to not knowing everything about everything. And the poets, on whose shoulders the future rests, might, late nights, thinking things over, begin to see some meanings that elude the rest of us. It is worth a try.

Lewis Thomas,
physician, philosopher, author

Fig. 8.4.   Schedule of Events, Excerpted from *Medical Ignorance: The Problem and the Challenge*, 1991, an International Conference, November 14-16, 1991, The University of Arizona College of Medicine, Tucson, Arizona.

flaunting our own naivité. In the College of Law, an advanced course on "AIDS and the Law" devotes a special segment to Ignorance, AIDS, and the

Law, where vexatious issues that transcend medical and legal theory and overshadow textbook knowledge are highlighted. And in the College of Agriculture, a seminar on Ignorance and the Environment titled "Anticipating the Future" explores possible future scenarios in the global environment and how ignorance and ignoreance are exerting unseen influences. Others have also experimented with ignorance-based instruction in higher education (Stocking, 1992).

Thus, ignorance as a pedagogical concept is easy to grasp and inexpensive to disseminate, popularize, and mainstream as an educational package because each subject matter has its own pertinent set of articulated and yet-to-be articulated questions. One can begin and end with questions, from the student perspective, rather than (or in addition to) simply lecturing on what allegedly is known. QQQ (Q^3; Questions, Questioning, and Questioners) Workshops and Courses have been initiated under recently awarded federal grants (Eisenhower Fund for Mathematics and Science Education) to assist Arizona's K through 12 science teachers (located in inner city and remote rural schools) in infusing curiosity and student questioning expeditiously and at low cost into science and interdisciplinary lessons and units, thereby transforming classrooms into sorely needed inquiry-based curricula. Even a Website on Ignorance now appears in cyberspace.

How much ignorance can a student or teacher tolerate? Some medical students, often less than dazzling performers in the traditional medical curriculum, are superb at mining and using ignorance-based learning. Often they are curious questioners but they are criticized for asking or are labeled troublemakers or dissidents. Some may not excel at multiple choice tests where pat answers are expected; and yet they thrive on the uncertainty and ambiguity of an ignorance-based curriculum. For such students, a self-motivated discovery pathway could work for 95% of what they need to learn in medical school including the facts, skills, and attitudes to perform at a high level. Other students, including some traditionally awarded top honors, experience difficulty and discomfort with generating original questions where no simple answer exists. Yet this educational task is probably more akin to the demands of the thoughtful practice of medicine. Some students put it all together—balancing knowledge and ignorance and functioning comfortably at the interface. It may be wise, therefore, to offer a choice of learning styles to the students but at least 5% of ignorance-based learning should be required to inculcate humility and resourcefulness yet not ruin a high grade point average!

Ignorance Evaluation: IQ (Ignorance Quotient) and Q Value Revisited

How should the ignorance curriculum be evaluated? How can acquisition of the desired attitudes, skills, and competencies to explore and value ignorance (the elusive ignorance quotient—IQ) be determined and short-term and future impact measured? Clearly not by short answer tests, but rather by the progression of questions—their number, depth, and fruitfulness. The questions a student raises at first are compared with those at serial time-points later in the course of exploration of a topic, patient work-up, or research experience, to determine, without directly requiring intermediate answers, how the questions have progressed. This evolution of questions—an important neglected area of evaluation research—is, together with what the student does about it, the crucial test of a student's ability to recognize and deal with ignorance.

Pre- and postself-assessment of attitudes, knowledge, and skills in recognizing and dealing with ignorance is carried out. Structured observation and evaluation of ignorance products by program faculty provide additional insight. Another source of data is student and participant feedback. Whereas some comments and suggestions reflect expected outcomes, others provide unexpected input often in unsolicited letters.

Medical Students. One CMI graduate, now an emergency room physician, listed a litany of questions that came to mind as he practiced emergency medicine. As the new man on the spot, his questions covered a whole gamut of concerns: "Is the patient stable or unstable? Do I have an IV? Are they on oxygen? What medicines are they on? Are they important, and so forth" And he continued:

> Medical ignorance abounds in the emergency department. It is precisely this active questioning and re-questioning that allows me to do a good job. It also has made me keenly aware of my limitations. Let's face it; 1 year of training no matter how good barely gains you admission to your own ignorance. I thank you for igniting the awareness of medical ignorance.

Another writes a research newsletter editorial entitled, "Stating One's Ignorance; A Lack of Knowledge, or a Quest For Knowledge."

Another, not an outstanding performer on standardized exams during the first 2 years of medical school, reported that after taking the ignorance course she:

> honored in three of the four rotations on the clinical clerkships . . . you told me that I presented patients well and others have now said the same. You also taught me to view things in questions. I do. You would be proud. I don't have a lot of information for face value on each of my evaluations but the professors, residents, etc. have mentioned my ability to ask good questions . . . I remember telling you, I never asked questions in medical school. You gave me the courage to do so and it has shaped my entire clinical learning experience.

Another stated:

> I learned that if our projects seem easy and we surely understand them, we are
> not really probing deeply; it is only when we become perplexed by all the new
> discoveries unfolding before us that we can safely admit to being deep into the
> realm of research . . . I truly gained an appreciation (and even a desire) for
> confusing and unexpected results. Not that I expected the unexpected, but rather
> I welcomed it when it came, and I eagerly probed to find out why it was
> unexpected and what it augured for the next set of experiments . . . I cannot
> predict where I will be in medicine 20 years from now, but I like that. And I
> know the lessons of ignorance, creativity, and fortitude engendered in me by
> these seminars will keep me traveling a meandering path.

Another student, now a successful researcher and board-certified
anesthesiologist on a medical school faculty, wrote:

> I particularly appreciated the exuberant atmosphere, the emphasis on mistakes
> and the breaking away from safe science, the potential fruit of a well-made
> mistake or the analysis of one that was unavoidable. The emphasis on ideas by
> stressing that medicine is a prisoner of a vast array of bias and dogma, that we
> are ignorant of what causes problems for our patients. We then are able to focus
> at least one eye somewhere over the horizon . . . it is also non-elitist; bread and
> butter clinicians can be part of this reform and I'm happy to have joined the
> forces of the enthusiastically ignorant.

Undergraduate Students. An undergraduate student, majoring in materials
science engineering and taking an ignorance seminar, was assigned the task of
simply recording an instance where ignorance helped or hindered him, a
common ignorance workshop exercise. He chose to compose an unsolicited
essay called "Ignorance is a Virtue, I Think," in which he observed:

> whether we like it or not ignorance is not only a part of life of every human
> being but is the only reason for living . . . you could obviously not know
> everything about everything in the universe nor could you possibly know
> everything about one specific object . . . you could take a rock, for example, and
> you could study its width, length, depth, weight, mass, density, durability,
> radioactivity, pliability, elasticity, color, composition, structure, surface area,
> center of gravity, yaw orientation, pitch orientation, roll orientation, atomic
> ionization energy, enthalpy, velocity, spin, etc. There is no end to what possibly
> could be known. Compared to the amount of knowledge that exists, the amount
> that even the most intelligent human knows is infinitesimal.

Minority High School Students. Summer minority high school student
research apprentices, often from disadvantaged home and school environments,

are another group encouraged to tap their ignorance alongside the experts. Many do not write well; some speak English poorly.

Yet even in the following run-on sentence from one high school student, who performed superior summer research, the impact of engaging the questioning process is clear. Reflecting on the questions she started with and those later developed by summer's end, she concluded:

> I found it amazing on how much is going on that I didn't know about and I'm glad I had the chance to uncover it although it has raised many questions—this will make me go out and find out the answers and it will also raise many more which is the way you learn about life.

A profound idea, indeed.

Another high school student reflected:

> I believe this will be an experiment of great importance. A lot of people tend to sometimes skip the questions, it sounds simple because they figure they have already been answered, but have they really? Many portions of this lab will answer many questions that is why I feel I have done a great deal to help science. I conclude with this: And that is that ignorance is an important factor. If everyone could admit this, we would live in a better world.

Still another high school student commented "with a more open mind and a bigger state of confusion than when I arrived [hardly something that students typically seek], I have learned more about my research project, medicine, people, life, and myself."

From a high school sophomore, who made a real science of her ignorance as she pursued geriatric research in a nursing home:

> This summer I ran upon many questions and got most of them answered. I had some particular questions that to me were important to understand like why the patients have the problems they did and why they were or weren't getting better. I had three different question categories. Questions that got answered, questions that got half-answered, and questions that didn't get answered.

She continued with examples, trying to explain why some questions didn't get answered.

One minority high school student began her 4-page ignorance essay (a summary of the questions with which she began and ended her research and the answers in between) with a quotation from Thomas Jefferson, "If a nation expects to be ignorant and free in a state of civilization, it expects what never was and never will be."   She then proceeded to challenge conventional Jeffersonian wisdom,

> This summer I had a very beneficial and enlightening research experience. I benefited from the realization that without ignorance, humans would never advance as a civilization. The joys and pains that result from discovery would be lost forever if humans were omniscient. At the same time I was enlightened by all the interesting things I learned through my first-hand experience with medical research.

K Through 12 Science Teachers.   A middle-school science teacher, who designed an ignorance-questioning curriculum component for her class summarized,

> I feel that my summer experience has had two main sections: Apoptosis [programmed cell death or cellular suicide] and everything else. I have been questioning both topics all summer. As far as apoptosis goes I now have a lot of known unknowns where I used to have unknown unknowns since I had never heard of apoptosis before. With everything else I have known unknowns where I used to have I just don't-care-to-know unknowns.

She then explained further:

> We encountered ponderings on the Internet . . . on the tapestry of truth, which is a wonderful thing, and in the question and answer and question session. We don't call it a question and answer session, we call it a question-answer-question-and-question session.

One teacher commented:

> [After this summer], I am more skeptical . . . more encouraged to let the students do brainstorming . . . I have seen timid students blossom . . . they are now more assertive and more willing to take changes. Students have shown lots of leadership and they learn to figure out things for themselves. [this] program [has been] is rejuvenating and challenging!

Another noted, "I learned research techniques and strategies and [am] able to teach this to my students [and] that science is not absolute [but] a continuous process . . . active search for several answers to a question and unexpected findings."

Thus, evaluation extends beyond participant performance and ignorance products to examining the empowerment process and the chain reaction that is set into motion by the questioning curriculum.

IGNORANCE REFLECTIONS

Nobel laureate Feynman (1988) also enjoyed musing in tune with the ignorance theme:

> When a scientist doesn't know the answer to a problem, he's ignorant. When he has a hunch as to what the result is, he's uncertain. And when he's pretty darn sure of what the result is going to be, he is in doubt still. (p. 245)

Nobel laureate Jacob (1988) expressed eloquently the exhilaration of the chase for answers to his questions (ignorance).

The Curriculum on Medical Ignorance even has its own anthem, "Yes, We Have No Pat Answers" (lyrics written by former University of Arizona resident surgeon now flow cytometry guru Dr. Howard M. Shapiro), sung to the tune of "Yes, We Have No Bananas":

> *Medicine has lots of words, from Latin and from Greek,*
> *We conceal our ignorance with classic double speak,*
> *So we go about our rounds explaining things away,*
> *Though with more humility we might come clean one day and tell you,*
> *"Yes, we have no pat answers.*
> *We have no pat answers today."*
> *What we have is congestion of question on question with certainty far away.*
> *With luck, we'll help our patients respire 'till we can retire,*
> *But yes, we have no pat answers, we have no pat answers today.*

As the information explosion (the Age of Information) shifts into the next phase, the real lesson of this century is that we never did, never will, and never should have pat answers. The coming Age of Ignorance and the ignorance explosion should prove a new age of enlightenment, where ignorance, failure, chaos, and unanswered questions emerge from the darkness and fulfill their potential for enriching lives and expanding future possibilities.

Alfred P. Sloan Foundation President Gomory (1995) summarized it well,

> We are all taught what is known, but we rarely learn about what is not known and we almost never learn about the unknowable. That bias can lead to misconceptions about the world around us . . . Science excels in creating the artificial and controllable increasingly knowable world . . . [yet] two limitations

may constrain the march of predictability. First, as the artifacts of science and engineering grow ever larger and more complex, they may themselves become unpredictable . . . And second, embedded within our increasingly artificial world will be large numbers of complex and thoroughly idiosyncratic humans. (p. 210)

ACKNOWLEDGMENTS

Supported in part by funds from the American Medical Association (AME-ERF), National Institutes of Health (HL07479—Short-Term Training in Professional Schools and R25RR10163—NCRR Minority Initiative: K-12 Teachers and High School Student Program), and Eisenhower Math and Science Education Act, Arizona Board of Regents (1995, 1997).

REFERENCES

Bauer, H. (1992). *Scientific literacy and the myth of the scientific method.* Chicago: University of Illinois Press.

Blum, D. (1990, April 11). Risk-taking encouraged: Failure 101, University of Houston Engineering professor offers an innovative and creative approach to design. *Chronicle of Higher Education, 36,* A15.

Cotton, P. (1991). Chaos, other non-linear dynamics research may have answers, applications for clinical medicine. *Journal of the American Medical Association, 266,* 12—18.

Drucker, P. (1992a, December 1). Be data literate: Know what to know. *Wall Street Journal,* p. A16.

Drucker, P. (1992b, July 22). Planning for uncertainty. *Wall Street Journal,* p. A12.

Feynman, R. P. (1988). *What do you care what other people think?* New York: Norton.

Gleick, J. (1987). *Chaos: Making a new science.* New York: Viking Penguin Inc.

Gomory, R. (1995). The known, the unknown, and the unknowable. *Scientific American, 272,* 120.

Ignorance is bliss to the world of computer design. (1995, January 9). *Inside Tucson Business,* p. 9.

Jacob, F. (1988). *The statue within: An autobiography.* New York: Basic Books.

James, W. (1971). Is life worth living? In J. K. Roth (Ed.) *The moral equivalent of war and other essays* (pp. 82–83). New York: Harper & Row.

Johnson, R. (1989, January 16). To pass this course, the students have to try their hardest to fail. *Wall Street Journal,* B1.

Kerwin, A. (1993). None too solid, medical ignorance. *Knowledge: Creation, diffusion, utilizations, 15,* 166-185.

Kobler, J. (1960). *The reluctant surgeon: A biography of John Hunter.* Garden City, NY: Doubleday.

Mulconrey, B. (1992, July 13). Manager's journal: Edison's greatest invention. *Wall Street Journal*, p. A12.

Meyers, N. (1995). Environmental unknowns. *Science, 269*, 358–360.

Peters, T. (1987). *Thriving on chaos: Handbook for a management revolution.* New York: Knopf.

Postman, N. (1995, July 25). Transcript of Public Broadcasting System, *MacNeill-Lehrer Newshour*, pp. 10-11.

Ravitch, M. M. (1987). *Second thoughts of a surgical curmudgeon.* Chicago: Yearbook Medical.

Regaldo, A. (1995). A gentle scheme for unleashing chaos. *Science, 268*, 1848.

Science. (1993, May 28). The unanswered questions. *260*, cover, 1209–1396.

Shattuck, R. (1996). *Forbidden Knowledge.* New York: St. Martin's Press.

Skrabanek, P., & McCormick, J. (1989). *Follies and fallacies in medicine.* Glasgow: Tarragon Press.

Smith, D. G. (1994). *The joy of negative thinking.* Philadelphia: Delancey Press.

Smith, L. (1990, June). Quoted in the *Chronicle of Higher Education, 36*, B1.

Smithson, M. (1989). *Ignorance and uncertainty: Emerging paradigms.* New York: Springer-Verlag.

Stein, H. (1993, June 11). The age of ignorance. *Wall Street Journal*, p. A10.

Stocking, S. H. (1992, August). Ignorance-based instruction in higher education. *Journalism Educator, 47*, 42–53.

Tenner, E. (1996). *Why things bite back: Technology and the revenge of unintentional consequences.* New York: Knopf.

Thomas, L. (1982). Medicine as a very old profession. In. J. B. Wyngaarden & L. H. Smith (Eds.) *Cecil textbook of medicine* (16th ed., p. xliii). Philadelphia: W. B. Saunders Co.

Witte, C. L., Kerwin, A., & Witte, M. H. (1991). On the importance of ignorance in medical practice and education. *Interdisciplinary Science Reviews, 16*, 295–298.

Witte, C. L., Witte, M. H., & Kerwin, A. (1994). Ignorance and the process of learning and discovery in medicine. *Controlled Clinical Trials, 15*, 1–4.

Witte, M. H. (Ed.). (1988). AIDA, Kaposi's sarcoma, and the lymphatic system: The known and the unknown. Special issue of *Lymphology, 21*, 1–87.

Witte, M. H. (1991). Medical ignorance, failure, and chaos: Bright prospects for the future. *Pharos, 54*, 10–13.

Witte, M. H., Kerwin, A., & Witte, C. L. (1988). Seminars, clinics, and laboratories on medical ignorance. *Journal of Medical Education, 63*, 793–795.

Witte, M. H., Kerwin, A., & Witte, C. L. (1989). *Medical Education, 23*, 24–29.

Witte, M. H., Kerwin, A., Witte, C. L., Tyler, J. B., Witte, A., & Powel, W. (1989). *The curriculum on Medical Ignorance: Coursebook & resource manuals for instructors and students.* Tucson: The University of Arizona College of Medicine.

Witte, M. H., Kerwin, A., Witte, C. L., Tyler, J. B., Witte, A., & Powel, W. (1996). *The curriculum on Medical Ignorance: Coursebook & resource manuals for instructions and students,* revised. Tucson: The University of Arizona College of Medicine.

Witte, M. H., & Shirai, T. (Eds.). (1990). AIDS, other immunodeficiency disorders, and the lymphatic system: Pathophysiology, diagnosis, and immunotherapy.

Lymphology, 23, 53–108.

Witte, M. H., & Witte, C. L. (1995). Epilogue: Beyond the sphere of knowledge in lymphology. In R. Ryan & P. S. Mortimer (Eds.), *Cutaneous lymphatic system: Clinics in Dermatology, 13,* 511.

Witte, M. H., Witte, C. L., & Kerwin, A. (1991, November). *Medical ignorance: The problem and the challenge.* Schedule of events for an international conference cosponsored by The University of Arizona Medical Center, Tucson, AZ and the Arizona Medical Association), Tucson, AZ.

Witte, M. H., Witte, C. L., & Kerwin, A. (1994). Ignorance and the process of learning and discovery in medicine. *Controlled Clinical Trials, 15,* 1–4.

Wu, A., Folkman, S., McPhee, S., & Lo, B. (1991). Do houseofficers learn from their mistakes? *Journal of the American Medical Association, 265,* 2089–2094.

Wurman, R. S. (1989). *Information anxiety.* New York: Doubleday.

APPENDIX

CMI Products
Publications, Presentations, Syllabi, and Media Coverage
1986-present
(M. H. Witte, A. Kerwin, C. L. Witte and collaborators)

Publications
1. Witte, M. H., Witte, C. L., & Leis, B. S. M. (1986). Shades of ignorance and the ignorance corner. *Lymphology, 19,* 29–30.
2. Kerwin, A. (1986). Ignorance and scientific progress. *Lymphology, 19,* 31–32.
3. Kerwin, A. (1987, September-October). Teaching about ignorance. *Critical Thinking News, 6,* 1.
4. Witte, M. H., Kerwin, A., & Witte, C. L. (1988). Seminars, clinics, and laboratories on medical ignorance. *Journal of Medical Education, 63,* 793–795.
5. Witte, M. H., Kerwin, A., & Witte, C. L. (1988). It has been said—On ignorance. *Perspectives in Biology and Medicine, 31,* 524–525.
6. Witte, M. H., Kerwin, A. & Witte, C. L. (1989). Curriculum on medical ignorance. *Medical Education, 23,* 24–29.
7. Witte, M. H., Witte, C. L., & Way, D. L. (1990). Medical ignorance, AIDS-Kaposi sarcoma complex, and the lymphatic system. *Western Journal of Medicine, 153,* 17–23. Featured in accompanying Editorial: Moser, R. H. (1990). Ignorance: Inevitable but invigorating. *Western Journal of Medicine, 153,* 77 and in *Internal Medicine News,* 1990, *23,* 3.
8. Witte, M. H., (1991). Medical ignorance, failure, and chaos: Bright prospects for the future. *Pharos, 54,* 10–13.
9. Kerwin, A. (1991). The education of an ignoramus. In K. G. Johnson (Ed.) *Thinking creatively* (pp. 157–170). Institute of General Semantics, Englewood, NJ..

10. Witte, C. L., Kerwin, A., & Witte, M. H. (1991). On the importance of ignorance in medical practice and education. *Interdisciplinary Science Reviews, 16,* 295–298.
11. Witte, M. H., & Witte, C. L. (1991). Medical education reform. *Journal of the American Medical Association, 265,* 3245.
12. Witte, C. L., & Witte, M. H. (1991). Ileus and ignorance. *Western Journal of Medicine, 158,* 532–534.
13. Kerwin, A. (1993). None too solid, medical ignorance. *Knowledge: Creation, Diffusion, Utilizations, 15,* 166–185.
14. Witte, C. L., Witte, M. H., & Kerwin, A. (1994). Ignorance and the process of learning and discovery in medicine. *Controlled Clinical Trials, 15,* 1–4.
15. Witte, M. H., Kerwin, A., & Witte, C. L. (1998). Curriculum on medical and other ignorance: Shifting paradigms on learning and discovery. In M. J. Intons-Peterson and D. L. Best (Eds.), *Challenges and Controversies in Applied Cognition: Memory Distortions and Their Prevention.* Mahwah, NJ: Lawrence Erbaum and Associates.
16. Witte, M. H., & Witte, C. L. (in press). Ignorance in infectious diseases: The case of AIDS and Kaposi sarcoma. *Infections in Medicine.*

Syllabi

1. Witte, M. H., Kerwin, A., Witte, C. L., Tyler, J. B., Witte, A., & Powel, W. (1989, Revised 1996). *The Curriculum on Medical Ignorance: Coursebook & Resource Manuals for Faculty and Students.* Tucson: The University of Arizona College of Medicine.
2. *Participant Workbook and Resource Manual:* QQQ Workshop #1, "Transforming Lessons from Teacher-Centered to Learner-Centered; from Passive to Active Learning; from Didactic to Inquiry-Based Pedagogy," 1995.
3. *QQQ Group Leader's Manual:* "Ignorance, Uncertainty, and QQQ1: Survival by Questioning, Questions Anyone?" 1995.
4. *Participant Workbook and Resource Manual:* QQQ Workshop #2, "Transforming Science Units," 1996.
5. *QQQ Group Leader's Manual:* QQQ Workshop #2, "Transforming Science Units," 1996.

Symposium/Conference Organizer

1. "Medical ignorance: The problem and the challenge" (organizer). University Medical Center, Tucson, AZ (an international working conference on how to recognize and deal with medical ignorance (cosponsored by Arizona Medical Association), November, 1991.
2. QQQ Workshop #1, "Transforming Lessons from Teacher-Centered to Learner-Centered; from Passive to Active Learning; from Didactic to Inquiry-Based Pedagogy," November, 1995.
3. QQQ Workshop #2, "Transforming Science Units," January, 1996.

Presentations (Lectures and Seminars)

Seminars and workshops at annual International Conference on Critical Thinking and Educational Reform, Sonoma State University, Sonoma, CA (an annual international conference attended by 800-1000 educators, all levels—K–12, university, professional), 1985–1996.

"Toward a curriculum on medical ignorance: No trivial pursuit," July, 1985.

"Ignorance: A powerful tool for teaching and learning critical thinking in the strong sense," and "Facing the unknown in medicine: An experiment to enliven medical and nursing education," August, 1986.

"Ignorance and critical thinking across the subject matter curriculum," and "Advanced ignorance," August, October, 1988.

"A syllabus for a curriculum on medical and other ignorance: Probing the depths of the unknown and chaos," and "Ignorance, thinking beyond the surface," August, 1989.

"Prescription for the 90's: Designing educational experiments in ignorance, failure, and chaos for students and teachers," August, 1990.

"Medical ignorance—The problem and the challenge: An international conference to teach students the intellectual framework to question, master content, discipline their minds, innovate, and save lives," August, 1991.

"Education is that which remains. . .Uses of ignorance," and "The gift of fantasy—Uses of ignorance," August, 1992.

"The unanswered question: The ultimate learning center," and "It pays to be ignorant: The cost and value of not-knowing," August, 1993.

"Ignorance, passion, and mess: Vital ingredients for education and industry," July, August, 1994.

"Thinking passionately: Ignorance, critical thinking, and the reluctant student," August, 1995.

"Don't vanquish ignorance: Use it wisely," August, 1995.

"Q value and the value of Q," August, 1996.

Seminars and Workshops at Medical Schools, Universities, Hospitals, and Professional Associations

"Curriculum on medical ignorance," Medical College of Pennsylvania Alumni Association seminar, Tucson, February, 1986.

"Curriculum on medical ignorance." Annual Medical Student Research Forum, University of New Mexico, Albuquerque, January–February, 1992.

"Medical ignorance" (Keynote speaker) and Workshop for Medical School Faculty to Promote Teaching Methods and Curricular Change, University of California, San Francisco, October–December, 1992.

"The curriculum on medical ignorance." Harvard Medical School, Boston, February, 1993.

"Curriculum on medical ignorance: A tool for curricular innovation." University of Maryland Schools of Nursing and Medicine as part of a Southern Regional Education Board project, Baltimore, June, 1993.

"Curriculum on Medical Ignorance: How to teach it and how to learn it." Audie L. Murphy Memorial Veterans Hospital and the University of Texas School of Medicine, San Antonio, June, 1993.

"Confronting ignorance: The art and science of teaching people how to question." American Federation for Clinical Research Science Education Workshop for Middle School and High School Teachers, Southern Section of the American Federation for Clinical Research, New Orleans, February, 1994.

"The ignorance revolution: Turning a bug into a feature." Association of American Medical Colleges Group on Business Affairs, Scottsdale, AZ, March, 1995.

"Curriculum on Medical Ignorance." 23rd Annual Predoctoral Education Conference sponsored by the Society of Teachers of Family Medicine, Orlando, FL, February, 1997.

Lectures

"Medical ignorance, AIDS, and elephants" (invited Earl of Litchfield Lecturer). University of Oxford and Visiting Physician, Radcliffe Infirmary, England, September–November, 1988.

"Medical ignorance, failure, and chaos: Bright prospects for the future" (commencement address). St. Louis University School of Medicine, Class of 1989, St. Louis, May, 1889.

"Lymphology, AIDS, and medical ignorance: A personal odyssey" (invited lecturer). Cetus Corporation, Emeryville, CA, August, 1989.

"AIDS, Kaposi's sarcoma, and medical ignorance: Reflections and reverberations" (keynote speaker). 12th Int'l. Congress of Lymphology, Tokyo-Kyoto, August–September, 1989.

"Medical ignorance and filariasis: Questions and more questions," Dermatology Rounds, All India Institute of Medical Sciences, Delhi, September, 1989.

"Medical ignorance, AIDS-Kaposi's sarcoma complex, and the lymphatic system" (plenary lecturer). Association of American Physicians, Western Section, AFCR, Carmel, CA, February, 1990.

"Curriculum on medical ignorance" (invited lecturer). University of Utah College of Medicine, Perspectives in Medicine (sophomore student lecture series exploring cultural issues in medicine not part of the traditional medical curriculum), March, 1991.

"Medical ignorance: The problem and the challenge" (invited speaker). Ro Chi Pharmacy Honors Society Convocation, The University of Arizona College of Pharmacy, Tucson, November, 1991.

"Medical ignorance and lymphology: A personal odyssey" (invited professors of medical and surgical ignorance). "Summer institute on medical ignorance and student research," and "Surgery: An unknowing discipline" (keynote lectures), Annual Medical Student Research Forum, University of New Mexico, Albuquerque, January–February, 1992.

"Medical ignorance and lymphology: A personal odyssey," and "Toward a curriculum on medical ignorance: Questions about questions" (invited Alpha Omega Alpha lecturer, and Spring Visiting Speaker Lecture), Spring Banquet, Medical University of South Carolina, March, 1992.

"The power of ignorance." 20th Annual Gold Headed Cane Lecturer, The University of Arizona College of Medicine, Tucson, October, 1992.

"A time to ponder" (invited speaker). The University of Arizona Women in Science and Engineering Program (WISE), Tucson, October, 1992.

"Toward a curriculum on ignorance for science and math teachers and students" (keynote lecturer). 3rd Annual Arizona State Teachers Science and Mathematics conference, Tucson, February, 1993.

"Towards a curriculum on medical (and all other) ignorance" (invited speaker). Symposium on Ignorance and Science, American Association for the Advancement of Science," Boston, February, 1993.

"Curriculum on medical ignorance," and "Feet, the true measure of man: Reflections on lymphedema" (Zelda Vicha Memorial Lecturer). Midwest Podiatry Conference, Chicago, March, 1993.

"The curriculum on medical ignorance: Its application in primary care teaching," 18th Annual Primary Care Update, Arizona Health Sciences Center, Tucson, March, 1993.

"Ignorance: A tool for exploring and exposing ethics and policy issues" (featured lecturer). 1st Intermountain Critical Thinking Conference, Institute for Ethics and Policy Studies Conference on Critical Thinking, University of Nevada, Las Vegas, June, 1993.

"Lymphedema, Kaposi sarcoma and medical ignorance." Department of Dermatology, Stanford University Medical Center, Stanford, CA, August, 1993.

"Ignorance Ward Rounds." Dean's Educational Rounds, The University of Arizona College of Medicine, Tucson, October, 1993.

"Curriculum on medical ignorance" (keynote lecturer). Ignorance and Intuition in Medical Practice, 2nd Annual Bergman Symposium, Maine-Dartmouth Family Practice Residency Program, Augusta, ME, March, 1994.

"Borders of scientific knowledge." Qu'est-ce qu'on ne sait pas? (What we do not know), UNESCO Philosophy Forum, Paris, France, March, 1995.

"Towards a curriculum on medical ignorance for the 21st century." Milwaukee Academy of Medicine, Milwaukee, March, 1995.

"Preparing for the age of ignorance." 14th International Conference on Human Functioning, Biomedical Synergistics Education Institute, Univ. of Kansas-Wichita, September, 1995.

"Medical ignorance, failure and chaos; Shifting paradigms for the 21st century," and "Questions and answers: Curriculum on medical ignorance." American Academy of Family Physicians, Anaheim Convention Center, CA, September, 1995.

"Insights into learning from the curriculum on medical ignorance." Basis of Learning: A

Hearst Festschrift" Conference. Indiana University, Department of Psychology, Bloomington, IN, April, 1996.

"Juggling and balancing knowledge and ignorance in medical education," (keynote speaker), 23rd Annual Predoctoral Education Conference sponsored by the Society of Teachers of Family Medicine, Omni Rosen Hotel, Orlando, FL, February, 1997.

"Questions, questioning, and questioners: An external evaluation," (co-presenters: Dr. L. Aleamoni, R. Duran, T. Villaescusa), The 1996-97 Dean's Forum on The Advancement of Knowledge and Practice in Education, The University of Arizona College of Education, Tucson, February, 1997.

"Medical ignorance: Preparing for the 21st century." Internal Medicine Grand Rounds, St. Joseph's Hospital, Phoenix, March, 1997.

"Curriculum on Medical (and Other) Ignorance: Shifting paradigms of learning, discovery, and living." Keynote lecturer, 1997 International Conference on Critical Thinking and Educational Reform, August, 1997.

Courses and Seminar Series

1. SURG 815V and SURG 896A; 3–4 week junior–senior electives. Seminars (twice weekly) and Clinics (full-time clinical) in Medical Ignorance, March 1985– .

2. Summer Institute on Medical Ignorance, for Medical Student Research Program and Minority High School Student Apprentice Program, The University of Arizona College of Medicine, 1988–.

3. Visiting Professor of Medical Ignorance (Distinguished Ignorami) Series, The University of Arizona College of Medicine, 1988–.

4. Seminar leader, Introduction to the Spirit of Inquiry: "Medical and other ignorance," UA Honors Seminar 295 (2 credits), Dr. Richard Kissling, course director, November, 1989. (Repeated August, 1990 as opening seminar and again in 1991, 1992, and 1993.) "Some perspectives on ignorance," August, 1996.

5. Seminar leader, UA Honors Engineering Seminars, Engr 196A: "Ignorance and the spirit of inquiry," Dr. Dunbar Birnie, Materials Science, Course Director, November 1990, 1995.

6. Pondering Rounds; 2nd Tuesday monthly, all University of Arizona community particularly Arizona Health Sciences Center. (open to medical, undergraduate and high school students, faculty, staff, and K–12 teachers), 1995–

7. Workshop leader, "Anticipating the future: Ignorance and environmental issues." Soil and Water Sciences 450, The University of Arizona College of Agriculture, February, 1995; March, 1997.

8. Course Instructor, Freshman Colloquium "Introduction to medical and other ignorance," Arts & Sciences 195A, (fall semester, one seminar weekly), 1995, 1996.

Grand Rounds and Ward Rounds in Medical Ignorance Series

University of Arizona College of Medicine/University Medical Center:

   a) Surgical Grand Rounds, "Medical student research and medical ignorance," March, 1989.
   b) Ignorance Rounds in Radiology, March 1991.
        Ignorance Ward Rounds, "Primary care update," Tucson, March, 1992.
        Surgical Grand Rounds, "Ignorance: A neglected field of knowledge in learning and practice," November, 1992.
        Dean's Educational Grand Rounds "Ignorance ward rounds," October, 1993.
   . All India Institute of Medical Sciences, Delhi, India: Dermatology, September. 1989.
   . University of California, San Diego College of Medicine VA Hospital, August, 1990.
   . University of New Mexico, Albuquerque, NM, January–February, 1992.
   . Loma Linda University School of Medicine, Loma Linda, CA, December, 1995.
   . Episcopal Hospital (Hahnemann Medical College-Medical College of Pennsylvania affiliate),

Philadelphia, PA, May, 1996.
. St. Joseph's Hospital, Phoenix, AZ: Internal Medicine, March, 1997.
. University of Minnesota, Minneapolis, MN: Internal Medicine, May, 1997.

Grant Support
AMA-ERF, Curriculum on Medical Ignorance Syllabus, January, 1988–
NIH #T35HL07479, Short-Term Training: Students in Health Professional Schools, May, 1981–April, 1988; May, 1981–April, 1988; May, 1989–April, 1994; May, 1994–April, 1999.
NIH #1-R25 RR10163 Minority Disadvantaged High School Student and K–12 Science Teacher Program, September, 1994-September, 2000.
Arizona Board of Regents, Eisenhower Math and Science Education Act: Questions, Questioning & Questioners: Workshops to Empower and Transform, March, 1995-January, 1996.
Arizona Board of Regents, Eisenhower Math and Science Education Program: The Arizona Questions, Questioners and Questioning Project (QQQ): Partnerships for Inquiry–Based K–12 Science Education Transformations, February, 1997-February, 1998.

Videotapes
1. Witte, M. H., & Witte, C. L.: Medical ignorance: The problem and the challenge. Proceedings of a conference, November, 1991, The University of Arizona, Tucson.
2. Witte, M. H.: The power of ignorance. 20th Annual Gold Headed Cane Memorial Lecture, October, 1992, The University of Arizona College of Medicine, Tucson.
3. Witte, M. H.: Ignorance rounds. Dean's Educational Rounds, October, 1993, The University of Arizona College of Medicine, Tucson.
4. Kerwin, A., Witte, M. H.: Questions, Questioning, Questioners (QQQ) Workshop #1, "Transforming Lessons from Teacher-Centered to Learner-Centered; from Passive to Active Learning; from Didactic to Inquiry-Based Pedagogy," November, 1995, The University of Arizona College of Medicine, Tucson.
5. Kerwin, A., Witte, M. H.: Questions, Questioners, and Questioning (QQQ) Workshop #2: "Transforming Science Units," January, 1996, The University of Arizona College of Medicine, Tucson.
6. Witte, M., and Summer 1996 K–12 science teacher researchers: Transforming Science Units: A televised planning conference, July, 1996.

Featured in Print Media
· "Mike Stuntz—UA Medical Student Research Program—Best of the West," *Arizona Health Center News*, January, 1989, p. 1.
· "Students Learn How to Benefit From Ignorance." *International Internal Medicine News, 23,* 3, 1990.
· "Tucson, Places to Practice," *M.D. Magazine*, September, 1991, pp. 65–72.
· "Doctors Learn About Medical Ignorance," *San Diego Daily Transcript*, October 1, 1991, p. 4A.
· "Medical Ignorance to be Explored at November Conference," *The University of Arizona Health Sciences News*, October, 1991, p. 1.
· "What's Up? Some Docs Will Learn How to Ask," *Memphis Commercial Appeal*, November, 1991, p. B1.
· "Medical Ignorance is Focus of Conference," *Lo Que Pasa*, October, 1991, p. 11.
· "Exploring Ignorance is Bliss," *American Medical News*, January, 1992, p. 29–30.
· "Ignorance, Medical and Otherwise," From the President, *Arizona Medicine*, January, 1992, p.4.
· "Turning Ignorance Into A Science," *Chicago Sun Times*, March 9, 1992, p. 12.
· "Better Living Through Ignorance," *Tucson Citizen*, March 10, 1992, p. 1b.

- "Professor Touts Ignorance as Bliss," *Blade Citizen*, Oceanside, CA, March, 1992.
- "Ignorance 101," *Physician's Weekly*, May, 1992.
- "Learning to Know What You Don't Know," *The New Physician*, Jan./Feb., 1993. p. 6.
- "Arizona Professor Offers Curriculum on Ignorance to Give Medical Education a Wake-Up Call," *The Chronicle of Higher Education*, January, 1993, p. A21–24.
- "Teen-agers are Already Doing Medical Research," *Tucson Citizen*, July 19, 1993.
- "Ignorance is Strength," *Lingua Franca-The Review of Academic Life*, April, 1994, p.7.
- "What Students Do Not Know Is What Counts in This Course," *Los Angeles Times*, April 12, 1994, p. A5.
- "Ignorama Mama," *The Tucson Weekly*, March, 1994, p. 4.
- "Medical Ignorance a Clue to New Knowledge," *University Heart Center Newsletter*, Spring, 1994.
- "Southern Section AFCR Sponsors Science Education Workshop for Middle School and High School Teachers," *AFCR Newsletter*, 6(3), June, 1994.
- "Popping the Cork on Ignorance," *Arizona Alumnus*, Fall 1994, p. 16.
- "Pursuing Careers in Research," *Arizona Daily Star*, July 24, 1995, p. 1B.
- "En Arizona, un professeur de philsophie enseigne l'ignorance aux étudiants en médecine," *Le Quotidien du Medecin*, March, 1996, p. 18.
- "The Anatomy of Medical Ignorance," *International Herald Tribune, Biannual Education Supplement*, February 11, 1997, p. 13,15.

and multiple press releases by the Arizona Health Sciences Public Affairs Office in local and regional Arizona media regarding individual K–12 science teachers and high school students in the Minority High School/K–12 Science Program and Summer Institute on Medical Ignorance during Summer 1995 and 1996.

Featured in Radio, TV Coverage
- "Curriculum on Medical Ignorance." In-depth interview, Medical Television Network, September, 1989.
- "The study of medical ignorance and how it relates to our health care," Arizona Illustrated, November, 1991.
- "Morning Edition" (on medical ignorance), KUAT Radio Talk Show, December 2, 1991.
- "Curriculum on Medical Ignorance," interview with Canadian Broadcasting Corporation for the Quirks and Quarks program aired May 1, 1993 to approximately 1/2 million Canadian listeners and 42 American public radio stations.
- "Curriculum on Medical Ignorance," interview with Canadian Equinox Science Radio with David Suzuki, February 15, 1993.
- "Curriculum on Medical Ignorance," interview with The Brigham Young University radio station, February 26, 1993.
- "Minority High School Science Teacher & Student Initiative," Arizona Illustrated, KUAT-TV June 30, 1993.
- "Reflexiones in Medical Ignorance" (a Spanish language show), KUAT-TV, July 4, 1993.
- "Curriculum on Medical Ignorance." Osgood Files, CBS Network Radio, June 3, 1994.
- "20th Anniversary Curriculum on Medical (and Other) Ignorance. Update 1996." Interview with Canadian Broadcasting Corporation (Jim Lebans) for the Quirks and Quarks program, aired April 9, 1996. Selected from best interviews over past 20 years.

9

Cognitive Technology

Douglas Herrmann
Carol Yoder
Indiana State University

Over the past 3 decades, cognitive psychology has generated a great
deal of research, so much that a number of basic and applied
researchers have recently developed ways to apply basic cognitive
theories to everyday problems. An especially important aspect of these
developments in applied cognitive psychology is that researchers have
not only developed applications but they have also developed
technologies, that is, applications that apply to more than one situation.
For example, the creation of a new method to enhance the recall
accuracy of eyewitnesses (such as guided recall) would be such an
application. A cursory examination of the literature indicates that
diverse cognitive technologies have been developed, for example,
assessment measures, memory improvement strategies, cognitive
rehabilitation strategies, devices that aid prospective memory,
cognitively oriented survey interviewing, and structured clinical
interviews of suspected victims of childhood sexual abuse. This chapter
defines cognitive technology and explains its importance to basic, as
well as applied research. It is shown how theories and methods lead
to the development of cognitive technology. Alternatively, it is also
shown how technology contributes to the development of basic theory.
Finally, consideration is given to the advantages of developing cognitive
technology in academia and to how basic researchers in academia
might begin an applied research program.

Cognitive psychology has grown rapidly over the past three decades. During this period, a sufficient body of basic cognitive research has accumulated such that many applied researchers have come to apply basic cognitive theories to everyday problems (Barber, 1988; Berger, Pezdek, & Banks, 1987; Gruneberg & Morris, 1992; Gruneberg, Morris, & Sykes, 1978, 1988; Herrmann, McEvoy, Hertzog, Hertel, & Johnson, 1996a, 1996b; Payne & Conrad, 1997). Although modern applications of cognitive psychology have developed throughout this period (Hoffman & Deffenbacher, 1992, 1993), it may be conceded that modern applied cognitive psychology did not gain momentum until the mid to late 1980s. Given the potential importance of new technologies, some psychologists have argued (Broadbent, 1985; Clegg, 1994) that psychology needs to be fully involved in the development of new products.

Some examples of cognitive technology that have been recently developed are summarized in Table 9.1. As can be seen from inspecting this table, a variety of memory problems have been addressed by researchers in their development of technologies. For example, assessment of memory capabilities now makes use of specially designed computer programs that, with the aid of large television monitors, measure memory performance with ecologically valid stimuli (Plude & Schwartz, 1996). Memory improvement systems and systems of cognitive rehabilitation have been developed to train skills in a framework of holistic self-care (Parenté & Herrmann, 1996). Prospective memory problems can be avoided to a large degree by making use of devices that trigger alarms that warn a person about upcoming appointments (Herrmann, Yoder, Wells, & Raybeck, 1996). Retrospective memory problems have been the target of interviewing procedures used for forensic purposes and for surveys. These interviews are carefully designed to elicit information that untrained interviews will not (Geiselman, Fisher, MacKinnon, & Holland, 1986). Carefully planned interviews that encourage subjects to think aloud indicate defects in the cuing capabilities of questions on surveys (Jobe & Mingay, 1991; Willis, Royston, & Bercini, 1991). Currently, many researchers are concerned with improving the technology of the clinical intake interview so that a false memory of supposed sexual abuse will not be implanted while actual memories of sexual abuse will not be suppressed by interview procedures (Miller, 1996).

The purpose of this chapter is to describe cognitive technology and explain its importance to basic, as well as applied, research (Dasgupta, 1996; DeVore, 1980). The chapter describes how theories and methods lead to the development of cognitive technology. Examples of cognitive technology are provided to demonstrate how such technology contributes to basic theory as well as guidelines about how to develop cognitive technology. Finally, on the

TABLE 9.1
Inventory of Cognitive Technologies:
Products or Services that Affect Cognitive Functioning

Cognitive Rehabiliation

Retraining Cognition. A cognitive rehabilitation program, presented in a book, that teaches people with neurological impairments to take care of physical states, emotional states, use of the social environment, use of the physical environment, and a wide variety of exercises that remedy cognitive processes (Parenté & Herrmann, 1996).

Iconic Memory Training of Road Signs. A method of rapid presentation of road signs that help prepare people who have suffered a neurological impairment to drive again (Hamid, Garner, & Parenté, 1996).

Education

Linkword Language Training. A method for the facilitation of language learning by the presentation of image mediators for vocabulary and grammar (Gruneberg, 1985, 1987).

Procedural changes in instruction of math and science (Sweller, 1989).

Graphic Design of Statistical Maps

Subtask Design of Statistical Maps. Design of statistical maps based on how visual and conceptual features of the map influence the reading of these maps (Lewandowsky et al., 1993; Pickle & Herrmann, 1995).

Interviewing

Cognitive Interviewing. Interview procedure designed to detect weaknesses in survey questions (Jobe & Mingay, 1991; Willis, Royston, & Bercini, 1991).

Police Interviewing Procedures. A combination of techniques (also called cognitive interviewing) used to help witnesses recall details of events (Geiselman et al., 1986).

Locating Misplaced Objects

Devices That Find Objects. Finds objects (such as a key chain) that have a radio wave emitting diode attached (Parenté & Herrmann, 1996).

Car Finder. Finds where the user parked a car by activating via a radio transmitter a remote-controlled horn (Parenté & Herrmann, 1996).

Memory Improvement

Memory Monitoring. Computerized equipment for people to access physical and emotional states, use of the social and physical environment, and task specific mental activities (Herrmann, Weingartner, Searleman, & McEvoy, 1992; West, 1989).

Memory Works. A CD that when played on a CD Rom (or a CDi played on a Cdi disk player) presents a memory improvement program that develops skills for remembering names, faces, facts, and figures (Plude & Schwartz, 1996).

Reminding

Telleminder. A computer–automated phone system for reminding people of medical appointments that the user might otherwise forget (Leirer, Morrow, Tanke, & Pariante, 1991).

Personal Data Assistants. Pocket-size computerized devices that can be programmed to trigger an alarm prior to appointments that the user might otherwise forget (Harris, 1980; Herrmann et al., 1996b; Kapur, 1995).

Medication Reminders. An organized pill box that triggers an audible alarm when medication is to be taken (Park & Kidder, 1996).

Digital Watches. Digital watches that remind (Naugle, Prevey, Naugle, & Delaney, 1988).

Information Filing Systems. Multiple varieties of these sytems (Lansdale, 1991; Lansdale & Edmonds, 1992).

---

assumption that some readers may be interested in exploring cognitive technology further, we discuss how basic researchers in academia might begin an applied research program.

Definition of Cognitive Technology

Cognitive technology may be viewed as a subset of applied cognitive psychology and human factors. This new field is concerned with the development of cognitive-enhancing products and procedures. A cognitive technology may be contrasted with a cognitive application. A cognitive application is the use of cognitive psychology for a certain situation whereas a cognitive technology is an application that facilitates a cognitive process in more than one situation.   One example of an application might involve changing the procedures of lineups in the south central police station in Terre Haute, Indiana to be based on a prototype theory of memory representation. If this police force shares its procedural change for effective lineups with others, the application becomes a cognitive technology.   If the procedural change is not shared, even though this police force is technically sophisticated, the line-up method remains an application.

Thus, for an application to become a technology, it must be shown to be transferable to another problem. The original application becomes the basis for another application. In developing a new technology, a primary goal is to enhance performance and to eliminate flaws. As a consequence a cognitive technology may play a role in the preparation of noncognitive products. For example, the use of cognitive task analysis may restructure the assembly of a product such as an airplane.   In this case, the contribution of the cognitive technology is hidden. Although the cognitive technology may be covert, assembly activities can be improved or altered to enhance productivity through applications of knowledge about human cognitive functioning. Industries have been doing this effectively for many years.

Although some disciplines have created new technologies that are in widespread use in this information age, it is often difficult to obtain current information on the extent of usage of applications.   The suppliers of the technologies may make this information commercially available only with specific marketing to niche markets.   Some applications are technology centered and may not address psychological and cognitive issues until technologies are operative (Clegg, 1994).   For example, reminding devices have been incorporated into automobiles only gradually and after many years (devices that turn high beams down, signal when gas and/or oil are running low, and signal when the keys are still in the ignition as the driver begins to exit the car without the keys).   Human cognitive limitations are often perceived as sources of error that should be dealt with as soon as possible in product design (Reason, 1988), leaving the use of cognitive psychology in design hidden from the user.

Examples of the Development of Cognitive Technologies

The development of a cognitive technology is typically a protracted process. To provide some appreciation of this process, we describe the recent development of two cognitive technologies.

Procedures for Designing Statistical Maps. Statistical maps shade geographic regions according to each region's value on some statistic. They are
used in a variety of fields to analyze the geographic influence on some
variable of interest. For example, statistical maps are used to determine
geographic patterns in the unemployment rate, the public's response to the
Census, or the mortality rate of particular diseases. However, the perceptual
characteristics of many maps sometimes exceed the human ability to interpret
these characteristics. In common parlance, many maps are too busy, thwarting
the desire to extract statistical data from the maps.

In the first half of the 1990s, the National Center for Health Statistics made
a coordinated effort to develop a theoretical framework to account for how
people read statistical maps. The reason for this effort was to develop
guidelines for the design of maps that report the mortality rates of various
diseases to the nation; these maps were to be assembled into an interdisease
atlas. An interdisciplinary team was formed to conduct the investigations that
would develop the guidelines. Pickle, a statistician, headed the team and
Herrmann was responsible for advising the team on the cognitive aspects of
statistical map reading (Pickle & Herrmann, 1995).

After careful study of the literature, it was evident that many articles in the
literature concerning statistical maps were consistent with the assumptions of
cognitive stage theory. Originally advanced over a century ago by Donders
(1868), cognitive stage theory assumes that a series of information processing
stages intervene between a stimulus and a response. In recent years, stage
theory addressed the selective influence of individual stages of information
processing (Sternberg, 1975) and whether stages occurred either successively,
in an overlapping manner, or in parallel (Rumelhart & McClelland, 1982).

The National Center for Health Statistics conducted a series of
investigations into statistical map reading with colleagues in universities. As
our team accumulated more and more data, stage theory turned out to be
enormously successful in explaining the reaction time data regarding the
reading of statistical maps (Hastie, Hammerle, Kerwin, Croner, & Herrmann,
1996; Herrmann & Pickle, 1996; Pickle & Herrmann, 1995). For example,
Sternberg (1966; 1975) concluded from the latency of recognition responses
that the process included an encoding stage, a memory search stage, and a
response stage where each stage involves qualitatively different kinds of
processes than the other stages. In similar fashion, our research found that
reaction time data were consistent with four separate stages of statistical map
reading: orienting to the map, reading the legend, integrating the map and the
legend, and extracting the relevant data from the map. Accuracy data also
indicated selective influence of different variables on these stages. In addition,
map-readers' self-reports also conformed to these stages. The evidence from

different measures and from different experiments suggested that the four stages were often executed sequentially.

Applying information processing stage theory to statistical map reading constituted a technology that was very helpful in identifying the design of maps for the atlas under development. Even prior to publication, spurred by conference presentations, the word about the model spread rapidly. We were asked to speak at several conferences where members of the audience often asserted that the model was just what they needed to guide their design process and to catch difficulties in map design before publishing the map.

Without the perspective of stage theory, developed by basic research in cognitive psychology, it is unlikely that our team would have recognized that statistical map reading unfolds in stages. Two decades of research on statistical maps had failed to recognize that map reading involves specific stages of information processing, probably in large measure due to the lack of input from a cognitive psychology perspective.

Procedures for Improving and Rehabilitating Memory. A second example of the development of a cognitive technology is provided by recent efforts to refine methods of memory improvement and memory rehabilitation. In the past 2 decades, several researchers and practitioners have sought to go beyond standard memory improvement methods and develop methods to influence other psychological modes that affect memory performance. A psychological mode is a factor that influences memory. For example, the psychological system is comprised of modes such as perception, comprehension, motivation, emotion, and attitudes. These modes serve particular psychological purposes but they also affect the memory mode. Thus, it was soon recognized that memory may be improved or rehabilitated by affecting as many cognitive and noncognitive modes as possible. Hence this approach has been called multimodal (Herrmann & Parenté, 1994; Herrmann & Searleman, 1990, 1992; Herrmann, et al., 1992; McEvoy, 1992; Parenté & Herrmann, 1996, West, 1985).

Clients are not only trained in mnemonic strategies to enhance cognition, they are also trained to control or enhance other psychological modes that affect memory performance. For example, memory-impaired clients are encouraged to take care of their physical state, manage their attitudes, manipulate their environment and monitor nutritional and chemical substances. Additionally, clients are equipped with external aids and taught social skills that facilitate cognitive performance. Thus, the multimodal approach improves memory performance by enhancing processes extrinsic to memory, including physical, chemical, and attitudinal states, and by imparting skills to manipulate the physical and social environment that in turn supports the effectiveness of memory strategies (Mullin, Herrmann, & Searleman, 1993).

This multimodal approach suggests a theoretical structure that facilitates the development of a technology to manipulate nonmemory modes to improve memory performance. This theoretical structure holds that nonmemory modes (physiological, emotive, social, perception of the physical environment) interface between memory and specific behaviors that communicate remembering, such as recalling a memory out loud or by writing down an account of a memory (Herrmann & Parenté, 1994; Herrmann & Searleman, 1992; Mullin, Herrmann, & Searleman, 1993). Although the theoretical structure originated to address an applied problem (i.e., of memory improvement and rehabilitation), this structure has been found to be relevant to basic theories of memory. For example, Zacks and Hasher (1992) and Intons-Peterson (1993) have separately pointed out that the model addresses a variety of important aspects of memory phenomena that basic research had overlooked. Searleman and Herrmann (1994) published a textbook that summarizes basic research findings in a multimodal context.

Research on the multimodal approach memory has provided a theoretical framework for explaining much of the unaccounted variance in memory research. The multimodal approach has sensitized basic researchers to consider the importance of noncognitive modes in memory performance. Considerable memory research has accumulated demonstrating that noncognitive modes can have a substantial influence on memory performance (Bendiksen & Bendiksen, 1992, 1996; McEvoy, 1992; Parenté & Herrmann, 1996; West, 1985).

In some cases, a noncognitive mode (such as attitude or emotionality) can change memory performance from success to failure. For example, highly stressful duties lead nurses to make considerably more memory failures than duties with little stress (Broadbent, Cooper, Fitzgerald, & Parkes, 1982). Where stress is extreme, such as a death in the family or the loss of a job, people are known to inadvertently shoplift goods from a store because they absentmindedly walk out of the store unknowingly holding the merchandise (Reason & Lucas, 1984). Malpass and Devine (1981) showed that memory for a staged act of vandalism could be enhanced by encouraging witnesses to explore their memory for their feelings at that time. On the other hand, Loftus and Marburger (1983) found a stressful viewing of a film of a hospital fire had a detrimental effect on episodic recall.

No one has conducted a comprehensive investigation of the relative effects of the different modes on performance, that is, providing estimates of percent of variance. However, the findings cited previously demonstrate that memory failures can be readily produced by noncognitive variables. Additionally, these findings demonstrate that attempts to develop a technology sometimes make discoveries that are useful for basic, as well as applied, research.

Paradigms for the Development of Cognitive Technologies

Cognitive technology has evolved from basic research and three other types of research. These different research strategies vary in how readily they can be applied to improving cognitive functioning. These three kinds of research include ecologically valid research, applicable research, and application research. The nature of these three kinds of research and what they contribute to the development of a cognitive technology is as follows.

Ecologically valid research assesses the degree to which fundamental principles inferred from basic research are observed in natural contexts. This kind of research uses stimuli that approximate real-life occurrences (Barker, 1968; Bronfenbrenner, 1977; Brunswik, 1957; Loftus, 1979; Neisser, 1976; Wright, 1997). Ecologically valid research sets up experimental contingencies using methods that are perceived as more realistic than those used in laboratories. This kind of research maximizes the possibility of participants responding or remembering as they might in real life without sacrificing experimental control. For example, a study that staged a crime in a classroom might be said to be ecologically valid in that it mimics an event that occurs in the real world. Thus, ecologically valid research is assumed to prompt responses that more closely parallel everyday activities than laboratory research often does.

As with basic research, a key goal is to isolate the effects of independent variables. Much ecologically valid or naturalistic research is conducted in order to develop knowledge that will be potentially useful when application research attempts to utilize this knowledge. Ecologically valid research is able to develop potentially applicable knowledge because this research deals with practical issues that impact everyday living. Nevertheless, ecologically valid research is not always readily generalizable to all applications. For example, a slide presentation that depicts a staged crime cannot be expected to affect a witness in precisely the same fashion as an actual crime (Loftus, 1979; Yuille & Cutshall, 1986).

Applicable research assesses the degree to which fundamental principles inferred from basic research may be applied to particular kinds of real world problems. For example, a study might investigate the effects of the presentation of mugbook pictures on witness recall of an individual who committed a staged crime. The presentation might include a front and side view of the protagonist. The protagonist might be presented early or later on in the mugbook sequence and depicted with pictures of other people having few or many similar characteristics. Participants might also be exposed to different instructional sets as well as different background information that might influence their expectations. The goal of the research might be to develop a procedure that eventually would be applicable to the use of mugbooks by police everywhere.

Applicable research is sometimes referred to as mission-oriented (Featherman, 1991). Because applicable research is designed to develop information about a particular cognitive application in real world settings, applicable research is expected to yield more findings that may be used to achieve a successful application than ecologically valid research often does (Herrmann & Gruneberg, 1993; Nogami, 1982). For example, an investigation that seeks applicable knowledge might use mugbook photos similar in size and quality to that used by most police departments in the hope that the recall of witnesses would influence actual mugbook procedures.

Application research seeks to solve a particular practical problem through development of a device or procedures. Application research is often based initially on ecologically valid findings and applicable findings and has the greatest chance to generalize to an actual applied situation because the research is designed specifically to accomplish this purpose. For example, a study that sought to influence mugbook procedures at the Greater Terre Haute Police Department (GTHPD) would deliberately try to mimic the conditions in which mugbooks are used by the GTHPD. Careful mimicry of conditions does not necessarily guarantee that application research will be successful in elucidating the processes that would be important to developing an eventual application. On the basis of application research, the resulting product or procedure may still not be effective because the critical variables had yet to be isolated. For example, a mugbook procedure developed from applied research might still be ineffective because the lighting in the viewing room is poor or because police harassment has rendered the local populace too afraid to cooperate.

Cognitive technology research involves developing an application that generalizes to two or more situations. Consequently, application research will usually be initiated in multiple contexts to assess generalizability. Suppose that the new GTHPD mugbook is shown to improve the recognition rate of felons and that the Greater Bloomington Police Department (GBPD) decides to consider adoption of the new improved mugbook procedure. If the GBPD finds the GTHPD mugbook procedure works better than the mugbook procedure they had been using, the new mugbook has the promise of being a cognitive technology. If several police departments also find the GTHPD mugbook procedures to be superior, then this mugbook technology might be adopted by other police departments. Thus, a cognitive technology is often the most sophisticated form of application, revised and refined to reflect contextual variations.

As with any kind of research, the final product rests on a series of investigations. Thus, the ecologically valid research with staged crimes and the applicable research on mugbook properties contribute to the body of knowledge that may result in an application. If the application is recognized as sufficiently goal enhancing, further development may result in a cognitive technology.

Alternatively, entrepreneurs and high-level administrators commonly demand an assessment of an application before investing in full-fledged product development. Application research presumes a logical and practical connection to everyday cognitive activities that is generally not articulated in ecologically valid research or by applicable research. Without evidence of application validity, further work on an actual application comes to a halt. Many basic and applied researchers believe that application validity provides the strongest support for the fundamental nature of a principle (Chapanis, 1967). If a principle fails to demonstrate application validity, the legitimacy of this principle is seriously challenged.

IMPORTANCE OF COGNITIVE TECHNOLOGY

To Society

Society usually does not appreciate the practical potential of most basic research. Indeed, basic researchers sometimes have difficulty appreciating the practical import of research outside their area of specialization. Similarly, society often fails to appreciate that some applied research projects are truly essential to potential technological developments. Applied researchers who work outside a particular application are often unprepared to judge the merit of an applied project.

Alternatively, society can judge the value of products and services. The more useful a product or service, the more valuable the public judges a field of science. Thus, as cognitive psychology grows in stature by providing useful technologies, society will become more and more willing to support grants for basic research and projects of applied researchers. From this perspective, the creation of applications and technology is as important as generating basic research. The public does not read our technical literature. To enlist the public's support, we need to dramatize the power of what has been discovered about cognitive psychology. A good application or an effective technology provides such drama.

To Applied Research

Applied research needs the support of society. Applications need to be publicized because of their utility to society but also to enhance the reputation of cognitive psychology and the fundability of our research (Smith, Randell, Lewandowsky, Kirsner, & Dunn, 1996). Although ecologically valid research suggests that basic theory may be useful over time, applied researchers may have little interest in such efforts because they need research that can be easily reconfigured into an application. Applicable research findings are more useful to applied researchers because these findings may be more readily translated to practical problems. However, such findings themselves do not guarantee that an application can be achieved.

Application research demonstrates the importance and utility of research because the product or procedure benefits society. Apart from demonstrating a particular researcher's creativity and skill in producing an application, each product potentially suggests to applied researchers other ways that similar applications can be developed. Indeed the applied literature and the word of mouth communication about applications may be as valuable to applied researchers as is the basic research literature pertinent to the initial development of an application.

To Basic Research

Basic research needs applications for much the same reason as applied research does: the support of society (Herrmann, 1998; Herrmann & Raybeck, 1997; Intons-Peterson, 1997). To be seen as valuable by society, basic research must produce evidence that the knowledge it generates leads to solutions of real world problems. Looking at funding opportunities today, it is clear that scientific disciplines that provide useful products enjoy societal support and funding (Miller, 1995). For example, the natural sciences receive more funding than the behavioral sciences in large measure because of their perceived societal utility.

Particularly when the world economy is poor and substantial segments of well-educated professionals lose employment because of cost-cutting measures, it is no longer adequate to claim that basic research need not be accountable. When effective applications are few, society will not support a science.

Basic research places a premium on controlling all but the targeted variables and consequently attempts to isolate effects of independent variables. Although this emphasis on scientific rigor has provided important understanding of cognitive processes, other approaches are necessary to insure our future. The more applications of cognitive psychology that are developed, the more that society will be willing to support cognitive research. Findings that are ecologically valid show other basic researchers that basic theory may be useful in the long run but these findings do not impress public policy makers and money managers. Applicable findings are somewhat more convincing but the public is likely to remain unimpressed. To demonstrate the power and utility of basic research, basic researchers need the applications and technologies developed by applied researchers.

The Role of Cognitive Technologies

An application of basic research to a particular situation demonstrates that basic and applied research can lead to a substantial change in the way that society does things. However, a single application in itself will rarely be enough to convince society to invest funds in basic and applied research. The more applications of cognitive psychology that are developed, the more that society will be willing to support cognitive research. Because cognitive technologies operate in multiple contexts, they are more likely to receive attention from the public. Thus, a combined goal of basic and applied research should be not only to develop particular applications but to develop applications that constitute technologies.

Some have further observed that we are now in the formative stages of an information age. During this time, it is incumbent on us to become fully involved in application and technology developments (Cooley, 1987). This is an important opportunity for cognitive psychology and our future may well depend on an appropriate response.

DEVELOPING A TECHNOLOGY RESEARCH PROGRAM

Readiness to get involved in applied research is partly a matter of luck. In graduate school, some people work in areas of basic research that are just a few steps away from application. Others find themselves in esoteric basic research where applications of this research seem as remote as Mars. If a researcher's efforts have focused on esoteric basic research, it may be useful to seek an application area that is consistent with one's skills rather than one's primary research.

Selection of an applied area should not, in our view, be dictated by financial concerns. The most important issue is making a contribution to society. As Miller (1969) said many years ago, psychologists sometimes should give psychology away. Alternatively, if psychologists get paid for the technologies they develop, such pay tends to increase the worth of all psychologists.

However, work can be rewarded in different ways. Some psychologists go into business for themselves and devote a substantial part of their lives to selling an application or technology. However, most basic and applied researchers are not interested in the particular challenges offered by business. Some researchers find an outlet for their application by taking a job in industry or government and convincing the organization involved to make use of an application. However, such contexts usually do not allow an individual to pursue a line of applied research suited to one's personal interests. Many times, researchers endeavor to get others to use their technology where the potential for immediate reward is absent.

Once people have conceived of the kind of cognitive technology appropriate to their skills, they will usually have identified the recipients of their applications and eventual technology. Consideration of one's expertise as well as who might benefit from an application of these skills may elicit the creation of an idea for a product or a service to be developed. For example, suppose someone is an expert at false memory research. A possible product that this person might develop could be software that trains people to better distinguish autobiographical facts that are verifiable from such facts that are not verifiable. Repeated attempts at distinguishing verifiable from nonverifiable facts might be expected to increase the ability to distinguish real memories from false memories (Johnson & Raye, 1981). As often occurs with practice, the individual involved improves in performance without necessarily becoming able to articulate what they have learned (Shiffrin & Schneider, 1977).

Such a piece of software might help therapists and researchers get insight into the state of recalling a valid memory and a false memory. This software might also help clients discover which memories are not trustworthy. By becoming more aware of the nature of true and false memories, clients might become more aware of internal properties of such memories. At a minimum, practice with the program might at least dispose clients to realize how difficult it is to determine whether a seemingly valid memory is indeed valid or false. It is doubtful that this software would put an end to the false memory debate and make the developer independently wealthy. Nevertheless, it is plausible that practice with such a memory discrimination program would be helpful to victims, relatives, and professionals who are caught in false-memory cases.

Once a person has developed a concept of a worthwhile product or a service, it is advisable to form a team to help in developing the concept further. This person might wisely ask a colleague who does similar research to check the theoretical appropriateness of the extensions of the person's expertise. A practitioner or potential user could be invited to join the team. This member will invariably raise realistic concerns about the product or service.

Reasons Why More Technology Research Should Be Conducted in Academia. It is customary to think that basic research occurs in academia and that applied research occurs in business, industry, or government. This division of labor makes sense to many people: basic research requires a think tank atmosphere whereas applied research should be close to the people, materials, and locations where applications occur. Although this situation is not likely to change soon, there is merit to considering the advantages of encouraging more technology research in academia (Gruneberg, 1996; Gruneberg, Morris, Sykes, & Herrmann, 1996; Herrmann, Raybeck, & Gruneberg, 1998).

The most important reason for having more technology research in academia is that the basic research world will learn sooner of applied research that challenges the assumptions of basic research. The sooner that basic researchers learn of the shortcomings of their findings, principles, or theories, the sooner they can progress with developing better findings, principles, or theories.

Also, because some topics of applied research are controversial, there are advantages to investigating these topics in academia. When academics engage in research, the project outcomes are often removed from proprietary interests that might otherwise foster biased decisions in the applied world outside of academia. For example, some people would agree that it is better to have cognitive rehabilitation treatments investigated by the companies who sell these treatments to families and hospitals. Alternatively, such investigations of cognitive technology might better occur in academia where researchers have no ownership of the treatments and therefore have no stake in the results. Thus, there appears to be some wisdom to arranging for academia to evaluate controversial technologies developed in other sectors of society.

CONCLUSIONS

Although cognitive technologies are on the increase, the absolute number of such applications is still small. As previously noted, the cognitive technologies in Table 9.1 represent just a sampling of recent and current technologies that have evolved from cognitive psychology. We believe that more cognitive technologies will be developed in greater numbers when cognitive psychology fully recognizes the important role that such technologies play in garnering financial support for ongoing basic and applied research. Increased efforts to develop technologies will result in more basic and applied contributions. Many of those psychologists who make such attempts will discover that creating a product or service is an exciting and satisfying intellectual challenge. Given the current economic and societal pressures of the age in which we live, we must reconsider our priorities. Clearly, the development of new technologies that aid a person's cognitive function is a worthy endeavor, pertinent not only to society but also to the welfare of cognitive psychology.

ACKNOWLEDGMENTS

We thank Mike Gruneberg and Doug Raybeck for influencing our appreciation of the issues discussed here.

REFERENCES

Barber, D. (1988). *Applied cognitive psychology.* London: Methuen.
Barker, R. G. (1968). *Ecological psychology.* Stanford, CA: Stanford University Press.
Bendiksen, M., & Bendiksen, I. (1992). A multi-dimensional intervention for a toxic solvent injured population. *Journal of Cognitive Rehabilitation, 10,* 20–27.
Bendiksen, M., & Bendiksen, I. (1996). Multi-modal memory rehabilitation for the toxic solvent injured population. In D. Herrmann, M. Johnson, C. McEvoy, C. Hertzog, & P. Hertel, (Eds.), *Basic and applied memory research: Practical applications* (pp. 469–480). Mahwah, NJ: Lawrence Erlbaum Associates.
Berger, D. E., Pezdek, K., & Banks, W. P. (1987). *Applications of cognitive psychology: Problem solving, education, and computing.* Hillsdale, NJ: Lawrence Erlbaum Associates.
Broadbent, D. (1985). Multiple goals and flexible procedures in the design of work. In M. Frese & J. Sabini (Eds.), *Goal directed behavior: The concept of action in psychology* (pp. 27–41). Hillsdale, NJ: Lawrence Erlbaum Associates.
Broadbent, D. E., Cooper, P. F., Fitzgerald, P., & Parkes, K. R. (1982). The Cognitive Failures Questionnaire (CFQ) and its correlates. *British Journal of Psychology, 21,* 1–16.
Bronfenbrenner, U. (1977). Toward an experimental ecology of human development. *American Psychologist, 32,* 513–531.
Brunswik, E. (1957). Scope and aspect of the cognitive problem. In R. Jessor & K. Hammond (Eds.), *Cognition: The Colorado symposium* (pp 1–27), Chicago: University of Chicago Press.
Chapanis, A. (1967). The relevance of laboratory studies to practical situations. *Ergonomics, 10,* 557–577.
Clegg, C. (1994). Psychology and information technology: The study of cognition in organizations. *British Journal of Psychology, 85,* 449–477.
Cooley, M. (1987). *Architect or bee?* London: Hogarth.
Dasgupta, S. (1996). *Technology and creativity.* New York: Oxford University Press.
DeVore, P. W. (1980). *Technology: An introduction.* Worcester, MA: Davis.
Donders, F. C. (1969). On the speed of mental processes. In W. G. Koster (Ed. & Trans.), *Attention and Performance II. Acta Psychologica, 30,* 412–431. (Original work published 1868)
Featherman, D. L. (1991). Mission-oriented basic research. *Items: Social Science Research Council, 45,* 75–77.
Geiselman, R. E., Fisher, R. P., MacKinnon, D. P., & Holland, H. L. (1986). Enhancement of eyewitness memory with the cognitive interview. *American Journal of Psychology, 99,* 385–401.

Gruneberg, M. M. (1996). *The reasons for conducting applied research in academe.* Unpublished manuscript, Swansea, Wales.

Gruneberg, M. M. (1987). *Linkword: French, German, Spanish, Italian, Greek, Russian, Dutch, Portuguese.* London: Corgi Books.

Gruneberg, M. M. (1985). *Computer Linkword: French, German, Spanish, Italian, Greek, Russian, Dutch, Portuguese, Hebrew.* Penfield, NY: Artworx.

Gruneberg, M. M., & Morris, P. E. (1992). Applying memory research. In M. M. Gruneberg & P. E. Morris (Eds.), *Aspects of memory: The practical aspects* (Vol. 1, pp. 1–17). London: Routledge.

Gruneberg, M. M., Morris, P. E. & Sykes, R. N. (Eds.). (1988). *Practical aspects of memory.* New York: Academic Press.

Gruneberg, M. M., Morris, P. E. & Sykes, R., (Eds.). (1978). *Practical aspects of memory.* New York: Academic Press.

Gruneberg, M., Morris, P., Sykes, R., & Herrmann, D. (1996). Creating t h e o r y versus applying theory. In D. Herrmann, M. Johnson, C. McEvoy, C. Hertzog, & P. Hertel (Ed.), *Basic and applied memory: Theory in context* (pp. 63–82). Mahwah, NJ: Lawrence Erlbaum Associates.

Hamid, M. S., Garner, R., & Parenté, R. (1996). Improving reading rate and reading comprehension. *Cognitive Technology, 1,* 19–24.

Harris, J. E. (1980). We have ways of helping you to remember. *Journal of the British Association for Service to the Elderly, 17,* 21–27.

Hastie, R., Hammerle, O., Kerwin, J., Croner, C., & Herrmann, D. (1996). Human performance reading statistical maps. *Journal of Experimental Psychology: Applied, 2,* 3–16.

Herrmann, D. J. (1998). The relationship between basic research and applied research in memory and cognition. In C. P. Thompson, D. J. Herrmann, D. Bruce, D. G. Payne, J. D. Read, J. D., & M. P. Toglia, (Eds.), *Autobiographical memory: Theoretical and applied perspectives.* Mahwah, NJ: Lawrence Erlbaum Associates.

Herrmann, D. J., & Gruneberg, M. (1993). The need to expand the horizons of the "Practical Aspects of Memory" Movement to applied research. *Applied Psychology, 7,* 553–566.

Herrmann, D. J., McEvoy, C., Hertzog, C., Hertel, P., & Johnson, M. (Eds.). (1996a). *Basic and applied memory: Theory in context* (Vol. 1). Mahwah, NJ: Lawrence Erlbaum Associates.

Herrmann, D. J., McEvoy, C., Hertzog, C., Hertel, P., & Johnson, M. (Eds.). (1996b). *Basic and applied memory: Practical applications* (Vol. 2). Mahwah, NJ: Lawrence Erlbaum Associates.

Herrmann, D., & Parenté, R. (1994). A multi-modal approach to cognitive rehabilitation. *NeuroRehabilitation, 4,* 133–142.

Herrmann, D., & Pickle, L. W. (1996). A cognitive subtask model of statistical map reading. *Visual Cognition, 3,* 165–190.

Herrmann, D. J., & Raybeck, D. (1997). The relationship between basic and applied research cultures. In D. G. Payne & F. G. Conrad (Eds.), *Intersections in basic and applied memory research* (pp. 25–44). Mahwah, N J: Lawrence Erlbaum Associates.

Herrmann, D., Raybeck, D., & Gruneberg, M. (1998). *A clash of scientific cultures: The relationship of basic and applied research.* Terre Haute, IN: Indiana State University Press.

Herrmann, D. J., & Searleman, A. (1990). A multi-modal approach to memory improvement. In G. H. Bower (Ed.), *Advances in learning and motivation* (pp. 175–205). New York: Academic Press.

Herrmann, D., & Searleman, A. (1992). Memory improvement and memory theory in historical perspective. In D. Herrmann, H. Weingartner, A. Searleman, and C. McEvoy (Eds.), *Memory improvement: Implications for memory theory* (pp. 8–20). New York: Springer-Verlag.

Herrmann, D., Weingartner, H., Searleman, A., & McEvoy, C. (Eds.). (1992). *Memory improvement: Implications for memory theory.* New York: Springer-Verlag.

Herrmann, D., Yoder, C. Y., Wells, J., & Raybeck, D. (1996). Portable electronic scheduling/reminding devices. *Cognitive Technology, 1,* 36–44.

Hoffman, R. R., & Deffenbacher, K. A. (1992). A brief history of applied cognitive psychology. *Applied Cognitive Psychology, 6,* 1–48.

Hoffman, R. R., & Deffenbacher, K. A. (1993). An ecological sortie into the relations of basic and applied science: Recent turf wars in human factors and applied cognitive psychology. *Ecological Psychology, 5,* 315–352.

Intons-Peterson, M. J. (1993). External memory aids and their relation to memory. In C. Izawa (Ed.), *Cognitive psychology applied* (pp. 142–166). Hillsdale, NJ: Lawrence Erlbaum Associates.

Intons-Peterson, M. J. (1997). How basic and applied research inform each other. In D. G. Payne, & F. G. Conrad (Eds.), *Intersections in basic and applied memory research* (pp. 3-24). Mahwah, NJ: Lawrence Erlbaum Associates.

Jobe, J. B., & Mingay, D. J. (1991) Cognition and survey measurement: History and overview. *Applied cognitive psychology, 5,* 175–192.

Johnson, M. K., & Raye, C. L. (1981). Reality monitoring. *Psychological Review, 88,* 67–85.

Kapur, N. (1995). Memory aids in the rehabilitation of memory disordered patients. In A. D. Baddeley, B. A. Wilson, & F. N. Watts (Ed.), *Handbook of memory disorders* (pp. 533–556). New York: Wiley.

Lansdale, M. (1991). Remembering about documents; Memory for appearance, format and location. *Ergonomics, 34,* 1161–1178.

Lansdale, M., & Edmonds, E. (1992). Using memory for events in the design of personal filing systems. *International Journal of Man-Machine Studies, 36,* 97–126.

Leirer, V. O., Morrow, D. G., Tanke, E. D., & Pariante, G. M. (1991). Elder's nonadherence: Assessment and medication reminding by voice mail. *The Gerontologist, 31,* 514–520.

Lewandowsky, S., Herrmann, D. J., Behrens, J. T., Li, S.–C., Pickle, L., & Jobe, J. B. (1993). Perception of clusters in statistical maps. *Applied Cognitive Psychology, 7,* 533–551.

Loftus, E. F. (1979). *Eyewitness testimony.* Cambridge, MA: Harvard University Press.

Loftus, E. F., & Marburger, W. (1983). Since the eruption at Mt. St. Helens, has anyone beaten you up? Improving the accuracy of retrospective reports with landmark events. *Memory & Cognition, 11,* 114–120.

Malpass, R., & Devine, P. (1981). Guided imagery in eyewitness identification. *Journal of Applied Psychology, 66,* 348–350.

McEvoy, C. L. (1992). Memory improvement in context: Implications for the development of memory improvement theory. In D. Herrmann, H. Weingartner, A. Searleman, & C. McEvoy (Eds.), *Memory improvement: Implications for memory theory* (pp. 210-231). New York: Springer-Verlag.

Miller, G. A. (1969). Psychology as a means of promoting human welfare. *American Psychologist, 24,* 1063–1075.

Miller, K. (1995). Why should federal dollars be spent to support scientific research? *Sigma Xi Forum: 1995 Vannevar Bush II Science for the 21st century.* Research Triangle Park, NC: Sigma Xi.

Miller, L. A. (1996). Can't we ever agree: A review of M. Pendergrast's (1995) *Victims of memory: Incest accusations and shattered lives. Cognitive Technology, 1,* 45–48.

Mullin, P., Herrmann, D. J., & Searleman, A. (1993). Forgotten variables in memory research. *Memory, 15,* 43–64.

Naugle, R. , Prevey, M., Naugle, C., & Delaney, R. (1988) New digital watch as a compensatory device for memory dysfunction. *Cognitive Rehabilitation, 6,* 22–23.

Neisser, U. (1976) *Cognition and reality.* San Francisco: Freeman.

Nogami, G. Y. (1982). Good-fast-cheap: Pick any two: Dilemmas about the value of applicable research. *Journal of Applied Social Psychology, 12,* 343–348.

Parenté, R., & Herrmann, D. (1996). *Retraining cognition.* Gaithersburg: Aspen.

Park, D. C., & Kidder, D. P. (1996). Prospective memory and medication adherence. In M. Brandimonte, G. Einstein, & McDaniel (Eds.), *Prospective memory: Theory and applications* (pp. 369–390). Mahwah, NJ: Lawrence Erlbaum Associates.

Payne, D. G., & Conrad, F. G. (Eds.). (1997). *Intersections in basic and applied memory research.* Mahwah, NJ: Lawrence Erlbaum Associates.

Pickle, L. W., & Herrmann, D. J. (1995). *Cognitive aspects of statistical mapping.* (Working Paper Series), Hyattsville, MD: National Center for Health Statistics.

Plude, D. J., & Schwartz, L. K. (1996). The promise of Compact Disc-interactive technology for memory training with the elderly. In D. Herrmann, C. McEvoy, C. Hertzog, P. Hertel, & M. Johnson (Eds.), *Basic and applied memory: New findings on the practical aspects of memory* (pp. 333–342). Mahwah, NJ: Lawrence Erlbaum Associates.

Reason, J. T. (1988) Stress and cognitive failure. In S. Fisher & J. T. Reason (Eds.), *Handbook of life stress, cognition and health* (pp. 238–256). New York: Wiley.

Reason, J. T., & Lucas, D. (1984). Absentmindedness in shops: Its correlates and consequences. *British Journal of Clinical Psychology, 23,* 121–131.

Rumelhart, D. E., & McClelland, J. L. (1982). An interactive-activation model of context effects in letter perception: Part 2. The contextual enhancement and some tests and extensions of the model. *Psychological Review, 89,* 60–94.

Searleman, A., & Herrmann, D. (1994). *Memory from a broader perspective.* New York: McGraw-Hill.

Shiffrin, R. M., & Schneider, W. (1977). Controlled and automatic human information processing II. Perceptual learning, automatic attending, and a general theory. *Psychological Review, 84,* 127–190.

Smith, W., Randell, M., Lewandowsky, S., Kirsner, K., & Dunn, J. (1996). Collaborative research into cognitive technology: The role of shared commitment, problem coherence, and domain knowledge. *Cognitive Technology, 1,* 9–18.

Sternberg, S. (1966). High-speed scanning in human memory. *Science, 153,* 652–654.

Sternberg, S. (1975). Memory scanning: New findings and controversies. *Quarterly Journal of Experimental Psychology, 27,* 1–32.

Sweller, J. (1989). Cognitive technology: Some procedures for facilitating learning and problem solving in mathematics and science. *Journal of Educational Psychology, 81,* 457–466.

West, R. (1985). *Memory fitness over forty.* Gainesville, FL: Triad.

West, R. L. (1989). Planning and practical memory training for the aged. In L. W. Poon, D. C. Rubin, & B. A. Wilson (Eds.), *Everyday cognition in adulthood and late life* (pp. 573–597). New York: Cambridge University Press.

Willis, G. B., Royston, P., & Bercini, D. (1991). The use of verbal report methods in the development and the testing of survey questionnaires. *Applied Cognitive Psychology, 5,* 251–267.

Wright, D. (1997). Methodological issues for naturalistic event memory research. In D. G. Payne, & F. G. Conrad (Eds.), *Intersections in basic and applied memory research* (pp. 69–88). Mahwah, N J: Lawrence Erlbaum Associates.

Yuille, J. C., & Cutshall, J. L. (1986). A case study of eyewitness memory of a crime. *Journal of Applied Psychology, 71,* 291–301.

Zacks, R. T., & Hasher, L. (1992). Memory in life, lab, and clinic: Implications for memory theory. In D. Herrmann, H. Weingartner, A. Searleman, & C. McEvoy (Eds.), *Memory improvement: Implications for memory theory* (pp. 232–248). New York: Springer-Verlag.

Author Index

Subject Index

A, B

Accommodation, *see* Compensatory mechanisms

Activity
goals and spatial memory, *see* Memory, spatial
and spatial memory, *see* Memory, spatial
and spatial thinking, *see* Memory, spatial

Aging, cognitive, *see* Cognitive aging

Alzheimer's disease, 50, 52

Amnesia, 8-9

Assimilation, *see* Compensatory mechanisms

Attribution errors, *see* Misattributions

Automatic influences of memory, *see also* Habit, 50, 52-53, 56-59 and Memory, processes, automatic, 8-9

Autosuggestion, 17-18

Beliefs about collaborative cognition, 63-66, 74-83
and accuracy, 63-64
and distortion, 63-64
about forms of, 65-66, 77, 79-81
self-efficacy, 74-77

C

Children's spatial memory, *see* Spatial memory

Cognitive aging, 65-69. 72-74
and beliefs about, 72-74
gains with aging, 65-67
losses with aging, 65-67
and memory, 65-67
practical cognition and aging, 68-69

Cognitive operations, 113

Cognitive rehabilitation, *see* Rehabilitation techniques, cognitive

Cognitive technology, *see* Technology, cognitive

Collaborative cognition, 63-64, 69-83
accuracy, 63-64, 69-71
distortion of, 63-65, 69-71
and expertise, 71-72
and memory, 69-83

Compensatory mechanisms, 67
accommodation, 67
assimilation, 67
remediation, 67
substitution, 67

Complex task, 114
tank gunnery, 114

For Product Safety Concerns and Information please contact our EU
representative GPSR@taylorandfrancis.com
Taylor & Francis Verlag GmbH, Kaufingerstraße 24, 80331 München, Germany